"As I celebrate 30 years of ordained ministry, I'm certain of two things: the work of God's healing ministry is deeply needed in our world, and it will not look like much of what we call 'church' 30 years from now. In this moment of swift transitions, I'm grateful for the ministry of FTE. The model of leadership and discernment that Stephen, Matthew, and Dori have developed there is a gift to all of us. Receive it and know that there is *Another Way*." —**William J. Barber II**, Pastor, Activist, and President of Repairers of the Breach

"We all want change of one sort or another, but as a result of increasingly divisive social and political factions, we had no organizing principle that we could agree upon. *Another Way* offers an opportunity for mutuality in hospitable spaces, storytelling, listening, reflection, and action. The process was hidden in plain sight: in our wisdom traditions, adages, stories, and creativity. Now that it has been tested in diverse settings and within a vibrant organization, I am excited about the possibilities. *Another Way* shows us how to move forward into an uncertain future, able to respond to challenges with heart and mind, and the dynamism necessary to thrive together." —**Barbara A. Holmes**, President Emerita, United Theological Seminary of the Twin Cities

"The practices you will encounter here are deeply rooted in ancient traditions that most of us have forgotten. *Another Way* offers alternatives to people who love God but have fallen out of love with religion. Here you will find a way of reengaging the Way of Jesus and exploring what that means, both at a personal and organizational level. Perhaps most importantly it grounds this exploration in voices and experiences of Black folk, addressing a long-standing gap in the literature on leadership, vocation, and the future of Christian faith." —**Richard Rohr**, OFM, Center for Action and Contemplation

"Brilliantly crafted, *Another Way* is a master class on facilitation and collaborative learning. Lewis, Williams, and Baker embody the vulnerability, intentionality, and thoughtfulness of leaders who have chosen another way. *Another Way* invites us to slow down and step off the frenzied hamster wheel of endless activity. The rhythmic voices of these three writers welcome us into deep engagement with self-awakening questions intended to aid in vocational discernment, organizational realignment, and communal empowerment. When you are ready to stop running from your purpose, sacrificing your well-being, and denying the changes occurring in and around you, settle in for this journey... choose *Another Way*." —**Gregory C. Ellison II**, Candler School of Theology, Founder of Fearless Dialogues

"In a world where communication has been reduced to 140-character sound bites, Stephen Lewis, Matthew Williams, and Dori Baker offer us *Another Way*, a way to sink into the silence of Beloved Community to allow the authentic to emerge from an experience of shared wisdom and trust. The authors welcome us into their own process of challenging notions of leadership, structure, and action and invite us to consider new ways of leading." —**Karen Oliveto**, United Methodist Bishop, author of *Together at the Table*

"The authors and their colleagues have transformed the Forum for Theological Exploration from a traditional funding organization to an intersectional, engaging, and lively incubator of the next generation of ecclesial leadership. FTE gatherings and fellowships are strategically building capacity, deepening conviction, and nurturing courage, especially with and for communities of color. This book shows how and why; must-read for anyone working toward a future for the church." —**Ched Myers**, Bartimaeus Cooperative Ministries, author of *Watershed Discipleship: Reinhabiting Bioregional Faith and Practice*

"This is a book that we have longed for! The wise authors guide readers to find new ways of being prophetic and compassionate leaders through countercultural, communal, soul-connecting, and life-honoring processes. The structure of the book itself serves as a powerful teaching tool as it embodies what the authors present as an alternative communal leadership model! This book is for leaders who truly care about people and our world!" —**Boyung Lee**, Senior Vice President for Academic Affairs and Dean of the Faculty, Iliff School of Theology

"This book is a manifesto for transformative, lifegiving, soul-soothing, spirit-led leadership. Confronted by the ways in which their work 'deepened the privilege of the privileged,' the authors invite us to accompany them as they explore assumptions, uncover toxic theologies, wade into hard truths, and experiment collectively to redefine leadership, rethink process and practices, and reimagine "the next most faithful step." A challenging and creative resource for all those seeking to build and sustain justice-seeking beloved communities joining God in the repair of the world." —**Janet Wolf**, Public Theology and Nonviolent Organizing, Children's Defense Fund

"I have been blessed to walk alongside Dori, Stephen, and Matthew for many years as friends, colleagues, and co-learners. Their deep commitment to the sacred art of hosting for justice and transformation is an inspiration to me. Their generosity of spirit and vulnerability have crafted this book, a text full of heart and inspiration, and a deep well from which we can drink together. Our times are calling for more stories and questions that help us give rise to a new form of spirit-infused and collective leadership. The territory and the future are unknown, but the imperative is clear. Let this book be your guide." —**Chris Corrigan**, global steward, Art of Hosting.

"FTE has long been a shining example of soulful, practical change-making, and this book embodies that wisdom with stimulating clarity. Dori, Matthew, and Stephen help us recognize the disturbingly individualistic nature of dominant leadership models and to rediscover ancient practices that awaken a deeper, more generative way of leading change. Whenever we ask 'Who am I?' it must be paired with its sibling 'Whose am I?' *Another Way* is rewarding reading for anyone eager to change the quality of presence within their organization." —**Casper ter Kuile**, co-creator of Sacred Design Lab and co-host of *Harry Potter and the Sacred Text* podcast

"A refreshing blend of story, theology, and practice. Lewis, Williams, and Baker challenge, guide, and invite readers to align their personal lives and the organizations they lead to imagine another way. Unlike business models of organizational change, *Another Way* reminds us God is and is in the process of vocational discernment and institutional alignment." —**Kathy Khang**, author of *Raise Your Voice: Why We Stay Silent and How to Speak Up*

This book is dedicated to...
a new generation of people—the dreamers, freedom fighters, artists, and warrior-healers—who refuse to accept things as they are as all that there is and pursue another way.

All that you touch

You Change.

All that you Change

Changes you.

The only lasting truth

is Change.

God

is Change.

— Octavia Butler
from *Parable of the Sower*

FOREWORD by
PARKER J. PALMER

Another Way

LIVING & LEADING CHANGE on PURPOSE

Stephen Lewis • Matthew Wesley Williams • Dori Grinenko Baker

Saint Louis, Missouri

An imprint of Christian Board of Publication

Cover design: Kate Morales, katemorales8@gmail.com

ChalicePress.com

Print: 9780827200838
EPUB: 9780827200845
EPDF: 9780827200852

Printed in the United States of America

Contents

Foreword

It's a privilege to invite you into a book written by three people I respect and admire, a book that comes from their experience leading the Forum for Theological Exploration (FTE) that does healing work in a wounded world. If that kind of work is on your agenda, you'll find this book a vital resource.

By happy accident, the path that led to this book began, in part, on the back porch of my home. Ten years ago, two of the three authors—Stephen Lewis and Matthew Williams—reached out to me for a conversation around shared concerns and visions. We spent a day with each other and a few close colleagues engaged in what the third author, Dori Baker, has described as "a lingering, sacred conversation that was in many ways the beginning of the journey described here."

A decade later, it's joy for me to introduce a book that contains a rich mix of personal stories, inspiring visions, challenging ideas, and practical methods for creating "safe space" for vocational discernment and sustenance among people of faith who want to lead change "in embedded systems of power and privilege." Equally important, FTE devotes itself to making sure that people without power and privilege not only have access to those spaces but feel deeply at home in them.

In the field of personal and social transformation, it's hard to find a subject more important than the one explored in this book. The spaces in which we gather are increasingly unsafe for deep and true speaking and listening, unsafe for the soul, as I suggested in lines I wrote fifteen years ago:

> We know how to create spaces that invite the *intellect* to show up, analyzing reality, parsing logic and arguing its case: such spaces can be found...in universities. We know how to create spaces that invite the *emotions* into play, reacting to injury, expressing anger and celebrating joy: they can be found in therapy groups. We know how to create spaces that invite the *will* to emerge, consolidating energy and effort on behalf of a common task: they can be found in task forces and committees. We certainly know how to create spaces that invite the *ego* to

put in an appearance, polishing its image, protecting its turf and demanding its rights: they can be found wherever we go! But we know very little about creating spaces that invite the *soul* to make itself known.[1]

In the absence of "soul spaces," we have little chance to show up for each other with what theologian Howard Thurman called "the sound of the genuine" in each of us.[2] When that sound is lacking, we will never hear the music of personal and social change.

As the authors explain in detail, *Another Way: Living and Leading Change On Purpose* centers on a set of practices set forth through the acronym CARE. These practices attend to four fundamentals that are often neglected, even in spaces formally designated as "spiritual" or "religious":

C = **C**reate hospitable space

A = **A**sk self-awakening questions

R = **R**eflect theologically together

E = **E**nact the next most faithful step

There's much to be said about the first three steps, and the authors say it here, clearly and well, offering commentaries and tools that give readers good guidance on what it would look like to take these steps in their own settings. They do the same with step number four. But because that step is the one that makes the CARE process different from group explorations that never find expression in grounded action, I want to say a few words about it.

In my experience, "enacting the next most faithful step" begins in the moment when you hear your soul's imperatives with a clarity that's beyond doubt. In that moment, you know intuitively that if you ignore or defy your soul, you do so at the risk of undermining your own identity and integrity. The dearth of CARE-type spaces in our society is driven by fear—the fear that if we were to listen closely to the truth within us, we would be called into the deep discomfort and hard work of personal and social transformation.

Here's an example of what I mean. Using methods similar to the CARE approach, I once facilitated a retreat for twenty-five physicians. In the middle of a challenging exploration of death and dying, one

[1]Parker J. Palmer, *A Hidden Wholeness: The Journey Toward an Undivided Life* (San Francisco: Jossey-Bass, 2004), 56.

[2]Howard Thurman, "The Sound of the Genuine" (Baccalaureate address, Spelman College, Atlanta, May 4, 1980). Speech edited by Jo Moore Stewart for *The Spelman Messenger* 96, no. 4 (Summer 1980): 2–3. The entire speech can be accessed here: www.uindy.edu/eip/files/reflection4.pdf.

physician said, "I work in a system that has me right on the edge of violating my Hippocratic Oath several times a week." As the others in the circle absorbed his words in silence, he spoke again: "You know, that's the first time I've ever said that to a group of fellow physicians." After more silence, this man spoke once more, this time from an even deeper and quieter place: "The truth is, that's the first time I've said that to myself."

When I heard his final statement, I realized that my physician friend was now on the horns of a dilemma. He had heard "the sound of the genuine" from the depths of his soul. Would he try to sweep under the rug what he'd heard, leaving him feeling alienated from himself? Or, when he left this safe space and went back to work, would he act on what he'd heard from within, manifesting his integrity in action?

This man opted for the latter. On returning to his workplace, using community-building tools he picked up at the retreat, he gathered a few colleagues who shared his dilemma, and together they created a penalty-free zone for the reporting of medical errors. It's the absence of such zones and the data they provide for systemic change that makes hospitalization the third leading cause of death in the U. S.

Though my story is not strictly a CARE story, it illustrates the power of circles that are safe for the soul to trigger moments of truth that—carefully nurtured and strategically pursued—can lead to organizational as well as personal transformation.

One of the most impressive features of *Another Way: Living and Leading Change On Purpose* is that the authors use their own organization as a case study in both the need and the potential for this kind of root-level change. Chapter 8, "Embodying CARE," includes these words:

> In 2012, the Fund for Theological Education[3] saw a crisis coming as it inched towards its sixtieth anniversary. In our own sphere, we recognized a drastic misalignment between our stated values and where our resources were deployed.

When you pick up a book about personal and social transformation and find that the writers use their own organization—and their own roles in that organization—to illustrate the honesty, the risks, and the struggles that transformation requires, you know you're holding a book you can trust. This is such a book.

— *Parker J. Palmer*

---

[3]The Fund for Theological Education was the original name of what is now the Forum for Theological Exploration.

Introduction

There's Gotta Be Another Way: Why CARE?

We three—Matthew, Stephen, and Dori—begin our time together in silence. Over the telephone, an expansive silence invites us to breathe, collect our scattered souls, and show up to each other in this moment, although we are five hundred miles apart.

Matthew ends the silence with "Thank you all." Stephen says, "I'd like to read something," and follows with these words of Howard Thurman: "We do not know each other yet. We have not dared to be silent together."[1]

So begins the practice, once again, of centering ourselves before stepping into a future that asks something of us.

This book is written by three people with very different backgrounds who share a common yearning and a common experience. The three of us yearn for a future in which all humans flourish and contribute to the earth's healing. We've experienced small spaces in which cocreating such a future seems possible, probable, and even surprisingly likely. These spaces begin with silence, slowing down, and remembering to be human.

Another Way: Living and Leading Change on Purpose centers on a group of practices we call *CARE*. CARE is an acronym for an approach that invites people to engage wholeheartedly in ways of leading profound change, ways that are deeply connected to people's inner well-being and to their communities of accountability. CARE consists of four adaptable moves. When creatively contextualized in a variety of settings, these moves allow people to find another way to lead and a deeper capacity to facilitate change in themselves, their communities, and the world.

We've seen this effect take hold in a crowded hotel ballroom among hundreds of activists, in a lecture hall filled with burned-out

[1]Howard Thurman, *The Inward Journey* (Richmond, IN: Friends United Press, 1961), 52–53.

power brokers, among board members of a nonprofit organization, in weekend retreats at woodsy church camps, and in seminary classrooms steeped in the assumptions of academia.

We've witnessed the results of CARE in young adults launching social enterprises to address eco-justice, CEOs who decide to invest resources in alternatives to the status quo, and change-makers who find the courage to approach difficult work in ways that align their passion, principles, and practices.

People who experience CARE-infused leadership sink into their honest selves and experience a mysterious relatedness among strangers. They come up out of a session led with CARE principles feeling changed, empowered, and able to take a next step. It is an effect at once deeply familiar and countercultural. It has a stickiness that reverberates in the communities to which people return. When we see it happening, we are reminded that people are built to experience community, to find joy in one another, and to create a better world out of a deep reservoir where the soul resides.

People who experience CARE-infused leadership sink into their honest selves.

When people first begin to practice another way, it can seem like driving on a dirt road instead of a paved highway. But once leaders begin to use the CARE practices regularly, they invariably begin to wonder how they ever led without them. We hear them remark on the results they see and on the joy they experience when they leave a gathering, believing again that they can change social structures that diminish human flourishing.

What Is CARE?

CARE grows out of our work at the Forum for Theological Exploration (FTE), a leadership incubator for the church and academy, at which Stephen Lewis is president, Matthew Wesley Williams is vice-president, and Dori Baker is senior fellow.

At FTE, we gather, convene, design, invite, create, explore, and play at the intersection of faith, leadership, vocational discernment, and social change. During the past sixty-five years, FTE has worked with more than six thousand young leaders discerning ways to make a difference in their communities through leadership in higher education, faith communities, and other public institutions. During the past fifteen years, we have worked with more than five hundred organizations and their leaders. These organizations are ones that intentionally accompany young leaders in their exploration and pursuit of lives of meaning and purpose or build capacity to lead positive change in their institutional context. In the last several years, FTE paid close attention to the needs of more than 1,200 diverse young leaders primarily between the ages of twenty and thirty called to serve as pastors, activists, and scholars, as well as to institutions that support, call, and hire them to lead.

We have discovered several noteworthy insights about the practice of leadership, the formation of leaders, and organizations' efforts to develop, hire, and retain the next generation of leaders. One important insight that is emerging from FTE's work with leaders and organizations is this: current practices are too individualistic and short-sighted. Organizations want better solutions to their leadership development and change-management challenges, but too many don't have enough time, the right personnel, or enough bandwidth to create and sustain meaningful change in their context. Individual leaders want to make a positive difference in their communities, institutions, and the broader world. However, they either don't know how to do so in meaningful ways or they don't fully understand that lasting, positive change requires collective and coordinated efforts of a team or community of leaders—not the lone efforts and aspirations of an individual.

These insights reflect a core corrective to established leadership norms. Instead of defaulting to the cult of individualism, we remind each other: If you want to go fast, go alone. If you want to go far, go together.

CARE is an acronym that spells out another way to live and lead change. It is an approach that helps us remember that people (and their ideas) are more powerful when they travel through periods of change together. It is a framework for how people can commit more fully to changing things they care about deeply in themselves, their communities, organizations, and the world.

As Parker Palmer indicated in the Foreword, the acronym goes like this:

C = **C**reate hospitable space

A = **A**sk self-awakening questions

R = **R**eflect theologically together

E = **E**nact the next most faithful step

In the pages that follow, we will introduce CARE and tell stories of people and organizations who have found these practices useful, even life changing.

We didn't invent the CARE practices. They aren't new. They come to us through many traditions, ancient and modern. They are fundamental to what it means to be human and to move through life together toward an uncertain future.

Again and again, we have synthesized, borrowed, and played with these practices among many diverse groups of people, some of whom identify as Christians, and others who eschew that label or what it has come to connote in twenty-first-century North America.

Over the years, this immersion took us to a small Presbyterian church in Greenville, South Carolina; a community center in Berkeley, California; a back porch in Madison, Wisconsin; and many other places across North America. On a deck overlooking the San Diego harbor, we decided to share what we've been learning about another way to lead, and to use this book to create a wider conversation about how people live and lead change on purpose. We invest a double meaning in the words "change on purpose," pointing both to change that is intentional and change that helps individuals and communities discover their "why"—the deep purpose of their existence. We use the acronym CARE, because "to care" is to attend deeply to one another's well-being. For us, the church exists to care, to lead lasting change for the good of all people, or else it loses its reason to be.

Though we three are grounded in the church, we recognize that many people experience "church" and "Christian" as largely negative, self-serving, or dehumanizing. Indeed, we also struggle daily with problematic portions of Christian tradition that we reject. CARE draws on forgotten roots of Christian faith and practice that are useful and necessary at this point in human history.[2] These roots hold particular promise for the development of leaders who work both inside and beyond the church and who want to be able to address the difficult issues confronting people, communities, organizations, and the world.

Who We Are

We are a team of two African American men and one white woman with a long history of wondering and struggling together over how our individual stories, vocational journeys, and hoped-for futures converge in the telling of this story. At times we will speak as a "we," but at other times as individuals. We recognize that varied opinions and divergent

[2]For more on this see: Peter Paris, *The Spirituality of African Peoples: The Search for a Common Moral Discourse* (Minneapolis: Augsburg Fortress Press, 1995); Barbara Holmes, *Race and the Cosmos: An Invitation to View the World Differently* (Harrisburg, PA: Trinity Press International, 2002), and *Joy Unspeakable: Contemplative Practices of the Black Church* (Minneapolis: Fortress Press, 2017); Richard Rohr, *The Universal Christ: How a Forgotten Reality Can Change Everything We See, Hope For, and Believe* (London: SPCK Publishing, 2019) and *The Naked Now: Learning to See as the Mystics See* (New York: Crossroad, 2009); Fabien Eboussi Boulaga, *Christianity without Fetishes: An African Critique and Recapture of Christianity* (Maryknoll, NY: Orbis, 1984); Charles Long, *Significations: Signs, Symbols and Images of Interpretation in Religion* (Minneapolis: Fortress Press, 1995); Marimba Ani, *Let the Circle Be Unbroken: The Implications of African Spirituality in the Diaspora* (Trenton, NJ: Red Sea Press, 1994).

viewpoints exist among the three of us, opinions and viewpoints that we need not attempt to reconcile, for this multiplicity is a strength borne of diverse worldviews, bodies, and experiences. We begin by introducing you to the parts of our individual journeys that prepared us for the work we do together through FTE, in hopes that you too will recognize the multiplicity of experience your team brings to your particular work.

Matthew writes:

I was born on the South Side of Chicago in the late 1970s to parents active in the church and in justice organizations working on issues related to poverty, equity, racism, and human freedom. Early on, my parents helped me to understand that service, protest, and organizing for change in the world are all expressions of active faith. They steeped me in the cultural and spiritual gifts of African-descended peoples and taught me how to drink from those rich ancestral wells. In so doing, they instilled in me a spiritual orientation that sees the inner life and the social world as two interdependent aspects of one and the same reality. For me, faith-rooted leadership is about social change, and change is rooted in the inner life. While I am the child of Reginald and Marcelle Williams, I am also the child of a long tradition of faithful women and men whose lives bore and bear witness to the fact that there is no task more sacred than the liberation of oppressed peoples. I accepted my call to ministry in this tradition at the young age of fifteen.

As a child, I witnessed my father's devotional practices and discovered my own in his library at home. The view out of that room was partially blocked by the red brick side of our neighbor's house, but it cleared the alleyway beyond that wall just enough to allow a shaft of occasional Chicago sunlight to illuminate my father's bookshelves. I would often stand in front of that endless wall of books and stare at the bindings. I would pull a few down at a time to allow them to talk to one another. Zora Neale Hurston, Tom Skinner, Linda James Myers, Frederick Douglass, W. E. B. Du Bois, and others spoke to me of my rich spiritual and intellectual lineage of love, faith, and struggle. This was the tradition to which I belonged, to which I would be accountable. I was blessed to be exposed at an early age to the life of the mind as a necessary element of Christian faith, human development, and the struggle for freedom, justice, and equity.

In that space, in conversation with those voices, I was learning how to practice being still, quieting my mind, talking to God, studying Scripture and history, and listening for the leading impulse of Spirit and my ancestors. These and other practices filled me with a sense of wonder and imagination and inspired me to believe that the wiles of evil systems would not have the last word—and that another world is possible. This was the contemplative space in which I began to discern my vocation.

I can see now that as I moved further through college, seminary, and into the public role of preaching and congregational leadership through my late teens and early twenties, I slowly began to lose touch with those contemplative practices and community rituals that had so filled my inner well. Prayer, meditation, and Scripture study too often became nothing more than performative tools I used to meet the endless demands of life in ministry.

After multiple bouts of leadership burnout by age thirty, I noticed that I was living out of a warrior-hero model of leadership that called for me to sacrifice my physical and mental well-being to serve the sacred needs of the community and the cause. My heroic self-understanding as a leader contributed to my cycle of burnout. Organizations such as churches, schools, and justice agencies that claim to be about the business of human flourishing often devour people in the process of trying to increase social good.

People, their well-being and wholeness, take a backseat to the "good" mission for which the organization exists. People, like interchangeable parts, are treated as a means to an end. Organizations tend to consume their leaders. Often subtly and unknowingly, those same leaders then sabotage the work of the organization. A deep dissonance often emerges between the way we work and the values embedded in the aims for which we struggle. The apparent message here is that our work requires of us a kind of fractured life, and this causes both the people and the collective mission to suffer. Our models of leadership and the methods by which we build and mobilize community conspire to drain the very life out of our leaders and the communities they serve, and thereby reinforce the death-dealing, soul-destroying realities we say we want to change.

For decades, I had a nagging sense that there's got to be another way to lead. With urgency, I began to explore ways to be in community with people who are seeking to live faithfully and meaningfully. It is that other way that I'm pursuing.

Stephen writes:

Born and raised in Charlotte, North Carolina, I grew up in an African American missionary Baptist church, where I was well acquainted with the idea that God has a purpose for everyone. As a six-year-old, I was drawn to myths and stories about healing and transformation. Some of this was directly connected to my prayers that God would heal my mother, who suffered from depression. But a lot of it was simply a natural curiosity I had about human quests and spiritual encounters, which seemed to be at the center of all these stories. Only years later, after a first career in finance, did I find myself returning to these stories, realizing they lie at the center of what matters most to me.

As a young professional, I found myself listening to the stories of colleagues as we traveled up and down sixty floors of a Charlotte skyscraper or waited at the busy intersection of Trade and Tryon Streets. I heard secret confessions of hopeful aspirations, dreams deferred, success followed by burnout, and the aching desire for something more than a career, money, and status. Despite working hard for these very things, once we got them, we all wanted more. The "more" we desired was to be better stewards of the one life entrusted to us. We wanted more meaning. We wanted more purpose.

Every day of all those years on my way to work I passed by the invisible people barely living in the shadows of Charlotte's booming financial district. Each day as I trekked the four blocks from the parking lot to my office, I wondered about God's purpose for the marginalized, forgotten, and abandoned. I wondered why Black and Brown people experienced deep faith and meaningful worship but lacked access to the kind of socio-political and economic power once leveraged by African -American church leaders and allies to improve the conditions of their community and city. I wondered why there appeared to be so much inequity in God's provision for Black and Brown people around the world. I began asking: What is the role of religion and religious institutions, particularly the church, in addressing the social conditions of marginalized people? How are they called to help develop solutions to address societal evils and injustices? What is their role in transforming communities and society?

What is the role of religion and religious institutions, particularly the church, in addressing the social conditions of marginalized people?

Over a lunchtime Bible study that I organized and led in the basement of nearby First Presbyterian Church, more of these questions emerged in the stories of twenty fellow sojourners searching for more in their lives. And gradually I felt a rumbling inside, inviting me to deeper questions about the meaning and purpose of my own life.

When I shared with my pastor my decision to pursue a call and attend seminary, he suggested I "be open." Those words unlocked doors.

They invited me to dive into the deeper truth of what mattered—what I cared deeply about—in my own life. I discovered there was something more to life than climbing the corporate ladder, making money, getting married, having kids, growing old, and then dying.

I came to believe that there is a future that mourns if we don't step forward courageously and use our lives on behalf of the greater good. For me that meant committing to shaping and advancing a different kind of religion. The word *religion* comes from the Latin *religare*, which means to reconnect. I have become committed to the forms of religion that rejoin and connect us to a profound wisdom. This kind of religion honors the unity of life that is deep within us and between us, a unity that transcends us, guides us, and even conspires with us to work on behalf of creating a better world. This led me to the work of inspiring and developing the next generation of faith leaders who will help shape a more hopeful future in which all people can live a life of meaning, dignity, and worth.

There is a future that mourns if we don't step forward courageously and use our lives on behalf of the greater good.

My collaborative friendship with Matthew began over a meal in suburban Atlanta in 2000. It became wildly fruitful during the fortunate circumstance of shared office space at FTE. Within these four walls near the campus of Emory University, we began to imagine a series of "what ifs": What if we helped people better align their espoused values with their leadership practices? What if we explored alternative ways of leading, ways that value collective wisdom and action? What might be possible if change-making leaders gain the tools to imagine and enact alternatives to the status quo?

The list went on.

What if we encourage young leaders to cultivate their inner life as a key discipline?

What if we invite young leaders of color into deep self-reflection—not alone, but with others, and in spaces that privilege trust and interdependence?

What if we explore together the steps that courageous change requires of us?

What if we could create opportunities for people to explore their call beyond the four walls of a church?

Those questions led us on a search for resources, specifically practices and processes that could help us to cultivate a different way of leading change. Among the many resources was the Center for Courage & Renewal founded by Parker J. Palmer, whose work helps people discover and sustain the deep connection between who they are and what they do in the world. In the work of the center we recognized some clues to an alternative. Both of us became facilitators of the center's processes and found numerous ways to begin to apply its practices, which are designed to help people align their soul and their role.

Our shared office became an incubator for new ideas and practices. Our exploration led us next door, into the office of our colleague Elizabeth Mitchell-Clement, whose bookshelf and brilliance exposed us to a world of ideas and frameworks. She challenged us to take seriously the instincts, intuitions, and intellectual urgings that were driving our desire to cocreate alternatives to the dominant models of leadership. At Elizabeth's urging, Dori's story-based method of theological reflection on vocation entered our work.[3]

As a result of these connections, into FTE's day-to-day life began to seep group practices of building trust, creating circles of deep listening, asking reflective questions, and using silence, writings, and reflections from authors to evoke shared truth. We created "Project Rising Sun," a two-year leadership academy for young pastors of color interested in learning how to lead change. This became the early laboratory in which the CARE practices first flourished.

Dori writes:

I grew up in rural Florida, where my exposure to religion was Sunday morning visits to Southern Baptist churches with my girlfriends, all of us still groggy after mostly sleepless sleepovers. There, I heard about a God who planned his son's life, death, and resurrection to save me. That never made any sense to me, but I was drawn to the story of an ancient wanderer, a man who spent a lot of time outdoors feeding and healing people. I also sensed belonging to something bigger than myself. My father, the son of Ukrainian immigrants, took me to midnight vigils at the Russian Orthodox church, which I remember as a blur of men in robes speaking a language I did not understand. Between the rule-based rigidity of the Southern Baptists and the incense-filled mysticism of Russian Orthodoxy, a deep curiosity about God began to form in me.

Questions about the connection between spirituality and justice slammed me during college as I trained to be a journalist. One winter, I covered a hard frost that ruined the local strawberry crop in the community in which I grew up. I noticed that beneath the diminished profits of wealthy (mostly white Baptist) farmowners hid a more devastating story—the situation of seasonal farmworker families (mostly of Mexican descent), whose very livelihoods depended upon

[3]Dori Grinenko Baker, *Doing Girlfriend Theology: God-Talk with Young Women* (Cleveland: Pilgrim Press, 2005).

the strawberry crop. I became acutely aware of the distance between my wealthiest and my poorest neighbors, and I became aware of the racial bias embedded in this reality. As the then-critical world of journalism continued to expose gaps in the religious worldview in which I swam, my curiosity about God grew more urgent. I left Florida to go to seminary in Chicago, not because I wanted to be a pastor—back then I didn't know female pastors existed—but rather to figure out for myself how God fit into the world of chaos, pain, and structural injustice that journalism revealed to me.

Seminary became a journey of scraping away at a pervasive image of God as an all-knowing white male obsessed with rules. Slowly, I came to recognize God as a mysterious life-force who answers to many names, always escapes description, and, more than anything, can be trusted as a compassionate presence in the midst of suffering and the seeming absence of hope. Along the way, I joined a local United Methodist church (UMC) that was living on the radical fringe of that denomination in the late 1980s. It was a nuclear-free zone making safe space for Central American refugees, welcoming queer and transgender folk, and advocating for the ordination and marriage of gays and lesbians. Here, in the presence of women mentors, I began to envision myself as a pastor and prepared for ordination.

A deep immersion in the writings of women and particularly women of color saved my life. In my last semester of seminary, I experienced an onset of unprecedented anxiety. Over a distinct three-day period, I became profoundly aware of the church as intricately entwined with racism and patriarchy. I found myself wondering if I could remain a Christian. Bereft of faith, I felt foolish for all the time and money I had spent in seminary. In this bleak midwinter, two images comforted me. The first was a tiny spark deep within me that I sensed was connected to the source of the universe. This faint glimmer of hope was reminiscent of the "divine spark" of which the Quaker tradition speaks. Accompanying this spark were the strains of spirituals, songs passed down by enslaved people. Having studied the spirituals in seminary, I knew that these songs interpreted the biblical story in a way that countered the dominating culture of their day. They took the very narrative white slaveholders twisted to condone slavery and turned it into life-giving sustenance for a people to rise up and seek freedom in the face of great danger.[4] The songs bounced around my brain, my heart, my spirit. Mingling with the inner spark, they worked a small miracle: on the fourth day, I got up out of bed, puzzled but grateful for what seemed like a mystical encounter. I rejoined my

[4]See Yolanda C. Smith, *Reclaiming the Spirituals: New Possibilities for African American Christian Education* (Cleveland: Pilgrim Press, 2004).

former self, knowing my next step was to pursue ordination so that I could take part in reforming a tradition from within. A year later Bishop Leontine Kelly, the first African American female bishop in United Methodism, laid her hands on my shoulders to ordain me into the priesthood.

Six months into my first parish, I found church leadership to be soul-shrinking. Busy weeks brought night after night of meetings, ego-driven committee members, and the corporate mandate to grow, grow, grow at all costs. In an effort to heal myself, I sought more embodied ways of leading, one of which included wilderness treks to the Boundary Waters Canoe Area. There for a brief two weeks each summer, I experienced another way, one in which we lived in community, preparing meals, hearing stories around the campfire, and contemplating the sun's daily path across the sky. These practices reminded me that church once revolved around nature's rhythms, rituals of care, and time spent hosting one another's humanity.

I found my vocation to be bridge building between the dying white institutions of Christendom and the liberating theologies emerging from scholars of color such as Katie Cannon, Kwok Pui-Lan, and Ada María Isasi-Díaz. Translating these theologies into the lived realities of contemporary girls and women became the focus of my first book.

Church once revolved around nature's rhythms, rituals of care, and time spent hosting one another's humanity.

I came to FTE in 2008, drawn by my work with youth and young adults around the practices of shared storytelling, deep listening, and reflecting together on meaning and purpose. I began to work with Matthew, Stephen, and other colleagues on a series of events called "Notice, Name, and Nurture" to support congregations in attending to the leadership potential of young people. These carefully invited, multiracial gatherings gave birth to temporary congregations who reveled in the diversity often lacking in their home congregations. Leaders reported back to us that practices they encountered at Notice, Name, and Nurture inspired them to change the way they began board meetings, led intergenerational fellowship, and nurtured volunteers engaged in organizing to improve their neighborhoods.

Matthew, Stephen, and Dori write:

Late one night, we walked through a makeshift gallery hung with colorful, three-dimensional depictions of the future that was emerging through the participants. We saw green spaces where people of all ages tended a garden; tables where plentiful food was shared among all; neighborhoods where expanded networks helped care for young and old. We heard ourselves saying "This stuff works. It really works!"

Matthew and Stephen began inviting the entire FTE staff into their shared history of experimentation and synthesis, action, learning, and reflection. We began thinking together about how to scale these practices for a wider audience. Along the way, we also began to use the practices to transform the very organization within which we were working.

Together, we've shared meals at the end of long days of learning, when we are miles from our homes. We've struggled deep into a conversation and resurfaced hours later, recommitted to articulating nuance, instead of settling for assumptions about one another's meanings. And we've debriefed the results of our collective efforts, sometimes bearing witness to failure, but often acknowledging those spectacular moments when grace sweeps in and uses one of us as a vessel of her larger purpose. We are not afraid of disagreeing and pushing one another toward greater clarity. We bring a sense of playfulness and joy to our collegiality.

Now we invite you to join us. Bring your authentic self into experimentation with these practices. Invite others into conversation about deep longings for a more hope-filled future. By engaging this work, you embody a response to the collective feeling that "There's got to be a better way to create a future that we all long to see."

Why CARE?

Why CARE?

Because there's got to be a better way of leading.

Social change is not merely a game of trade-offs in which we sacrifice personal and communal well-being for the pursuit of shared ideals. We need not live divided, believing a better world is possible while daily resigning ourselves to reproducing social realities we say we don't want.

We are not doomed to remain in leadership loops that rely on the illusion that all we need to achieve our aims is that one special person to take us to the promised land. We need not follow leaders who envision and embody their vocation only as heroes, martyrs, and saviors, and inevitably fall into predictable patterns of burnout.

Because there *is* another way.

Institutions and organizations *can* learn to respond courageously to the increasingly complex challenges facing the communities they serve. Young people growing up in these communities *can* find ways to make a difference with their lives. Organizations *can* find ways to reimagine their role in cultivating the kind of leaders we need now.

People are not the means to the ends in social change. Human beings are the ends. The well-being of all creation is the end. There *is* a better way of leading. We've seen it. We experience it. And it never ceases to amaze us.

CARE is an invigorating intervention. It invites us to reimagine how we engage in change at personal, organizational, and communal levels by revisiting our understanding of leadership and purpose. Purpose is inextricably tied to the enterprise of leadership. In fact, it is the seedbed from which leadership springs. What might be different if we began to explore these fundamental notions out of a new framework?

We are not the first to call into question dominant modes of thinking and talking about leadership and vocation. We are part of a great cloud of witnesses who believe there is another way.

We hope that this book pushes further conversation and action among people who, like us, believe that people's lives depend on us enacting alternatives. We invite you to imagine what practices of leadership look like when vocation is something that emerges not simply from individual soul-searching but from the shared soul of CARE-full community discernment.

We are part of a great cloud of witnesses who believe there is another way.

Why CARE Works

The CARE practices work because people are hungry to make a difference in the world. The hundreds of young adults we gather each year tell us over and over again that they long to discover their purpose and make a difference. They long for others who will accompany them on this journey. They want to stop pretending they have it all figured out. They want room to learn from failure. They want safe places to share their vulnerability. They want freedom to roam around at the edges of disciplines and traditions, seeking a fertile space where new ways of doing life can be born.

The move toward leadership grounded in self-awareness and honesty is fragile, however, because it runs counter to strong currents in our culture. These currents teach us to think that for "strong leaders," independence trumps interdependence; coercion is superior to collaboration; the all-knowing expert is wiser than the collective wisdom of a community; and success is measured by a test score or a tax bracket.

The CARE practices remember other ways of living and leading. These ways of living and leading, fragile at first, become muscular with practice. Where once we walked into a room full of strangers unsure of their willingness to engage in these practices with us, we now anticipate and welcome friends around the world longing to practice another, better way of leading.

Is This Book for You?

This book is for people who ask:

- How do I lead in pursuit of what I'm *for,* rather than getting stuck in what I'm against?
- How can I learn to lead in life-giving ways?
- When I get greater clarity about me and my call, how do I take steps to move in that direction?
- How do I mobilize my organization to be present in the world differently?
- How do we adapt faithfully to the complex shifts in our environment?
- How do I keep on leading change without burning out?

As you can imagine, these questions appeal to a wide cross section of people. We often find they attract people who feel like misfits born at the wrong time. When they find each other, they share a spark of recognition and report the feeling of coming home.

You may be:

- an individual who aspires to discover your own life of meaning and purpose, figuring it out for the first time, or once again,
- a guide or facilitator who, by role or by nature, helps others discover meaning and purpose,
- a leader of an organization who wrestles with how to create lasting and positive change in your context.

You may find yourself living out more than one of these roles simultaneously. Maybe you are a young person who already facilitates soul-filled practices of discernment among your peers. Maybe you are an entrepreneur launching a social enterprise. Maybe you are the leader in a congregation, institution of higher education, or community organization who names, notices, and nurtures the gifts of young people in your midst.

This book is also for people in any of the above categories who long to become who they were meant to be, *but don't want to go it alone.* It is for young adults who are motivated by their faith to make a difference in the world, including those who are motivated by their faith tradition, and some who call themselves "spiritual but not religious." It is for all those people who have said to us: "I want to do x, y, and z in my context, but seminary (or my MBA or PhD) didn't prepare me to lead change."

CARE awakens and sustains leaders, inviting their inner wisdom, their intuition, and their integrated selves into the task of leading change—in themselves, their communities, and the world. It grows out of the life and ways of Jesus, and it reflects ancient cultural traditions and ancient wisdom of the African diaspora. It draws from the time-honored practices of faith communities in which ordinary people inherit and reinvent ancient spiritual traditions. It borrows from benevolent thinkers such as Parker Palmer, Paulo Freire, Howard Thurman, Otto Scharmer, Ella Baker, Margaret Wheatley, Thich Nhat Han, Richard Rohr, and Peter Senge, who themselves have lifted up and revisited strains of wisdom from ancient traditions and cultures.

In the chapters that follow, you will meet some of the thinkers and doers named above. Some of them we tracked down in real time, sitting with them to ask how their work intersected our own, and asking them to help us understand emerging networks of change innovators.

You will see what CARE looks like up close and personal, through the lenses of our own trial-and-error attempts at using the practices. We don't always get it right. In fact we acknowledge that we will never get to a place of always getting it right. We frequently need to stop, breathe, reorient ourselves, and remember that continuing to practice self-awareness in our leadership is a lifelong journey. Grace extended toward us and others is a necessary companion.

CARE awakens and sustains leaders, inviting their inner wisdom, their intuition, and their integrated selves into the task of leading change.

How to Read This Book

In the coming prelude, Matthew describes a moment when he experienced a new kind of space in which to discern his next steps as a leader. This serendipitous exchange lasted only a few minutes and happened unexpectedly, but it altered the course of Matthew's future. Revisiting this moment helps us imagine how the CARE practices mindfully invite such moments into our living and leading.

The subsequent eight chapters alternate between "show me how" chapters that walk through each one of the four CARE practices in turn, and "think it through" chapters that reflect on concepts embedded within the practices. We have organized the book this way because our thinking informs our practices and vice versa. However, readers hungry to begin using the practices may choose to read the practical chapters (1–3–5–7) in order, going back later to read the conceptual (2–4–6–8) chapters in between. Other readers might be curious about the underlying sources and would benefit by turning directly to the conceptual chapters.

In this book, you will find:

Another Way Manifesto

Think of this as a new default setting. Because the leadership ways embedded in CARE are countercultural in most places, we state these declarations up front and revisit them regularly. They remind us of what we know by heart and what we can trust as we do the work of leading change in ourselves, our organizations, and our world. We refer back to them at the end of each chapter.

Chapter 1 *C*: Creating Hospitable Space

We invite you inside the brain of a facilitator, who begins to trust the countercultural moves of CARE while leading a high-powered team through a difficult process of change. Here we walk through the first step in CARE: creating space where souls feel welcome to drop down, slow down, and enter into new ways of being together.

Chapter 2: The Inner and Outer Tug of Call and Purpose

Why am I here? What is my life's purpose? Embedded in these questions are the concepts of call and purpose, which lie at the core of leading change for good. In this chapter, we consider the world as an "inescapable web of mutuality." Such a communal worldview reshapes "call" and "purpose" from hyper-individual quests to radical interdependency between self, community, and God. This helps us understand how the CARE practices support people as they follow the tug from their present reality into an imagined future in which all can flourish.

Chapter 3 *A*: Asking Self-Awakening Questions

The stories of our own lives connect us to our deep passion. How do we uncover the stories that lie dormant within us, ready to inspire and sustain us as we lead change? Here we turn to the second practice in CARE: Asking Self-Awakening Questions. This practice puts us in touch with what we really love, what we care deeply about, and what motivates our acts of courage. Learning to listen and lead from a deep, awakened center is especially important when our leadership challenges structures that undergird exploitation, oppression, or brutality. Self-awakening questions create dialogue that leads persons and communities to wake up and "stay woke."

Chapter 4: The Work Our Souls Must Have—Vocation and Leadership

In this chapter, we pause again from the CARE practices to reflect more deeply on concepts embedded within them, this time turning to vocation and leadership. For too long, leadership has been seen as the role of the elite few who are called to create change. Because this messianic view of leadership is so deeply embedded in our culture, here we practice telling and retelling other stories, stories that help us imagine a future in which cocreators follow their inspired dreams, stepping into leadership roles that help a better future emerge.

Chapter 5 *R*: Reflecting Theologically Together

Here we explore a particular tradition of theological reflection as an indispensable discipline for leaders and communities that seek to lead change for good. Within the CARE approach, theological reflection engages and critiques inherited ways of reading sacred literature and social life, enabling us to glimpse alternatives to the status quo. This approach, driven by focused dialogue and careful attention to our embodied experiences, also stimulates imagination and insight into particular next steps that leaders can take to build experimental alternatives or to help change ineffective and unjust systems.

Chapter 6: Liberating Leadership

This chapter explores a way of revisioning leadership that evolves from experiences within the prophetic Black church tradition and the broader Black freedom struggle. This kind of leadership we call "liberating leadership" because it dismantles the dominant forms of living and leading that reinforce the oppressive norms of empire. It helps to create alternative ways of being that open new, expansive possibilities for communities to flourish. Liberating leadership undergirds CARE. Simultaneously, the CARE practices help to create conditions in which "liberating leadership" can emerge.

Chapter 7 *E*: Enacting the Next Most Faithful Step

Enacting our next most faithful step is a practice of transforming insight into reflective action. Here we emphasize immediate action that enables us to unearth, test, and reflect on our assumptions and actions in pursuit of a new heaven and new earth. Each word used to describe this practice suggests a set of critical questions that should inform our action. This chapter walks us through an experience of designing preliminary prototypes of solutions to intractable community problems.

Chapter 8: Embodying CARE

Age-old wisdom flows from deep root to trunk to flowering branch. Purpose grows out of necessity.

While using these practices with our institution's external partners, we began using them in our own organization. In this chapter, we recap the practices through stories, highlighting moments when we used the CARE practices to transform our organization. You will see here how the practices come into play not as universal, linear steps, but rather as context-specific iterations that weave into and around again and again, more like a dance than a forced march. The practices become more familiar with use, and our failures become learnings that feed aspirations in the next go-round. We end this chapter by reviewing our Another Way Manifesto—a statement to which return again and again to ground us as we lead.

At the end of each chapter, we pose a set of questions for you to use in quiet reflection as you journal, in conversation with peers, or as you build an intentional learning community. These questions will help you think about how this chapter directly affects you as you live out your leadership role, whether you are:

- **an individual learner or leader** who aspires to discover your own meaning and purpose, figuring it out for the first time, or once again
- **a guide or facilitator** who, by role or by nature, helps others discover meaning and purpose
- **an organizational leader** who wrestles with how to create lasting and positive change in your context

Our Hope

We hope that as you read this book, you find yourself drawn more purposefully to a community of seekers who know there's got to be another, better way. Across history, we see people with their backs up against the wall finding strength in community, refusing to give in, seeking creative alternatives, and trying something new. Some of it works! Walls fall. Life-giving structures emerge. Age-old wisdom flows from deep root to trunk to flowering branch. Purpose grows of necessity. And it is all deeply communal, part of the collective "work our souls must have."[5]

The pursuit of alternatives is urgent. We wrote this book slowly over a three-year period while paying attention to what was going on around us and within us, both the tragedies and the life-giving responses. These included:

Across history, we see people with their backs up against the wall finding strength in community, refusing to give in, seeking creative alternatives and trying something new.

- massacre of worshipers at Mother Emanuel Church in Charleston, South Carolina
- rise of the Black Lives Matter movement and Kaepernick's NFL protest
- targeted violence against LGBT communities
- proliferation of mass shootings
- rise of white nationalism, such as the white supremacy on display in Charlottesville, Virginia
- Women's March and the #MeToo movement
- travel ban against Muslims
- detention and deportation of immigrants and refugees at the United States–Mexico border
- Standing Rock resistance to the Keystone oil pipeline
- clarion call of climate change voiced by scientists and the experience of weather-related catastrophes

It was a disruptive era within the church as well, including:

- death of institutions
- continued unveiling of widespread sexual abuse by Roman Catholic priests, Southern Baptist clergy, and clergy of many other denominations
- rupture of centuries-old denominations

[5]emilie m. townes, "Ethics as an Art of Doing the Work Our Souls Must Have," in *Womanist Theological Ethics: A Reader,* ed. Katie Geneva Cannon, emilie m. townes, Angela D. Sims (Louisville: Westminster John Knox Press, 2011), 35. Townes is quoting Katie Geneva Cannon, who frequently used this phrase as a definition for vocation. Townes expanded on this phrase in a speech entitled "womanist understanding of vocation," given on April 13, 2015 at an FTE event in Nashville. It is archived at www.leadanotherway.com

The list goes on. These social upheavals are outcroppings of systems all of us inhabit and internalize. They have catalyzed thousands of young people to rise up, using their gifts as poets, prophets, politicians, and protesters to work for change. The change they seek is not small, simple, or insignificant.

As we were writing, we became increasingly clear that we, too, are part of a movement of people pursuing transformed ways of being. Tweaking the status quo is a dead end.

Our hope is that this book will be one among many sparks for conversations that lead to action. Some might call that the work of cocreating the conditions in which a new heaven and a new earth will emerge. This hope requires of us a deep reckoning with the beliefs, habits, and practices through which we have cocreated the world as it is. It also requires that we cultivate new ways of relating to ourselves, one another, and creation for the emergence of "another, better way."

We wrote this book for leaders, dreamers, and change-makers like us who are yearning for alternatives to the status quo. Here we unpack and offer the best of what we've learned together. This exploration is a work in process. It is and will continue to be an unfinished journey.

In the next section, we invite you into a moment of necessity that gives birth to purpose through a story from Matthew's vocational unfolding. This prelude sets the stage for CARE as a rhythm of stories and reflections or—as our former colleague Elizabeth Mitchell Clement often reminded us—big questions, small journeys, between meals, as life happens.

Questions for Reflection

For the individual learner seeking meaning and purpose:

1. In this chapter the authors tell stories about times in their individual journeys when they were challenged to stay connected to something larger than themselves that drew them into leadership. Spend a moment reflecting on your own journey. When have you experienced or felt connection to something larger than yourself, calling you into a role or identity? When did you feel most alive in that connection or call?

2. Stephen writes, "There is a future that mourns if we don't step forward courageously and use our lives on behalf of the greater good." How does this idea resonate with you? What will the future mourn if *you* do not live out *your* purpose?

3. What was one challenging idea you encountered in this chapter? What made it so?
4. What was one helpful idea you encountered in this chapter? What made it so?
5. What is one thing you take with you from this chapter that might make a difference in the way you explore your own sense of purpose?

For the guide/facilitator helping others find meaning and purpose:

1. Matthew writes, "After multiple bouts of leadership burnout by age thirty, I noticed that I was living out of a warrior-hero model of leadership that called for me to sacrifice my physical and mental well-being to serve the sacred needs of the community and the cause. My heroic self-understanding as a leader contributed to my cycle of burnout." How do the people you accompany or the people you know who are seeking to create change express their burnout? What causes contribute to the burnout of leaders in your context? What resources (e.g. stories, lived examples, resiliency practices) exist in your context to help leaders cultivate their inner life in community or to create more sustainable activism?
2. Dori writes, "Six months into my first parish, I found church leadership to be soul-shrinking." In what ways are the communities in which you live and work soul-shrinking or soul-expanding? What is your role in contributing to the care of souls in these environments?
3. How might a young person watching you describe the way you lead? How intentionally do you invite others into shared leadership?
4. What was one challenging idea you encountered in this chapter? What made it so?
5. What was one helpful idea you encountered in this chapter?
6. What is one thing you take with you from this chapter that might make a difference in the way you mentor or create community?

For those leading organizational change:

1. The authors reflect, "We are reminded that people are built to experience community, to find joy in one another, and to create a better world out of a deep reservoir where soul resides." Is it part of the culture of your organization to help people connect their soul with their role? What are the challenges to bringing this awareness to your workplace? Who are the potential conversation partners for you as you seek to live and lead on purpose?
2. Collective wisdom and meaning-making is necessary to solve complex global problems such as climate change, vast economic inequity, and systemic injustices. How are organizations in your sector (nonprofit, business, higher education, religious, etc.) exploring a more communal understanding of leadership and more collaborative approaches to work?
3. What was one challenging idea you encountered in this chapter? What made it so?
4. What was one helpful idea you encountered in this chapter? What made it so?
5. What is one thing you take with you from this chapter that might make a difference in the way you lead change within your organization or within your sector?

For all:

1. Review *Another Way Manifesto* on the next page. Which sentences stand out to you after reading this chapter?
2. We are building an interactive playlist to accompany each chapter. You can find it on Spotify at **Another Way: The Book.** The song we recommend for this chapter is "We've Come a Long Way to Be Together" by Bernice Johnson Reagon. Please add to the playlist as you are inspired.

ANOTHER WAY MANIFESTO

THERE IS A FUTURE THAT MOURNS IF YOU AND I DO NOT STEP INTO OUR PURPOSE.

VOCATIONAL DISCERNMENT IS A DANGEROUS DANCE THAT REQUIRES RISK AND COURAGE. IT MAY LEAD YOU WHERE YOU DID NOT PLAN TO GO AND INSTIGATE PROFOUND CHANGE IN SELF, OTHERS, AND THE ENVIRONMENT.

CULTIVATE YOUR OWN INTERIOR LIFE AND ITS COMMUNAL SOURCES. LEADERS WHO LACK AWARENESS OF THEIR INNER SOURCES TEND TO REPRODUCE WHAT ALREADY EXISTS.

LEADERSHIP IS A COMMUNAL PRACTICE THAT BUILDS THE CAPACITY OF A TEAM, COMMUNITY, OR ORGANIZATION TO ENVISION AND ENACT A FUTURE INFORMED BY THE PAST AND THE DIVERSE PEOPLE AROUND US.

LEADERSHIP IS MORE ABOUT PUBLIC LISTENING THAN PUBLIC SPEAKING.

DIALOGUE IS AN ESSENTIAL LEADERSHIP PRACTICE AND A CORE PROCESS FOR CHANGE.

CREATE SETTINGS ON PURPOSE TO ENGAGE THE WISDOM OF THE ROOM VERSUS A "SAGE ON STAGE."

BETTER CHOICES EMERGE WHEN THE PARTS OF A LIVING ORGANISM ARE CONNECTED TO THE WHOLE.

STRENGTHEN YOUR CAPACITY TO EMBRACE MYSTERY BY THINKING ABOUT, PLAYING WITH, AND ADAPTING TO UNCERTAINTY, BECAUSE IT, LIKE DEATH, IS INEVITABLE.

IN THE FACE OF UNCERTAINTY AND DESTABILIZATION, GIVE YOURSELF PERMISSION TO PRIORITIZE EXPERIMENTATION AND PROTOTYPING. PAY ATTENTION TO HISTORY, POWER, JUSTICE, AND EQUITY OR YOU WILL MERELY MAKE CHANGE WITHOUT MAKING A DIFFERENCE.

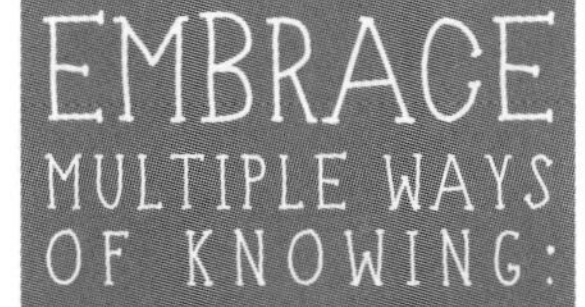

SING, DANCE, MOVE, TAKE A MEDITATIVE WALK, AND ENGAGE OTHER EMBODIED PRACTICES. INTEGRATING THESE WAYS OF KNOWING MOVES US PAST THE PLACES WHERE WE GET STUCK.

THE **WISDOM OF OUR ANCESTORS AND DESCENDANTS IS ALWAYS PRESENT AND AVAILABLE TO US,** SO REMEMBER TO WELCOME THEM AS WE FACE THE MOST DIFFICULT TASKS OF OUR LIVES.

LEARN FROM MULTIPLICITY. MOST OF US ARE MORE THAN ANY ONE THING SIMULTANEOUSLY. **APPRECIATE THE COMPLEXITY OF OTHER STORIES AND PERSPECTIVES.**

CULTIVATE **NEW POSSIBILITIES THAT EMERGE BY RESISTING THE TYRANNY OF EITHER/OR.** HOLD THE PARADOXES THAT SHAPE OUR COMMUNAL LIFE WITH PATIENCE AND CURIOSITY.

A downloadable version of this manifesto can be found at www.leadanotherway.com

Prelude

An Alternative Space for Discernment

Sitting Still Together

Matthew writes:

As I walked hastily toward the intersection of Peachtree and Baker Streets in downtown Atlanta, I had no idea that I was approaching a vocational crossroad. In my final year of seminary, I was carrying anxiety about my future like a piece of heavy luggage. I was hoping that the event to which I was hurrying would help me figure things out. The setting was the industry trade show for religious scholars, the 2003 Annual Meeting of the American Academy of Religion and the Society of Biblical Literature. Organized to host thousands of presentations, lectures, and speeches, it is a study in busy-ness, an avalanche of stimulating choices: to participate is to be in one session always feeling as if I want or ought to be in another as well.

I rushed onward with an inner whirlwind of questions: What's next for me? How do I get a bead on what I am really called to do and be in the world? Will I live up to the expectations of my parents, professors, and mentors? What mentors should I model? What will be my next most faithful step in figuring out what I will do with my life in light of my sense of purpose, passion, and call?

Though I was deeply connected to faith-rooted traditions of justice and liberation, I was perplexed about what I would do after seminary. I knew what I cared about, but I didn't know what I wanted to *do*. How could I both earn a living and contribute to the causes and communities that I loved? At the time I saw only the two potential paths my mentors prodded: congregational ministry or religious scholarship. While I cared deeply about the life of the church and religious scholarship, I was beginning to get a nagging feeling that neither the pastorate nor the professorate was what I really wanted. By that time I had already served in congregational ministry, but had burned out more than once. I also loved the life of the mind, but I couldn't figure out how to whittle down my multiple intellectual interests to a single research project that I wanted to pursue for the next five to seven years. Both of those roles made me feel like David wearing Saul's armor. But if not these paths, what else? These were the paths I knew best, but each stirred up its own inner resistance.

This nagging anxiety had me at a rushed, breathless pace. If only I attended enough sessions, heard enough scholars, encountered as many new ideas as possible, I thought I would get a clue as to what most enlivened me. Having just grabbed a sandwich to eat before the next session, I stood at the intersection of the two streets and literally stumbled into my next teacher.

There he sat, legs dangling on a half wall in front of the hotel, head slightly cocked to the right, still and silent, seemingly looking off into the distance. I burst into his quietude, excited to find him alone and potentially available to dispense some advice. "Dr. Harding!"[1] I called out as I approached him. He nodded slowly and responded kindly, "Hello." I started in, the pace of my introduction mimicking my harried heart rate. "My name is Matthew Williams, I am a student at the Interdenominational Theological Center. May I ask you a question? I'm trying to figure out my next steps and I'm hoping you might give me some advice." With another kind nod he gave me permission to proceed.

I explained my vocational dilemma. Then I added, "And I know Howard Thurman was a friend and mentor to you. He has been a major spiritual mentor for me as I have been trying to figure this out. Is there any advice you can give me?"

"Matthew," he responded slowly, signaling that he now knew me by name. "Stick with Howard." He took a deep breath and after a seemingly endless pause he continued, "He'll help you."

Then I waited, listening for an additional outpouring of wise advice, but he was done with words. That was it. Then he invited me to join him sitting on that half wall. And I did.

For the next few moments, Dr. Vincent Harding and I sat still together. No words passed between us, but profound communication was taking place. As we shared that space, my heart rate began to slow, and I sank down into a rhythm of thought and feeling that allowed the burdensome luggage I carried to lighten. I was slowly and suddenly aware of being present to myself and to the moment. I felt deep

[1]Though in general throughout this book we do not include honorific titles, here we follow the African American cultural tradition of honoring elders in this way.

gratitude and a sense of peace I had not felt in a long time. After a few moments, I said to Dr. Harding, "Thank you."

"You're welcome," he replied, still sitting peacefully on the wall.

As I walked away, my heart rate was slower, my breathing calm, and my pace relaxed. I no longer felt the need to be in more than one place at that moment. I chose one session and stayed there, rather than hopping from place to place.

Something about my encounter with this man had changed my rhythm, my thinking, and my energy. I was different as a result of sharing his space and being in his presence.

Dr. Harding's response to my anxious breathless request for vocational advice was to offer me a space to be fully present to my questions and myself. There on a half-wall in front of a hotel, he created a holy alternative space—a stark contrast to the environment of the massive gathering we were attending. He offered me the gift of experiencing, if only for a moment, a different frequency born of another way of being in the world.

If I had experienced this with someone else, I might have dismissed it as a nice moment with no real relevance to my vocational questions and passion for social justice. But this was Dr. Vincent Harding—legendary activist, scholar, and sage. His writing and leadership advanced the cause of human freedom through the prophetic traditions of Black religion and culture.[2] Having had this experience with Dr. Harding, I began to explore the connection between his contemplative way of being and the power of his social witness. What is the relationship between the holy alternative he helped me experience and the impact of his prophetic life and leadership?

Before that experience, I had not considered non-anxious presence or the use of silence as resources from which I could lead, let alone make the most meaningful choices of my life. In retrospect, I am aware that I was striving after the "right thing to do." I'm also aware that the depth of my commitment to the causes I cared about was something I always felt I had to prove to others and to myself. This experience with Dr. Harding awakened in me the possibility that I could discern and live out my call from a different inner place, not a place of striving or proving, but simply a place of being.

I asked myself questions: I can participate in justice-making and social healing without the burden of vocational anxiety? I can do the work I care about from a place of inner quiet and stillness? My contribution to fostering love, justice, and peacemaking can derive from a source deeper than anger? I don't endlessly have to prove my

[2]For more on the life and work of Vincent Harding, see www.veteransofhope.org/founders/vincent-gordon-harding/.

commitment to the causes I care about by piling on exhausting activity? I can actually prune my commitments by spending time listening to the source material of my soul while remaining in constant connection to community?

Those few moments with Dr. Harding were enough of an opening for me to begin to ask such questions and explore the possibilities they would reveal.

CHAPTER 1

C: Creating Hospitable Space

In the story you just read, Matthew's encounter with sage, scholar, and activist Vincent Harding unfolded unexpectedly and quite naturally. At just the right moment, in just the right way, an intervention occurred that shifted Matthew's future trajectory, opening a way that allowed him to be true to himself.

We don't have to wait patiently for such a serendipitous encounter with a holy messenger. We ourselves can mindfully create the conditions that allow us to midwife one another and a future that wants to emerge.

In this chapter, we describe a way of inviting those kinds of moments for both individuals and organizations. Here we focus on the first step in CARE—**Creating Space**, a space into which we welcome others in order to find head-heart-and-body knowing, to slow down the norms of efficiency, and to enter into new ways of creating a future that calls forth collective wisdom.

Living and Leading Vignette

We begin with a story, again from Matthew, years after his encounter with Vincent Harding and the ensuing journey toward mindful leadership practices he pursued within his role at FTE. He reflects here upon a time when he used the CARE practices to lead a group gathered to unearth and address systems that embed white privilege in the process of becoming a scholar in religion and theology.

Matthew writes:

Subtle insurgency. This was the aim of the design. Academic environments feed on hierarchy, rank, power struggles, and intellectual warfare. In this kind of environment, it is a countercultural task to design a space that invites scholars to drop their center of gravity from their heads to their hearts, to engage one another in ways that bypass normal professional patterns. We convened these scholars and leaders to address a field-wide challenge. The situation that drew us together one participant described like this: "The consensus which gave rise to the structures of which we are a part is fractured."[1]

On its face, the meeting was about the landscape of doctoral theological education and how it tends to the cultivation of scholars of color. We invited leaders to discern what it would take to eliminate the persistent deficit of scholars of color in this sub-field of higher education, especially in light of the so-called 2040 moment when whites will no longer represent a majority in this country or in its seminary classrooms.[2] We gathered to address a complex issue.

What do we do when the norms, assumptions, and basic ideas about our shared work begin to disintegrate? We knew we were convening stakeholders in the field of theological education who were living into an uncertain future.

We needed to create space for a different kind of conversation to take place, a space in which human beings:

- Slow down and enter a humane rhythm that allows us to see ourselves and one another
- Listen with attention to bodily sensation and gut feeling
- Suspend ego-driven patterns of critique and judgment
- Call on deeper ways of knowing to discern the present and the future
- Notice and operate from an underlying interdependence

The subject of our gathering was *merely* institutional and field-wide transformation. No big deal. More than thirty diverse gatekeepers and power brokers, academic executives, and organizational heads were present. The entire system was represented in one room, and it was my role to help the parts of that system to discern the stakes and figure out a future for the field.

---

[1]Juan Martinez, "What Does 2040 Mean for Doctoral Theological Education?" (speech given at FTE National Consultation on Doctoral Theological Education, Christian Theological Seminary, Indianapolis, April 18, 2013).

[2]The 2040 moment refers to the projected point at which whites will no longer make up a majority population in the United States. Because of current trends in the church and academy, that moment will happen much sooner in graduate schools of theology. Our aim in this meeting was to start a frank and bold dialogue to begin to unearth the unseen elements of the field that give rise to racism, unjust economic models, epistemologies, class bias, power, institutional identities, cultures, and values. See www.pewsocialtrends.org/2008/02/11/us-population-projections-2005-2050/ and www.fteleaders.org/pages/calling-for-more-than-we-have-got-thus-far.

So, we **sit face to face.** We gather around small bistro tables, large enough only for notes and conversation, small enough for each of us to be conspicuous and unavoidable. There is not enough space for laptops and phones, which operate as human shields. We have to show up to be here.

We start our time together in **silence.** It's true, isn't it, that often when we come into a room we are not yet fully in that room? So, we invite silence—extended silence that is long enough to feel unusual and possibly uncomfortable for those of us who earn our stripes by the words we speak and write. Silence asks us to become fully present to ourselves and one another.

Silence asks us to become fully present to ourselves and one another.

My thank you breaks the silence. The room feels different. "Don't speak unless you can improve upon the silence" it seems to say.

Each step is an invitation to deeper engagement with ourselves and one another. We have to show up. So, our next move is to determine *how* we will choose to show up. It is fundamentally a human thing. When groups gather, **shared guidelines**—tacit and explicit—determine how people will relate to one another. We use the concept of covenants to establish how we will be present, engage with, and experience one another. We draw from a set of guidelines we call Covenants of Presence.[3]

And now, I'm still nervous. I've never led a meeting like this with academics, let alone academic executives. Will this work? Will they check out? Will they see this as hokey, feel-good stuff? *Trust the process.* I coach myself. *This is designed for human creativity and innovation. At the end of the day, these people are human beings and the ordinary modes of engagement are unacceptable. Trust the design.*

So we visit the covenants, speaking them aloud together . . .

Speak your truth . . .

Turn to wonder instead of judgment . . .

Slow down and pay attention to the stuff beneath the words . . .

We come as equals.

---

[3]Our Covenants of Presence are adapted from the Touchstones used by the Center for Courage & Renewal and the book by Margaret Wheatley, *Turning to One Another: Simple Conversations to Restore Hope to the Future* (San Francisco: Berrett-Koehler, 2009). They can be found at www.leadanotherway.com.

We own these statements and voice them into the room slowly, changing the space that exists within these four walls and between each breath.

Then I ask people to tell a story prompted by these two questions: "Why does this work matter to you? How did you come to care about this?" I watch as people, now operating at a perceptibly slower pace, turn to one another and begin to dip into their memory banks—those deep places where we know about racism, ethnicity, power, class, and gender through multiple layers of our own lived experience. Those things that we often avoid talking about locate us within the issues we've come together to address. As people begin to share their pain, passion, and hopes, the mood in the room shifts again. It feels different. Now we couldn't get the participants to stop if we wanted to. *It's beginning to work*, I tell myself. *Trust the design.*

Mindful Moves of Creating Space

During this difficult-to-facilitate meeting, Matthew choreographed five specific moves that include: sitting face to face, sharing silence and stillness, establishing shared guidelines, slowing down, and turning to story.

It is tempting to revert to conventional methods of gathering people: bring in an expert, hire a keynoter, and let them talk. When you change the game plan this significantly, you open yourself to ridicule. What if people remain fortressed behind their façades of professionalism, or worse, give way to their fears of losing scarce resources in a competitive environment and clam up or perform business-as-usual? What if the change you are asking people to imagine is change they resist, resent, or deeply distrust? After all, you are inviting people to give up power, relinquish privilege, and build new structures that are bent toward justice.

Chances are that many of these factors are at play. But if we, as leaders, keep doing the same things we've always done in the same ways we've always done them, we will keep getting the same results. We are well aware those results are not working.

CARE emboldens leaders to make the necessary countercultural moves to allow new solutions to our most pressing problems to emerge. The gathering Matthew recounts above resulted in such new solutions: a redesign of $1 million of programming and the birth of an institutional network committed to removing systemic barriers to the thriving of scholars of color in the theological academy.

One reason CARE practices work in situations like this is that they draw on sources of wisdom that shift the way people see, think, feel, and act together. These sources arise from specific cultures, but echo throughout many. We'll talk more about those sources later. For now, it's enough to remember that despite façades of protection we put in place for good reason, most human beings yearn for connection. We long to dive deeply, to go beyond the surface of things. But we've become accustomed to defense mechanisms that keep us operating at a safe distance from one another, which is well below our collective potential.

Despite façades of protection we put in place for good reason, most human beings yearn for connection.

And so, when we design a CARE experience, we begin by creating a space that invites people to lean into that yearning for connection: we invite them into their humanity. These opening moments of Matthew's leadership vignette reflect five intentional interventions that grow out of the first practice of CARE: creating hospitable space.

- Sitting Face to Face
- Sharing Silence and Stillness
- Establishing Shared Guidelines
- Slowing Down
- Turning to Story

Let's look briefly at each of these interventions that collectively form the C of CARE. Why can we trust the process in which we employ them? How do these micro-moves add up to more than the sum of their parts? From whom do we draw in remembering these ancient, human-forming practices?

Sitting Face to Face

In our work, we use World Café (www.theworldcafe.com) and other group processes designed to host meaningful conversations. Authors Juanita Brown and David Isaacs tell the origin story of World Café about a gathering of twenty-four people in their California home on a day when an unexpected downpour moved them indoors. Improvising, they set up TV tables in their living room. A friend put down red-checkered tablecloths. Playfully, Juanita decided each table needed a vase of flowers to complete the café look. Someone added crayons and paper. Instead of moving into a formal conversation as planned, Juanita and David encouraged their guests to gather around these small tables to begin chatting about a set of meaningful questions. Later, they asked people to switch tables, continuing to share what was bubbling up from the small, intimate conversations. As themes from each round of smaller conversation were fed into the larger group's reflection, David and Juanita observed a collective wisdom emerging. Somehow, they had become wiser together through this process of dialogue that drew forward the collective experience and expertise of the gathered group.

The World Café process was born of this impromptu innovation. It has become a global movement that consists of creating a welcoming space, inviting conversation partners, and posing questions that move people into the heart of the matter around which they seek change.

Juanita and David remember that first event: "The energy in the room is palpable. It is as if the very air is shimmering." When people from the small tables join others to share what they've drawn and discussed, "it is as if the intelligence of a larger collective Self, beyond individual selves in the room, has become visible to us. It feels almost like 'magic'—an exciting moment of recognition of what we are discovering together that's difficult to describe yet feels strangely familiar."[4]

Similar to the bistro tables used in World Café, Peter Block talks about sitting "knee-to-knee"[5] and Meg Wheatley talks about "turning to one another."[6] The point here is that we configure physical space to invite people to sit in way that doesn't allow us to be anonymous or to overlook one another. We know that such group processes are not new; they simply help us remember fundamentally human principles. Most people are moved by eye contact. It is a joy simply to be heard by someone; it can be gratifying to listen deeply to another person. The small tables, crayons, and flowers used in World Café are simply props, aesthetics that invite different ways of relating to each other. This creates the conditions for new and unusual conversations to arise. We could similarly ask people to turn to one another or to take a walk outside in groups of twos or threes.

This approach to creating space for social change focuses its attention at the level of the molecular bond rather than the atom. Neither hydrogen nor oxygen can be water alone. They have to come together to form a bond in a particular way for them to make a new substance. It's not about the hydrogen and oxygen atoms individually; it's about the way those atoms come together that makes water. Creating

---

[4]Juanita Brown and David Isaacs, *The World Café: Shaping our Futures Through Conversations That Matter* (San Francisco: Berrett-Koehler, 2005), 15.

[5]Peter Block, *Community: The Structure of Belonging* (San Francisco: Berrett-Koehler, 2009), 151-162.

[6]Margaret Wheatley, *Turning to One Another: Simple Conversations to Restore Hope to the Future* (San Francisco, CA: Berrett-Koehler, 2009), 4.

space is about paying close attention to relatedness—the way we come together—as the ground condition from which new conversations, identities, and realities may emerge.

Sharing Silence and Stillness

The late Howard Thurman is a twentieth-century spiritual guide whose ideas you will encounter throughout this book. Reading his works immerses the reader in the world of a deep-thinking mystic; listening to his recorded voice moves one into the mystery itself. [7] He speaks at a pace that allows for silence between words. The listener can savor an idea, dwell with it, befriend it, before moving on to the next. Observers say that Howard Thurman would often create discomfort in people gathered to hear him speak. While standing at the podium, he would pause, relaxing into a long, spacious silence. People who had not experienced him before might wonder, "Is he okay? Is there something wrong?" But when he finally broke the silence and began to speak, his speech seemed to weigh more. Each word fell in its own time, resounding with meaning in the listener's ear.

Taronda Spencer, a member of Spelman College class of 1980 to which Thurman addressed his "Sound of the Genuine" remarks,[8] reflected on the day Thurman spoke at her baccalaureate:

> Before he started, he stopped and paused. He was in meditative thought. He is kind of draped over the podium and it was a long pause, maybe a minute. We don't know if he's sick? We're anxious! All of the sudden this man rises up and gives us the most amazing speech we'd ever heard. We still talk about it.[9]

We have come to trust the power of that kind of silence, despite our own cultural indoctrination to maximize each moment. This shift was embodied on one occasion when we were leading a two-day training course in the CARE practices for a group of three hundred United Methodist pastors in Virginia. The first time we invited them into silence, a few people immediately pulled out their smartphones to check email, texts, and social media. The next time, we began by gently describing the culture of busy-ness that ensnares us in visions of our own import. We drew attention to the possibility that a silent, slow, sabbath moment might indeed be good for one's soul. At the end of the

---

[7]Howard Thurman, *The Living Wisdom of Howrd Thurman: A Visionary of Our Time*, (Sounds True, 2010) available on audiblebooks.com

[8]Howard Thurman, "The Sound of the Genuine" (Baccalaureate address, Spelman College, Atlanta, May 4, 1980). Speech edited by Jo Moore Stewart for *The Spelman Messenger* 96, no. 4 (Summer 1980): 4. The entire speech can be accessed here: www.uindy.edu/eip/files/reflection4.pdf.

[9]Taronda Spencer, personal interview with Dori Baker, December 15, 2013.

event, a young pastor told us that after overcoming the temptation to check his phone, he allowed this immersion in silence to impact him, bathing him in a respite that soothed a constant rumble he experiences as prevalent among his twenty-something peers.

The classical cellist Yo-Yo Ma echoes the great mystics when, in an interview with Krista Tippet, he talks about the silence that exists between one note and the next. "Could the next note be part of the first note? Or could the next note be a different universe?" he muses. "You know, have you just crossed into some amazing boundary and suddenly the second note is a revelation?"[10]

That moment of revelation born of silence is never guaranteed, but we have learned that *chosen* silence creates the conditions in which those kinds of holy moments can slip in, perhaps snatching us up unaware into an experience of delight, truth, or beauty.

We recognize a tension here. People have used silence to oppress one another. People who have experienced being marginalized know what it is like to be "silenced" rather than to choose silence. For that reason, we also invite people into "stillness" or "quiet." Contemporary scholar Kevin Quashie calls us to consider the distinction between "quiet" and "silence," introducing quiet as a metaphor for the inner life and an alternative to the frame of resistance in Black culture. Quiet is the place where imagination flourishes, where a person's vulnerabilities, hungers, desires, and ambitions are free to imagine future possibilities.[11]

Establishing Shared Guidelines

In his book *A Hidden Wholeness,* Parker Palmer writes that, "A small circle of limited duration that is intentional about its process will have a deeper, more life-giving impact than a large, ongoing community that is shaped by the norms of conventional culture."[12] We learn through our work with the Center for Courage & Renewal that establishing the norms of a gathering at the beginning of its work together can completely transform an individual's ability to disarm, engage, and lean into a conversation, even one that may bring challenge, conflict, or difficulty. The difference rests in giving people a chance to take these norms one at a time, look at them, think about them, and determine together what they need to be fully present.

---

[10]Yo-Yo Ma, "Music Happens Between the Notes," interview by Krista Tippet, The On Being Project, https://onbeing.org/programs/yo-yo-ma-music-happens-between-the-notes-jul2018/.

[11]Kevin Everod Quashie, *The Sovereignty of Quiet: Beyond Resistance in Black Culture* (London: Rutgers University Press, 2012), loc. 66–69, Kindle.

[12]Parker Palmer, *A Hidden Wholeness: The Journey Toward and Undivided Life* (San Francisco: Jossey Bass, 2004), 75.

So, once we've gotten a sense that people have truly arrived, we deepen the space by looking at guidelines we call Covenants of Presence. In our work with the CARE practices, we've adapted what the Center for Courage & Renewal calls "Touchstones." We've made them our own, and we encourage people to choose from these covenants—or add their own—to meet the needs of the group they are assembling. We learned to avoid a long list that can begin to feel like a burdensome set of rules. Instead, we choose to revisit the ones that seem to be important on a given day. They include aspirations such as:

- Believe it's possible to leave refreshed and renewed,
- Shift from certainty to curiosity,
- Learn to respond to others with honest open questions,
- Listen generously,
- Welcome discomfort and dislocation.

Sometimes we ask for volunteers to read them aloud, one covenant at a time, choosing the one that is particularly attractive or challenging to them. Sometimes we ask people to read them silently and subsequently to name the one that stands out for them. We ask if these are covenants to which we can all agree, and whether there are additional covenants folks need in order to be fully present. In this way, the covenants become a sacred agreement that create a container in which we hold each other accountable. One young adult participant, Cassidhe Hart, later shared that, "When I first encountered this at the forum in 2013, I had a mini conversion experience. I had come into the room holding past experiences where my peers' inner wisdom had not been invited to be present in meaningful ways. Hearing my peers read these covenants into the room sparked hope and joy in my generation and their capacity for leadership."[13]

As an agreement of how we are going to be present, the covenants may be counterintuitive to the ways we typically act with our families, colleagues, or friends. The norms of the spaces we inhabit are automatic. We implicitly give our assent to inherited ways of being together. Changing these patterns—that is, mindfully creating space that is different than our habits dictate—is a radical departure from everyday ways of being together. The covenants create the conditions for us to have conversations we otherwise could not have.

Shortly after we started sharing these covenants at events across the nation, we began hearing back from people about the transformation

[13]Cassidhe Hart, in discussion with Dori Baker, March 7, 2019.

they witnessed as they took them back to their local contexts. "I began using the covenants at the beginning of committee meetings," one community organizer told us, adding: "It completely changed the way people treated each other." A pastor who founded a neighborhood-based nonprofit near Houston, Texas, found the covenants useful at the start of meetings, where they shifted the focus away from individual egos and toward a shared hope of creating real change. "I began starting every board meeting for our nonprofit with a shortened version of your covenants. It was amazing how people's attention tuned in, how they were able to hold a space that was gracious, hospitable, and open to unexpected outcomes," he recounts.[14]

Over time, we realized that one of the favorite covenants is the one we list last. It says, "Believe that it is possible for us to emerge from our time together refreshed, surprised, and less burdened than when we came. Believe that this time can provide renewal, refreshment, and possibilities; that seeds planted here will bloom in time to come."[15]

Mysteriously, simply setting such an intention can become a self-fulfilling prophecy.

Slowing Down

A fourth important characteristic of the meeting Matthew described is the cadence, rhythm, and energy a leader brings; it is a commitment to slowing down. Slowing down long enough to create a human-centered space matters as we help people follow their own sense of meaning and purpose into living and leading change.

Addressing a group of leaders who've come together for a day's work, Stephen begins like this:

> I live in Atlanta, Georgia. We have an interstate that goes around metro Atlanta called I-285. The posted speed on that interstate is 65 mph, sometimes 70. One of the things I notice is that you can drive 75 mph and people will pass you by at a much faster speed. We are moving very fast! I recognize that when I am going that fast, I can only see so much. However, I notice that when I slow down to 35 mph, as I'm pulling into my neighborhood, I begin to see more. I can see the tree line and the changing foliage. I can see the distinctions and the diversity within the forest surrounding my neighborhood. I can see more when I slow down.

---

[14]Interview conducted by Dori Baker with John Morris, pastor of St. Mark's AME-Zion Church in Dallas, Texas, June 2, 2012.

[15]Covenants of Presence, www.leadanotherway.com

> Silence or moments of pause are great gifts, particularly for those of us who have children or lead busy lives pulled in multiple directions. We rarely give ourselves time to pause and gather ourselves. Just as you gather flour to make bread or dirt to make clay, we need to gather our fragments into a whole. It's a rare gift that we take for granted and that we don't often pursue. So in just a moment, we're going to take a moment to pause. I invite you into a time of centering. A breathing space. A place for us to pause so that our souls can catch up with our bodies to be present in this moment.

Stephen then shares these words from Howard Thurman:

> Can we get still enough, not quiet enough—but still enough—even in the midst of our busyness. Can we find moments of stillness to just be . . . to listen to the sound of the genuine that is within each of us. I don't know if you can—but this is our assignment.[16]

After a few minutes of silence, Stephen asks:

> What words or phrases from that particular text moved you? What spoke to you? Find a landmark from that text or from the stillness that followed that you don't want to lose as you move forward in the day. Take a moment to journal.

The kind of slowing down Stephen facilitates in this storied exercise changes the way we relate to each other in a dramatic way. It creates space for us to be human—to be able to hear each other and to be able to enjoy one another. The quality of our being present is directly tied to our ability to slow down and be with each other, and this affects the quality of the work we will do together. Slowing down begins to create a bit of distance from our regular workaday worlds: we begin to breathe and think and engage in ways we normally don't when we are in the constant, stress-filled grind of everyday life. In this kind of created space, we become freer to explore, imagine, engage, and be present to one another.

The quality of our being present is directly tied to our ability to slow down and be with each other, and this affects the quality of the work we will do together.

---

[16]Howard Thurman, "The Sound of the Genuine" (Baccalaureate address, Spelman College, Atlanta, May 4, 1980). Speech edited by Jo Moore Stewart for *The Spelman Messenger* 96, no. 4 (Summer 1980): 2–3. The entire speech can be accessed here: www.uindy.edu/eip/files/reflection4.pdf.

Turning to Story

Finally, we invite people to turn to the stories of their own lives. There is no better way to move people past dogma, ego, and defenses than to invite people to tell a story. As soon as they begin, we see them make eye contact and invite deeper engagement. They become real. If we've taken care so far to create an inviting and soul-holding space, people are ready now to step into it. This is the threshold between Creating Space and the next step in CARE, Asking Self-Awakening Questions. In later chapters we'll talk in more detail about why story is central to CARE. For now, let's examine the qualities and challenges of creating mindful, intentional space.

What Kind of Space Is This?

The cumulative effect of these interventions is a liminal time/space that is qualitatively different from the everyday space most of us inhabit. Four characteristics of such time/space that we've witnessed are:

- increased potential for interpersonal safety (and risk)
- an invitation to step out of the invisible norms we inhabit
- a dawning awareness of our potential for wholeness and connection
- renewed energy for the possibility that alternatives may emerge

Increased potential for interpersonal safety (and risk)

The notion of "safe space" is problematic, particularly when bringing together people of vastly different life experiences and perspectives. In our work, we bring together diversities in age, spirituality, gender norms, political persuasion, ethnicity, sexual orientation, dis/ability status, socioeconomic and educational levels. The space we are creating is not necessarily safe; some would call it dangerous space. We sometimes call it "brave space," emphasizing the need for courage to confront mental models that may need to change.[17] Because of this, we often include in our Covenants of Presence a statement that encourages constructive conflict. It encourages participants to welcome diverse perspectives and seek to understand and learn what is at stake for the other person. Because we are not all alike, it is only through listening with curiosity and

[17]Brian Arao and Kristi Clemens, "From Safe Spaces to Brave Spaces: A New Way to Frame Dialogue Around Diversity and Social Justice," in *The Art of Effective Facilitation,* ed. Lisa M. Landreman (Sterling, VA: Stylus Publishing, 2013), 135–150.

without judgment that together we can construct an alternative perspective that embraces what's at stake for all.

Even when we succeed in creating boundaries for a certain level of safety, we know that this space is not necessarily without conflict, challenge, or a difference of perspectives, opinions, and ideas. The validation of multiple perspectives has its limits. As Robert Jones Jr. writes, "We can disagree and still love each other, unless your disagreement is rooted in my oppression and denial of my humanity and right to exist."[18] Once we have created the conditions, each person has agency around what they share, but even then, the risk of hurting or being hurt remains.

Entering spaces that allow for levels of vulnerability does not come naturally to most humans anymore. It is an intentional, mindful, learned behavior that takes practice, practice, and more practice.

Entering spaces that allow for vulnerability does not come naturally to most humans anymore.

Invitation to step out of the invisible norms we inhabit

In his book *Out of Babylon*, Walter Brueggemann constructs a metaphorical parallel between sixth-century Babylon, to which the biblical Jews were exiled, and contemporary U.S. culture. Both are empires with totalizing norms. Brueggemann writes, "Empires like Babylon lack both patience and tolerance toward those whose ultimate loyalty belongs to someone or something other than the empire itself."[19]

The kind of space we create through CARE, in addition to inviting people *into* a new reality, invites people *out of* an implicit reality so thoroughly pervasive that it is akin to the water in which we swim. This reality goes by different names, but its primary characteristic is an emphasis on exchange, transaction, and utilitarianism. Our society's dominant and implicit reality assumes that relationships exist for the purpose of extracting resources for private or personal gain. It fosters little to no sense of interdependence or connection, except as it serves the goal of gain. All of creation, including people, other living beings, and the earth itself, become resources to exploit. Relationships are simply a means to an end. This ideology obscures a basic fact underscored in ancient scripture and new science: *all of life is one*. We exist inescapably in a vast web of interdependent life.

[18]Robert Jones Jr. (@sonofbaldwin), Twitter, August 8, 2019, https://twitter.com/SonofBaldwin/status/633644373423562753. See also Robert Jones Jr., *The End of White Christendom* (New York: Simon and Schuster, 2017).

[19]Walter Brueggemann, *Out of Babylon* (Nashville: Abingdon Press, 2010), loc. 310-11, Kindle.

A dawning awareness of our potential for wholeness and connection

Creating space gives scope to the collective intelligence that exists among those who are in the room. Our collective wisdom is necessary. When we create the space, this collective wisdom becomes available to solve the most pressing problems we face. In this space, we engage in a democratic process at a micro level.

Creating space is also a way in which we connect with each other at a deeper level. In Thurman's words:

> Now if I hear the sound of the genuine in me and if you hear the sound of the genuine in you it is possible for me to go down in [my spirit] and come up in [your spirit]. So that when I look at myself through your eyes having made that pilgrimage, I see in me what you see in me. [Then] the wall that separates and divides will disappear, and we will become one because of the sound of the genuine makes the same music. [20]

In other words, "When I go down in me, I come up in you." The ultimate aim of creating space is to get to this "one," this whole, that lies latent within our separateness. We have the capacity to create a kind of wholeness, a kind of collectiveness that reinforces our bond of connection to one another. That wholeness exists over against the ways in which we live our lives in fragmentation.

Creating space mirrors ancient ideas that stem from the African concept of *ubuntu*, succinctly captured in the Zulu greeting *"Sawu Bona"* translated "I see you," and its response, *"Sikhona,"* which means, "I am here." It suggests that "Until you see me I do not exist." A person is only a person through the humanity of other people.

We sometimes invite people into a reenactment of this greeting. At the start of a meeting, we will ask people to sit in a large circle. We'll invite one person to begin by choosing any one person in the room to "see" into existence. She makes eye contact with a person and walks across the room, introduces herself to the person she has seen, and sits down. As each person is seen, he turns to "see" another person. The process continues until everyone has been seen. This exercise removes the automatic "Hello, how are you?" from the room, replacing it with a potentially more meaningful personal connection. It brings into being a particular unique temporary engagement.

Out of the busy-ness of our normal lives, we all show up so that we can be the container for a different kind of collective wisdom

---

[20] Thurman, "Sound of the Genuine."

that is available to us in this moment.[21] All of this is in service first to our shared humanity, but it also creates a better outcome: the whole is better than the sum of its parts. No longer can we say who is the smartest person in the room, because the room itself—the gathered whole—is the smartest.

Renewed energy for the possibility that alternatives may emerge

No longer can we say who is the smartest person in the room, because the room itself – the gathered whole – is the smartest.

Matthew tells about an experience he had after his first retreat with the Center for Courage & Renewal. He shared with a friend that he was fascinated by the way the group process and an intentionally designed space facilitated surprising vulnerability and intimacy among strangers. His friend replied dismissively, 'Yeah, but that was just a retreat. It's not the real world."

In one sense Matthew's friend was right. It can be less risky to share some things with a stranger than with the people with whom you live, work, play, and make a life. That's why bartenders and barbers know the intimate details of the lives of their regular customers. We live in a *real world* where too often the spaces and systems—work, church, business, health care, criminal justice—in which we live are designed to help us avoid intimacy and vulnerability. Instead, they structure our relationships in ways that often produce xenophobia, exploitation, disconnection, and distraction from our inner lives. Yes, that's the "real world."

But in another sense his friend was dead wrong. Matthew recovered from his dismissal and responded, "What is the real world? What I experienced was real. Because I experienced it, I know it's possible." What was different about the experience of the retreat was that it was intentionally designed to invite people into a different kind of conversation with themselves and thereby with one another. It was an alternative space and micro-reality that sustained Matthew in the conviction that the dominant reality is not the only one. Another way is possible. Another world *is* possible.

Ultimately in the CARE practices, creating space is about cocreating conditions where Spirit-inspired alternatives to the current reality may emerge. Peter Block suggests that alternative futures are cocreated one room at a time.[22] The way we design and practice being, discerning, and

[21]For more on collective wisdom, see https://ssir.org/articles/entry/the_dawn_of_system_leadership.

[22]Block, 2009.

working together has the potential to do one of two things: reproduce reality as it is or invite us to imagine and embody a reality distinct from the dominant one.

Gregory Ellison repeatedly observes "Once you see, you cannot not see."[23] It is nearly impossible for someone to convince a person that war is inevitable if that person has experienced nonviolent conflict transformation and sustained peace in community. To know in our cells the experience of an alternative is to embody the possibility that the status quo is not the only game in town. The current reality has been intended, designed, cocreated, and sustained. Likewise, alternatives can and must be discerned, designed, cocreated, and sustained. We create space for those alternatives to emerge.

Going Forth

Think about those seminary presidents and executives we visited at the beginning of the chapter, or call to mind leaders of the civil rights movement. Leading change in embedded systems of power and privilege is lonely work. Innovators and change agents grow weary. Like wilderness survivors, they get by with a drop of rainwater lingering on a leaf, while knowing that somewhere nearby there must be a river. The CARE practices are about ways of hosting people so that they can be like water, a life-giving substance that refreshes parched places and sustains a beautiful determination to thrive.

In the next chapter, we turn to the notions of call and purpose, showing how they grow richer when seen from a communal worldview. Is leadership just about the chosen few? Is it a scarce commodity? Are certain people simply born for it? We think there is another way. The world needs multiple and diverse leaders to address the complex challenges it faces now. Cultivating these leaders within a communal approach to call and purpose welcomes dialogue with the elders, ancestors, and traditions that gave us birth. Access to these deep sources of knowing sustains the struggle for a new and more hopeful future.

Questions for Reflection

For the individual learner/leader seeking meaning and purpose:

1. This chapter begins with a prelude—Matthew's story of a chance encounter with sage and activist Vincent Harding. Harding created an alternative kind of space in which Matthew was invited to slow down, breathe more deeply, and release

[23] Gregory C. Ellison II, *Fearless Dialogues: A New Movement for Justice* (Louisville: Westminster John Knox Press, 2017), 12. See also www.fearlessdialogues.com

his burden of vocational anxiety. Can you recall a time in your life when someone created such a space for you? Do you currently have a friend or mentor who creates space for you to discern what you care about from a place of inner quiet and stillness? If not, how might you go about finding someone like this?

2. It is countercultural in many of the spaces we inhabit to sit still, quiet our phones, and invite a restful moment of silence or sabbath. What makes these acts challenging in the contexts you inhabit? What might you or your peers need to do to overcome these challenges?
3. What was one challenging idea you encountered in this chapter? What made it so?
4. What was one helpful idea you encountered here? What made it so?
5. What is one thing you take with you from this chapter that might make a difference in the way you create space to explore your own emerging questions and deep longings?

For the guide/facilitator helping others find meaning and purpose:

1. This chapter begins with a prelude—Matthew's story of a chance encounter with sage and activist Vincent Harding. Harding created an alternative kind of space in which Matthew was invited to slow down, breathe more deeply, and release his burden of vocational anxiety. How do you create space for others to slow down, listen to their inner truths, or let go of anxiety?
2. Do you remember a friend or mentor who helped you find direction at a crucial point in your life? What characterized that encounter? What are some of the practices you cultivate to host yourself before hosting others?
3. What was one challenging idea you encountered here? What made it so?
4. What was one of the most powerful or helpful ideas you encountered here? What made it so?
5. What is one thing you take with you from this chapter that might make a difference in the way you mentor, create community, or make yourself available to others?

For those leading organizational change:

1. Organizational cultures predict how people show up for each other. Attempting to change a culture to be more humane can be extremely challenging. Like Matthew's inner critic, voices real or imagined might respond dismissively or accuse you of trying to create "kum ba yah" moments. How does it feel when you consider risking vulnerability? What bubbles up if you imagine using your power to convene a more CARE-infused gathering? What experiences can you call upon to remind you of the benefits of taking such a risk?
2. How might you nurture more curiosity among your people and peers about leading in ways that welcome collective wisdom and shared meaning-making?
3. What was one challenging idea you encountered here? What made it so?
4. What was one of the most powerful or helpful ideas you encountered here? What made it so?
5. What is one thing you take with you from this chapter that might embolden you to create space for people to slow down, connect, share stories, or encounter one another more deeply?

For all:

1. Review *Another Way Manifesto*. Which sentences stand out to you after reading this chapter?
2. We are building an interactive playlist to accompany each chapter. You can find it on Spotify at **Another Way: The Book.** The songs we recommend for this chapter are "Holding Space" by Mayyadda and "People Get Ready" by the Impressions. Please add to the playlist as you are inspired.

CHAPTER 2

The Inner and Outer Tug of Call and Purpose

In a real sense all life is interrelated.
All [humans] are caught in an inescapable network of mutuality,
tied in a single garment of destiny.
Whatever affects one directly, affects all indirectly.
I can never be what I ought to be until you are what you ought to be,
and you can never be what you ought to be until I am what I ought to be . . .
This is the interrelated structure of reality.
—Martin Luther King Jr.[1]

In this chapter, we pause from the CARE practices themselves to think through three concepts woven throughout this book: call, purpose, and vocation. Seeing the world as an "inescapable network of mutuality" expands our understanding of call, purpose, and vocation from the Western focus on the individual self to a focus on communities. This helps us understand how the CARE practices support people who want to follow the tug from their present reality into an imagined future in which all can flourish.

Olive Schreiner's story of a dream provides a way into understanding one's purpose within a communal story. We retell the story this way:

[1]Martin Luther King Jr., *I Have a Dream: Writings and Speeches that Changed the World,* ed. James M. Washington (San Francisco: Harper Collins, 1992), 84–85.

A woman walking out of a desert approaches the steep, high bank of a river where an old man meets her. She is seeking the land of freedom. He tells her it is before her, but she sees nothing but a fast-flowing river and a steep and slippery bank. He encourages her to look beyond her initial vision, and when she shades her eyes she can see—on the other shore—the land of freedom. She wonders how she will get to this land of trees, hills and sunshine: there is no bridge, the water is deep, the banks are steep and slippery, and no one has managed to cross the river before. She determines to go. But in a moment of hesitation, she blurts out: "For what do I go to this far land which no one has ever reached? Oh, I am alone! I am utterly alone!"

And the old man, says to her, "Silence! What do you hear?"

She listens intently and says, "I hear the sound of feet, a thousand times ten thousand and thousands of thousands, and they beat this way!"

He says, "They are the feet of those that shall follow you. Lead on! Make track to the water's edge! Where you stand now, the ground will be beaten flat by ten thousand times ten thousand feet."

The old man explains how locusts cross a stream. First one descends to the water's edge and is swept away. But as others quickly follow, their bodies pile up to build a bridge over which the rest can pass.

And she says, "Over that bridge which shall be built with our bodies, who will pass?" He says, "The entire human race." At that, the woman grasps her staff and turns down that steep and slippery bank to the river.[2]

In stories of people who create lasting change, we often hear about a gentle, persistent tug—a pulling out of deeply tangled threads from which come questions such as Why am I here? What is my life's purpose? Embedded in these questions are the concepts of call and purpose, which lie at the core of leading change.

Call and Purpose

In Schreiner's dream, the woman called by a vision is searching for freedom. The last line in the dream suggests that the woman's call—and perhaps our own—is connected to the call of a community that is searching toward a common vision. The story also suggests that pursuing a call is not without sacrifice. Schreiner's dream offers a corrective to the ways we sometimes understand purpose and call—as something heroic, solitary, glorious, and self-evident—by suggesting that sometimes we are unsure and need trusted elders to encourage us

[2]Olive Schreiner, *Dreams* (Matjesfontein, Cape Colony, South Africa, 1890). The Project Gutenberg E-Book1439. www.gutenberg.org/files/1439/1439-h/1439-h.htm#link2H_4_0005.

to follow the path we *think* we're called to pursue. We need others to help us imagine the way forward.

George Santayana suggests that "imagination needs a soil in history, tradition, or human institutions, else its random growths are not significant enough and, like trivial melodies, go immediately out of fashion."[3] In light of that, we explore the soil—the multiple conversation partners throughout history and in our current contexts—out of which we imagine call, purpose, and vocation.

Though in everyday discourse we often use the words "call" and "purpose" interchangeably, we take a moment here to think about the distinctions between them and how they relate to the concept of vocation. Here are our working definitions of call, purpose, and vocation:

> **Purpose** is the *telos* or end to which a life aims. Purpose is the answer to the question Why am I here? Toward what end is my life pointing?
>
> **Call** is the episodic, time-bound expression of purpose, as it bubbles up over the course of a lifetime.
>
> **Vocation** is the long arc of a life spent searching for purpose and acting out call, and it applies to individuals as well as collectives. While vocation often appears more clearly as one looks back, discerning one's next steps toward a life of meaning and purpose is the ongoing work of vocation.

In chapter 4, we will robustly imagine vocation through the lens of a communal worldview, but for now we want to emphasize that listening for one's call, living a life of purpose, and discerning a vocation are part of *every* human life, not a luxury reserved for the privileged few.

Our colleague Patrick Reyes illustrates this in his vocational autobiography *Nobody Cries When We Die*. Grounded in the social location of a Mexican-American growing up in Salinas, California, Reyes reflects that as a child, his first call was to stay alive. In the face of daily assaults on his humanity, he remembers the exact moment when God called him—through caring others and elders—to stay alive. Reyes describes that call to endure and persist through violence, oppression, and marginalization as a "call to life."[4]

---

[3]George Santayana, *The Wisdom of George Santayana* (Philosophical Library, 2010), loc. 41, Kindle.

[4]Patrick Reyes, *Nobody Cries When We Die: God, Community, and Surviving to Adulthood* (St. Louis: Chalice, 2016), 2.

Like Reyes, we push back against a strain of thought that has sequestered notions of call to be primarily about serving in the church. Similarly, we push back against notions of human development that assume young adults encounter a psychosocial moratorium in which to figure this out. For most people, call, purpose, and vocation are wrapped up in the everyday struggles, joys, and surprises of living.

A long lineage of conversation partners help here. Historically, the word *call* has held a specifically religious association. The origin of the word lies in its Latin root *vocatio*, which means a call or summons. In biblical understanding, God was the caller of one who responded to a life of faith. The Hebrew Bible notes that prophets were among those who spoke for and were called by God. The New Testament carries this tradition forward: Jesus calls his followers from their occupations to journey with him and become disciples.

Notably, sixteenth-century theologian Martin Luther redefined the term *call* to include not only religious but also nonreligious occupations. This thought gave believers the ability to interpret Scriptures about calling more broadly than being about just a religious profession. This broadening signals God's interest in the larger concerns of the community and endows each person with particular gifts and a purpose in service to the common welfare of society.

Whereas *call* emphasizes the One doing the calling, *purpose* describes one's unique role in life, one's role in society. But such purpose is not only about an individual's self-serving desires. Purpose is also concerned with the meaning and impact of an individual's life when viewed from a larger perspective than one's own. Derived from the Greek word *telos*, purpose points toward an end or ends. Toward what end is the woman in Schreiner's dream searching for the land of freedom? For what purpose am I called to use my gifts?

William Damon, a scholar of human development, defines purpose as an intention to accomplish something meaningful that has consequences in the world beyond oneself. Within this understanding, everyone can pursue a purpose and have an impact on their families, communities, organizations, and the broader society.[5] Damon's definition of purpose further broadens Martin Luther's, making purpose accessible to individuals who are seeking to understand their life in meaningful but nontheistic ways.

However, we lose something when we fail to wrestle with the *subject* of a call: that is to say, *who or what* is calling us. Contemporary

---

[5]William Damon, Jenni Menon, and Kendall Cotton Bronk, "The Development of Purpose During Adolescence" in *Applied Developmental Science* 7, no. 3 (2003): 119–28. Also cited here: web.stanford.edu/group/adolescence/cgi-bin/coa/sites/default/files/devofpurpose_0.pdf.

theologian David Cunningham offers an expanded definition of call that teases out this important nuance. He suggests that a call acknowledges something beyond us that calls us beyond ourselves for others.[6] While Cunningham understands that "something" to be God, his definition suggests that the caller in our lives could take on various forms—individuals, communities, social ills, or the cries of the marginalized. Not everyone is going to agree that "the caller" is God; some people will simply feel called to respond to a need in the world. Some people are less concerned with "who" does the calling; others find that naming the "who" helps sustain their activism over the long term.

Take the contemporary example of the Black Lives Matter movement. During the past few years, people have protested across the United States in response to police officers killing unarmed Black children, women, and men. These killings and the attention drawn to them by protests *call* many people to work toward solutions that will improve the distrust between the African American community and law enforcement.

Many people consider this *call* to be a religious one. Through other people and circumstances, God calls people to get involved in human affairs beyond themselves. When the U.S. Justice Department's investigation uncovered that in Ferguson and nearby municipalities intentional disproportionate ticketing and jailing of Black and poor residents was being used to help fund the city's budget, attorneys and other public servants felt called by their faith in God to engage in action to change those systems.

Recall that the Latin root of the word *religion* is *re-ligare,* meaning to reconnect. Thus, religious leaders are called to reconnect us to the profound, inescapable mutuality of life that is deep within us and between us. That which transcends and guides (if not conspires) with us to work on behalf of shaping a more hopeful future is religion—whether organized, disorganized, or organic. This future assumes that all of us, not just religious leaders, have a calling and that we are all called to participate in shaping the world beyond ourselves.

In a culture that privatizes religious experiences, it is important to acknowledge when it is God who calls us to engage passionately in civic life. This naming serves as a corrective to both privatized visions of call and to the notion that God is separate from our everyday lived realities. In this framing, God and the community in which we

---

[6]Stephen Lewis, conversation with David Cunningham, Professor of Religion, Hope College, August 28, 2019. See David Cunningham, *At This Time and In This Place: Vocation and Higher Education* (New York: Oxford, 2016)

'live, move and have our being' sustain us, giving us energy to stay in the fight longer.

One's call and one's purpose grow out of one's imagination, passions, interests, experiences, and contexts.

In these examples, call and purpose have to do with matters beyond "me, myself, and mine." They are distinct from ambition, point to that which is beyond self-serving, and are deeply connected to the well-being of the larger society.

In this book, we use *call* and *purpose* interchangeably, reflecting the ways we hear people using the terms in and out of religious communities. One's call and one's purpose grow out of one's imagination, passions, interests, experiences, and contexts: all of these are clues that help us discover how our unique gifts are pulled forth for the world over the course of our lifetimes, in ways that began long before us and continue long after us.

What about Passion?

Passion comes from the Latin word *passio,* which means to suffer or sacrifice. It's the same word used to describe the suffering or crucifixion of Jesus. Passion elicits questions like: About what do I care deeply? What am I willing to sacrifice? What are the limits of my sacrifice?

In *This Bridge Called My Back,* women of color name the multiple oppressions that stem from racism, sexism, and classism and remind us that some people have been required to sacrifice more than others.[7] While pursuing a call can sometimes be costly, it does not necessarily require one to suffer. Passion for a cause can cost too much, and it's important to steward one's own health and well-being. We all know people who have not paced themselves, who have given too much of themselves to a cause, leading to exhaustion, bitterness, or burnout. Audre Lorde writes: "Caring for myself is not self-indulgence, it is self-preservation, and that is an act of political warfare."[8] Here Lorde responds to the burden women of color often carry in service to the well-being of the larger community.

We need to remind ourselves that while Jesus's call eventually led to his crucifixion, it was an of act of the state, not his calling, that killed him. Similarly, Martin Luther King Jr. followed a call that put him at odds with the powers that be. It wasn't his calling that killed him, but rather the forces that could not abide the social change that he and other leaders of the civil rights movement embodied.

[7]Cherríe Moraga and Gloria Anzaldúa, eds., *This Bridge Called My Back: Writings by Radical Women of Color,* 4th ed. (Albany State University New York, 2015).

[8]Audre Lorde, *A Burst of Light and Other Essays* (Mineola, NY: Ixia, 2017), 130.

One way to think about the relationship between purpose, passion, and calling is to consider how these terms inform each other. Sometimes passion unveils a call. Other times a call illuminates or clarifies an already existing passion we have. Purpose focuses the energy of our passion and the trajectory of our call. Oftentimes, our passions can expand our imagination of a call. Our call can redefine our sense of purpose in life. How we explore and live out of this cyclical dynamism depends on our history, context, experiences, opportunities, and assumptions.

Elizabeth Gilbert, author of *Eat Pray Love,* wrote a lesser-known book called *Big Magic: Creative Living Beyond Fear.* In it, she cautions that overemphasizing passion can turn up the volume of anxiety. Curiosity, she says, is a good alternative. Curiosity is a

> friend that teaches us how to become ourselves. And it's a very gentle friend, and a very forgiving friend, and a very constant one. Passion is not so constant, not so gentle, not so forgiving, and sometimes not so available. And so when we live in a world that has come to fetishize passion above all, there's a great deal of pressure around that. And I think if you don't happen to have a passion that's very clear, or if you have lost your passion, or if you're in a change of life where your passions are shifting or you're not certain, and somebody says, "Well, it's easy to solve your life, just follow your passion, . . . it just makes people feel more excluded, and more exiled, and sometimes like a failure.[9]

People discover their purpose as a result of listening and responding to the needs, cries, passions, and longings in their lives. Many of us would agree with African Methodist Episcopal Bishop John Hurst Adams, who writes, "I wasn't struck by lightning, and didn't fall off no mountaintop. I think I was groomed and nurtured, and I was converted."[10] That nurturing can be subtle and can take years to manifest.

Matthew's friend Michael tells a story. While walking out of worship one day, the pastor grasped his hand a little longer than normal and said, "Have you ever thought about ministry?" In the moment, Michael brushed off the question, but it haunted him. He came back

[9]Elizabeth Gilbert, "Choosing Curiosity over Fear," interview with Krista Tippet May 24, 2018, The One Being Project, https://onbeing.org/programs/elizabeth-gilbert-choosing-curiosity-over-fear-may2018/.

[10]John Hurst Adams, "The Law Student Who Became Bishop," in William H. Myers, *The Irresistable Urge to Preach: A Collection of African American "Call" Stories* (1991; Eugene, Oregon: Wipf and Stock, 2015), 17. Also quoted in William H. Myers, *God's Yes Was Louder Than My No: Rethinking the African American Call to Ministry* (1994; Eugene, Oregon: Wipf and Stock, 2015), 35.

to it years later and heard it amplified as he answered a call to become a pastor. Similarly, Stephen remembers being gently but firmly grabbed by the elderly hand of congregation member Mother Mary Pearson, who said, "God's hands are on you. I just can't wait to see what will happen." That moment had impact: "Her hand on mine, her words, they continued to stir in me, quickening my attention, even as I continued to consider how to make a living," Stephen remembers. In both of these examples, the outcome was a call, eventually, to leading through organized religion.

But a call can just as easily be to become a teacher, a community organizer, or an artist. Dori's father, the son of Ukrainian immigrants, remembers the moment he received his call to become a social worker. At the age of fourteen, he awoke one morning in the doorway of a business near his home, having run away from a violent argument between his parents the night before. He decided then to dedicate his life to young people finding themselves in similar situations.

Call can arise from deep pain in one's life or from approaching the world with curiosity, which Gilbert describes as an impulse that "just taps you on the shoulder very lightly and invites you to turn your head a quarter of an inch and look a little closer at something that has intrigued you."[11]

The CARE practices lead people to explore, be curious, and remember that they, like the woman in Schreiner's dream, are not alone. The CARE practices invite people to tell stories about their own inner tugs and outer calls in spaces that have been explicitly created to hold them with care, within a community of other seekers.

To refresh your memory, the acronym CARE stands for:

Create Hospitable Space

Ask Self-Awakening Questions

Reflect on Meaning and Purpose

Enact the Next Most Faithful Step

By design, these practices reinforce a worldview in which people are not separate entities driven solely by selfish ambition, but rather are part of a collective energy that, when freely shared and received, becomes a powerful source of sustainable change in the world. The CARE practices help us move beyond these limitations—ones we don't even realize we're operating within—to imagine our call and purpose as part of a collective movement.

---

[11]Ibid.

Limiting Perspectives around Call and Purpose

Stephen often shares that he has never come across anyone in all of his travels who did not want their life to matter. Indeed, it is our experience that almost every conversation that dives deep—whether it be with the person at a bus stop or the DMV—often leads back to the human longing for meaning and purpose.

However, the ways in which we typically talk about call and purpose in the United States tend to be problematic. At least eight limitations, primarily derived from Western sensibilities, restrict our ability to host meaningful conversations that could help people clarify their own sense of purpose and call in life. Here we describe each type of limiting perspective and then widen the view.

Limiting perspective #1. Call is individualistic. Too often, we limit discussions about call to center around a single individual, as if that individual is disconnected from their community. For instance, we are accustomed to hearing "What is your calling or purpose in life?" This individualistic perspective is especially operative when people reserve the word *call* specifically for individuals pursuing a religious role, such as a minister, priest, or missionary.

Another way: "What is our shared purpose?" or "What are the different ways we are called to work together to accomplish the community's purpose?" This would acknowledge that people can be called to serve the common good through a variety of roles and relationships—a portfolio including paid work along with the multiple ways we play, volunteer, coach, and create with others.

Limiting perspective #2. Purpose is confined to a once-and-for all profession. Often purpose has become synonymous with a person's career or how one makes a living. "I was called to be an activist," or "My purpose in life is to become a doctor." Religious institutions consumed by their own survival often co-opt the terms to address changes in their workforce, including identifying the next generation of leaders, who they assume will fill positions left behind by retirees.

Another way: Purpose is a dynamic, unfolding journey. On one hand, purpose includes discovering professions that are aligned with one's gifts and contributions to the world. On the other, purpose speaks to so much more than one's profession or the limitations imposed by the future leadership needs of current institutions.

Limiting perspective #3. Call is too idealized and extracted from what breaks our hearts. Dominant understandings of call are often sterile and stripped of any association with real sacrifice or suffering, implying that there is little to no cost related to answering a call. During a recent conversation on vocation, a white, upper-class mainline pastor confessed that as a young person responding to a call to ministry he was always certain of a safety net provided by his family and network of support. As a result, he said he never felt risk associated with his call, except the likelihood that he would not be as highly paid as most of his friends.

Another way: Responding to a call often involves some form of risk in service to a larger community or issue. Activist Bree Newsome knew this kind of risk. She answered a public cry to remove the Confederate flag from the South Carolina statehouse, knowing that such an action might make her vulnerable to public scorn and possible violence from Confederate sympathizers. When we scan the lives of people who seem to be living purposefully, we discover frequent sacrifices they made to be faithful to their call. The old man in Schreiner's dream speaks of the bodily sacrifice that some people make on behalf of others in pursuit of their calling.

Limiting perspective #4. Purpose is about choice. Conversations around purpose tend to carry two diametrically opposed assumptions: either we have agency to choose what we want to do with our lives, or we don't have any choice in the matter. Neither point of view is completely correct.

Another way: In truth, purpose involves a paradox. There are times when purpose chooses us, life experiences prepare us, and we respond. At other times, we choose our purpose by responding to an impulse or crisis when we are not even fully aware of the ways in which that moment may spark our call to a larger purpose. Purpose is a dance, a cocreative tension in which people are active participants in a dialogical, communal process, rather than passive responders operating in isolation.

Limiting perspective #5. Call is without prejudice. We hear "You can be anything you want to be." However, preferences, biases, and prejudices determine who gets to pursue their call, who does not, and who does so in spite of opposition. Marginalized people have a long history of negotiating a tangled web of oppressive systems in order to pursue their purpose. Access to opportunities, resources, and support are available to some and limited or denied to others. Purpose is always being mediated: discerners mediate between their own courage and the anxieties that derive from their community of accountability, as well as the prejudices, assumptions, and limitations enforced by others.

Another way: We can intentionally build spaces designed to attend to the needs of marginalized communities. We can create opportunities and pathways for people within historically marginalized communities to pursue their purpose, passion and call in ways that don't require them to endure harmful and oppressive environments and people.

Limiting perspective #6. Purpose is a privilege. Some people consider finding one's purpose a privilege of the middle and upper class. After all, who has time to sit, ask questions, and reflect on the meaning of life when life is volatile and traumatic, consumed by the many demands vying for one's attention?

Another way: To working-class people and communities addressing the basic needs of survival, discerning one's sense of purpose is not a set-apart task or luxurious privilege; rather it is wrapped up in the necessities of existence. It is grounded in everyday realities, sometimes as elemental as surviving to adulthood.[12] Purpose emerges not only in the midst of an individual's human development, but also when communities call up leaders in the midst of oppression and struggle, as one conversation partner offered: "Didn't Sojourner Truth have a calling? Didn't Nat Turner pursue a purpose?"[13] Finding one's purpose is a flesh-and-blood concern for all people. The goal of finding purpose must be kept close to the ground if it is to gain any traction and hold meaningful significance in the lives of everyday people.

Purpose emerges not only in the midst of an individual's human development, but also when communities call up leaders in the midst of oppression and struggle.

Limiting perspective #7. Discussions about call often are abstract and categorized in binary, universal categories—such as community leader, parent, caregiver, and so on—as if they look the same from one community to the next, or as if the categories accurately capture the complexity, expansiveness, or hybrid ways people live out a call.

Another way: Everyone is shaped by their contexts. As a result, call grows out of and is shaped by one's history, exposure, experiences, and assumptions. As discerners pay closer attention to their world, they will become more aware of the unique dimensions that either liberate or confine their understanding of call.

Limiting perspective #8. Purpose only applies to individuals. Frederick Buechner said "the place God calls you to is the place where your deep gladness and the world's deep hunger meet."[14] Howard Thurman said, "Don't ask yourself what the world needs. Ask yourself what makes *you* come alive and then go do that. Because what the

---

[12]Reyes, *Nobody Cries When We Die.*

[13]Delano Douglas, in conversation with Dori Baker, October 3, 2017.

[14]Frederick Buechner, *Wishful Thinking: A Theological ABC* (New York: Harper & Row, 1973), 95.

world needs is people who have come alive."[15] Both of these quotations are often used to focus on individuals exclusively, as if institutions and communities do not also have purpose in service to a larger good.

Another way: Organizations have purpose too. Because the majority of the world's resources are locked up in institutions, it is crucial that we widen the focus, so that organizations also seek purpose in service to a better world. New forms of for-profit and nonprofit businesses are emerging through which people are seeking to make a positive impact on the world. Businesses, congregations, and nonprofits that take seriously Buechner's statement and Thurman's imperative are more likely to bend their will and resources toward a greater purpose.

At least one of these eight limiting perspectives tends to be present in every conversation about call and purpose, subtly reinforcing a dominant Western worldview and limiting our imaginations. Important correctives lie in non-Western worldviews and can be helpful to those who desire to lead change.

Widening the Concept of Call and Purpose

In the community where Stephen grew up in Charlotte, North Carolina, most people seemed to know, care for, and look after one another. Its members shared a communal identity, belonging, and dignity. Parents fed their kids a consistent diet of self-determination and giving back to the community. Stephen remembers feeling that he was part of a wider community that was part of him wherever he might go. He was shaped by ideas such as:

- You are the answered prayers of a community.
- You sit under trees you did not plant and drink from wells you did not dig.
- Your life is not simply your own.
- You are leading your life on behalf of and connected to a larger community, so don't embarrass your community.

These ideals were nurtured and reinforced by family, church, and the wider community that valued an interconnected sense of community among members over and against rugged individualism. His experiences and sense of community are not universal and are far from being perfect. They represent only one expression of a diverse African American community in the United States. While a communal

[15]Quoted from a personal conversation with Howard Thurman in Gil Bailie, *Violence Unveiled:Humanity at the Crossroads* (New York: Crossroad, 1994), xv emphasis added.

sensibility varies and wanes with each passing generation, some sense of it is retained by many African Americans.

African Americans possess a wide range of expressions of community. This communal sensibility is present among families, religious communities, block clubs, and neighborhoods. While there is a shadow side of any community, at its best the African American community reflects Martin Luther King Jr.'s words, with which we opened this chapter: "Whatever affects one directly, affects all indirectly. I can never be what I ought to be until you are what you ought to be, and you can never be what you ought to be until I am what I ought to be."[16] King's words acknowledge a strong sense of interdependence among African Americans as well as other people engaged in the long history of human and civil rights. This community ethic is the buoy that has kept afloat many African Americans in the treacherous sea of struggle in the United States.

This notion of community emerges from the multigenerational memory of African and African diasporic people. This memory is shaped by a long and complicated history in which African diasporic peoples have retained and recovered their ideas and practices of community, even in the face of colonization and enslavement. One of the concepts that describes this communal sensibility is *ubuntu.*

Ubuntu, as well as its derivatives *ntu* (living force or Spirit) and *buntu* (grace), are Southern African philosophical and theological concepts that are concerned with what it means to be human. M. Fulgence Nyengele says, "*Ubuntu* is the substance and core of being a person and speaks particularly about the fact that we cannot be fully formed as human beings in isolation."[17] Rather, we have to participate and be actively engaged in a community with others. It is only through our communal participation and interaction with other people that we begin to develop trust, compassion, caring, humility, kindness, and forgiveness, which are all qualities of what it means to be human and humane toward others. Similar to the fruit of the Spirit, *ubuntu* is possible because *ntu* or Spirit "orients persons toward life-giving choices, actions and behaviors."[18] Fulgence Nyengele suggests that it is only through *buntu* or grace that people are able to mature fully into what it means to be human in our interactions with others. Therefore, "*ubuntu* promotes and enhances the abundance of human life in the community and beyond. [It] embodies the spiritual quest for human dignity, integrity, social harmony, and interconnectedness; and as such

[16]King, *I Have a Dream,* 84–85.

[17]M. Fulgence Nyengele, "Cultivating *Ubuntu:* An African Postcolonial Pastoral Theological Engagement with Positive Psychology," *Journal of Pastoral Theology* 24, no. 2 (Winter 2004): 4–18.

[18]Ibid.

it is a major goal toward which communities orient their members and a communal life into which they are socialized."[19]

Ubuntu is one conceptual garden out of which a more expansive understanding of purpose and call can sprout. In chapter 4, we will return to an African-derived perspective to enrich the vocational imagination of leaders hoping to create lasting change for the good of their communities and the world.

Into and Out of the Desert

The woman in Schreiner's story makes tracks toward the river after coming out of the desert. The desert, in Christian scripture and tradition, is often a place of soul-searching. Jesus retreated to the desert to connect to his own authenticity, to confront the powers aligned against him, and to gain clarity about his own call. Similarly, the desert fathers and mothers—Christian monastics who retreated into the deserts of Egypt, Syria, and Palestine during the first four centuries after the execution of Jesus—retreated to the wilderness to seek another way of being.

In a recent conversation with René August, a priest in the Anglican Church of Southern Africa and veteran South African anti-apartheid activist, we explored the image of the desert as a place people go to seek enlightenment or spiritual renewal. She helped us imagine that the desert is not simply a place of isolation and solitude: it is also a place of violence and danger. Outside the protection of the city walls lie bandits, robbers, and wild animals, as well as the threats of starvation and thirst.

When asked: Where are the deserts in our lives that call us?, August answered: The inner cities of South Africa are a kind of desert. People are called to go to these particular places—not to seek solitude but to be in solidarity, to create better oases in the places where people are suffering.[20]

Asking questions of Scripture in this way, August reminded us of the many activists, pastors, and scholars we know who are called to the heart of the city. For some of them, the call emerges from the city in which they live; for others, the call is more like Paul's Macedonian experience related in Acts 16—a call to a different city to which they have relationships of accountability and connection. Like the desert fathers and mothers, contemporary leaders answer inner and outer tugs to go to hard places in community, where they become clear about who they are and what they're called to do and be.

---

[19]Ibid.

[20]Stephen Lewis, conversation with René August, October 17, 2017.

The desert is a metaphor for the places into which we are called, places perhaps of solitude, suffering, or solidarity, where we can listen deeply to our inner voices and keep moving toward our emerging future. The woman in Schreiner's dream is coming out of the desert, following an inner and outer tug to create a future of freedom for herself and all of humanity. With the help of her elder, she moves forward, in the direction of her calling.

Awakening Purpose

Cultivating an imagination of the world as an "inescapable web of mutuality," especially through the lens of Schreiner's story, wildly expands our understanding of call and purpose, removing the limitations we've been considering to reveal a rich and nourishing landscape.

When focused only on the material realities of what she is trying to do, the woman in the dream sees only the harsh obstacles. Like contemporary activists, she is in danger of being worn down. She sees only the slippery shores and the raging river before her. But the view changes when she enters into dialogue with her wise elder. He is the whisper in her ear, the tap on her shoulder, asking her to consider realities beyond her view. He greets her at the edge of the desert. In community, she awakens to a new vista and is able to see the distant shores of a better future.

In dialogue with our own elders—our ancestors, our neighbors, the traditions that gave us birth—we access deeper sources of knowing. This communal approach to call and purpose creates an interior architecture that can sustain the day-to-day grit of our struggle for a new and hopeful future.

In dialogue with our own elders – our ancestors, our neighbors, the traditions that gave us birth—we access deeper sources of knowing.

Such a worldview gathers together the interdependencies of self, community, and God. This often invisible interdependence is what sustains our visible, material work in the world: it is the inner and outer tug of call and purpose. This unseen relatedness between the self, the community, and God provides the necessary scaffolding to manifest the work for which we are called. This fundamental truth heightens the importance of a leaders' attention to their inner life, which we begin to explore in the next chapter.

What would it mean for us to support leaders who've been called to the most vulnerable places of our contemporary reality to seek the land of freedom? It would mean supporting people's awakening. It would mean calling on the wise sages. It would mean standing in the liminal spaces between the desert and the river's edge, helping others see the future while also hearing echoes of the past.

With this worldview and approach to call and purpose in mind, we turn now to the second set of practices in CARE, that is, ***A: Asking self-awakening questions.*** By design, such practices reinforce a vision of radical interconnectedness as crucial to our ability to live into purpose and cocreate a desirable future.

Questions for Reflection

For the individual learner/leader seeking meaning and purpose:

1. This chapter names eight limiting perspectives on call and purpose, then turns these perspectives around to look at them another way. Which of these limiting perspectives most influenced you? What messages might be limiting your imagination about your purpose? Of which of these limiting perspectives might you choose to let go?

2. A recurring theme you will encounter in this book is the importance of cultivating access to your deeper sources of knowing. These may come from your ancestors, your family, your neighbors, the traditions that gave you birth, or the intentional communities where you find shared values. What practices do you have for remembering, reconnecting, and replenishing from your own deep wells?

3. What was one challenging idea you encountered here? What made it so?

4. What was one of the most powerful or helpful ideas you encountered here? What made it so?

5. What is one thing you take with you from this chapter that can help you envision your call, your purpose, or your vocation as part of a larger web of mutuality?

For the guide/facilitator helping others find meaning and purpose:

1. Of the eight limiting perspectives on call and purpose named in this chapter, which hold most influence in the culture/

context in which you lead? Which are the most damaging or least helpful to the people you accompany?

2. The authors ask, "What would it mean to support leaders who've been called to the most vulnerable places of our contemporary reality to seek the land of freedom? It would mean ... standing in the liminal spaces between the desert and the river's edge, helping others see the future while also hearing echoes of the past." How have you stood in those spaces? What stories, language, or imagery from your context illuminates the communal tug of purpose and call?
3. What was one challenging idea you encountered here? What made it so?
4. What was one of the most powerful or helpful ideas you encountered here? What made it so?
5. What is one thing you take with you from this chapter that might help you make visible the "unseen relatedness" between the self, the community, and the larger web of mutuality?

For those leading organizational change:

1. Can Olive Schreiner's dream be helpful as a metaphor for organizational change? Does the history of your organization bear witness to those who have gone before, the ones who laid the groundwork for the positive change you seek today?
2. The clearer the organization gets about its own purpose, the more its people can get clear about their own alignment with the organization. When an individual discovers their purpose to be at odds with the purpose of the organization, how might you express deep gratitude and help that person to pursue places where their soul and role can be more aligned? To what degree can you help the organization remain responsive to the evolving purpose of its people?
3. What was one challenging idea you encountered here? What made it so?
4. What was one of the most powerful or helpful ideas you encountered here? What made it so?
5. What is one thing you take with you from this chapter that might help you tend to the interconnectedness of your individual and collective purpose?

For all:

1. Review *Another Way Manifesto.* Which sentences stand out to you after reading this chapter?
2. We are building an interactive playlist to accompany each chapter. You can find it on Spotify at **Another Way: The Book.** The songs we recommend for this chapter are "River" by Ibeyi and "Painted on Canvas" by Gregory Porter. Please add to the playlist as you are inspired.

CHAPTER 3

A: Asking Self-Awakening Questions

Whom can I ask what I came to make happen
in the world?

—Pablo Neruda, The Book of Questions

"But who do you say that I am?"
Matthew: 16:15

When someone asks about what you really love, what you care about, and what inspires you to create change, they help awaken you to your own deep center. From there, you gain access to the passions that can help you create change. In the last chapter, we saw the ways in which a hyper-individualized worldview co-opts the very words we use to talk about meaning and purpose. Here, we practice putting flesh on a communal worldview by engaging the second practice in CARE **A: Asking Self-Awakening Questions.** This is a deeply dialogical process by which to discern ways of living, acting, and leading change on purpose.

Living and Leading Vignette

Dori writes:

Sitting in a corner of a large paneled room at Harvard Divinity School, I fight the urge to take off my black suede boots.

I am preparing to facilitate a conversation among eighty spiritual innovators, most of whom are Millennials successfully creating community around a highly particular need they recognize among their "spiritual but not religious" peers. Among these young leaders are people who identify as Buddhist, Christian, Jewish, atheist, agnostic, secular humanist, or as holding multiple religious belongings.[1] We are midway through a three-day gathering. We've been getting to know one another and our contexts, and now is the time to begin listening more deeply to what may be emerging among us.

Finally, I listen to what my intuition is saying. "Dori, take off your boots. You are about to be standing on holy ground." The boots stay off as I move to the center of the circle. In my blue socks, connected and grounded, I remind the room of the space we've been creating. I gesture toward the Covenants of Presence from the day before. I invite everyone into a few moments of silence and a few deep, refreshing breaths. I begin to ask a series of questions about what may be emerging among us, questions that create an air of expectation:

What if there is something that wants to emerge in our gathering that can only happen if we pause, sit still for a moment, and invite one another into a time of questions?

What if there is no expert in the room? What if the room itself is the expert? What if there is something that wants to emerge in our gathering that can only happen if we pause, sit still for a moment, and invite one another into a time of questions?

Then, I slowly read these words, penned by a Quaker named Douglas V. Steere in post–World War II England:

> Have you ever sat with a friend when in the course of an easy and pleasant conversation the talk took a new turn and you both listened avidly to the other and to something that was emerging in your visit? You found yourselves saying things that astonished you and finally you stopped talking and there was an immense naturalness about the long silent pause that followed. In the silent interval you were possessed by what you had discovered together. If that has happened to you, you know that when you come up out of such an experience, there is a memory of rapture and a feeling in the heart of having touched holy ground. [2]

---

[1]Casper ter Kuile and Angie Thurston convened this gathering as a follow-up to their report *How We Gather* and published their findings as *December Gathering: Notes from the Field,* which can be found at www.howwegather.org/reports.

[2]Douglas V. Steere, *Gleanings: A Random Harvest* (Nashville: Upper Room, 1986), 83.

Steere vividly captures a memory most of us can summon. He goes on to say: "To 'listen" another's soul into a condition of disclosure and discovery may be almost the greatest service that any human being ever performs for another."[3]

Over the next few minutes, I introduce a practice, animated by questions that invite people to imagine that moments like the one Steere describes don't only happen by accident. We don't have to wait for "holy listening" to arise spontaneously. We can actually create the conditions that welcome it. The thirty-six hours that this group has spent together created exactly those conditions. Now, a few powerful questions will invite us to discover what wants to awaken among us.

I give the following instructions[4]:

Choose a partner and decide which of you will go first. Together we'll have a few minutes of silence to ponder a question. Then one of you will take a deep breath and begin to speak. You may talk about whatever arises for you in response to the question. Trust what comes up. There's no need to censor yourself or try to create a neatly packaged story—just go where your heart leads you. Your partner will abide by our covenants, will remember that your story belongs to you, and will hold it in confidence.

Partners, you will only listen. You are a calm attentive presence, listening avidly to what is emerging. Only listen, using body language if necessary, but try not to speak.

After a few minutes I will ring a bell to stop you. You may not be ready to stop talking or to stop listening. More words, ideas, and questions might be bubbling up. That's okay. You can revisit them later. For now, we'll trade places and the listener will become the speaker. Got it?

The question I invite you to answer is this: In the last day and a half, when did you feel most alive?

Sit in silence with this question and see what it awakens for you.

After a few minutes, I break the silence to invite these young leaders to begin sharing and listening. A buzz fills the room. After a few minutes, I ring a bell. The buzz diminishes. Speakers become listeners, and the cycle begins again.

At the end of these six minutes, I know the urge to take off my boots was well heeded. I am standing on holy ground. I sense that the room has dropped into a place of presence, an alive awareness that almost always happens when people are invited into this kind of

---

[3]Ibid.

[4]A guide to leading this exercise can be found at www.leadanotherway.com

attentive collective inquiry. That feeling is confirmed when, after a few moments of journaling come to an end, the microphone passes from one person to another: the "room itself" begins to voice the wisdom that our guiding questions stoked. They say the following:

- I feel a quality in the room right now . . . a generosity of spirit.
- I now know that we can do things we didn't know we could do.
- I feel a siblinghood of risk-takers.
- We are pulling out an authenticity from within.

Mindful Moves of Asking Self-Awakening Questions

Each one of us carries around a universe of life experiences that shape the way we act, feel, learn, and lead. Most of the time those memories operate implicitly, working under the surface to direct our energies, both positively and negatively. How do we uncover the hidden stories, memories, and knowings that drive us? How do we bring them to mindful awareness, so we can choose what will inspire and sustain us as we lead change?

When we create environments for exploration, we offer each other opportunities to search the deeper meaning of our lives and hear one another into fuller expression of what we already know, or into new knowings that are emerging from our ongoing experience. This is a form of tending to the inner life—that unseen, intangible place from which call awakens.

The story at the beginning of this chapter illuminates five mindful moves that invite people to enter creatively into **A: Asking self-awakening questions.** These moves are:

- **Creating Space** by revisiting the first of the CARE practices, remembering that we gather with intentionality to invite silence, sit face-to-face, tell stories and slow down, reintroducing the Covenants of Presence if time has passed since their introduction.
- **Employing a muse** to invite the simultaneously playful and serious expectation that we are connected to deep sources of wisdom and to something larger than ourselves, something to which our authentic selves desire to awaken.
- **Discerning questions that are truly self-awakening,** questions that move us to a place of inner exploration, discovery, and creativity that we cannot access alone.

- **Letting the questions breathe** in a way that holds mystery and defies tidying up lingering uncertainties.
- **Catching what surfaces** through journaling, holy listening, harvesting, or a dialogue-based process such as World Café or Open Space Technology.

In the vignette above, self-awakening questions moved a large group to tap into their collective wisdom. Self-awakening questions were an intentional part of the design of the gathering. Asking self-awakening questions can also become habit-forming: once in our tool kit, we find ourselves turning to them in one-on-one conversations and informal circles. We begin to lead with listening, waiting, and wondering—rather than knowing, telling, and displaying our own expertise. As a result, the public spaces we create, such as workshops or classrooms, become spaces that invite soul expression and expansion. Let's look at each of these moves.

Revisiting C: Creating hospitable space

Our default patterns of relating to one another are strong. Because creating hospitable space and sharing attuned presence with one another is countercultural, the first mindful move is to repeat non-anxiously the invitation for our whole selves to be present, physically and relationally.

We remind people to slow down, breathe, and become fully present to themselves and the people in the room. If we constructed a centering table on the first day, we now light the candle on it. We might add to the items on the table by bringing in a piece of nature that reflects our surroundings: a seashell, an azalea flower, or a rock that reminds us of the geographical space we occupy and the physical space we are cocreating each time we reconnect. We also add items of significance—symbols of our places of origin, our own ancestral lineage, or a commitment made during our time together.

The Covenants of Presence introduced in chapter 1 create relational space, a distinct way of showing up for one another as human beings. We sometimes embody this reality by enacting the aforementioned Zulu greeting "*Sawa Bona*" (I see you) and the response, "*Sikhona*" (I am here). Recall that this greeting derives from the understanding that: "Until you see me I do not exist. You see me into existence." We enact this ritual, actually walking around the room from person to person, taking turns seeing and being seen. This practice embodies a communal worldview, literally seeing each other as equals and acting out the decision to welcome our collective wisdom.

Employing a muse

As preparation for self-awakening questions, we might introduce a song, an interactive group exercise, or a poem that, like a muse, opens us to images, metaphors, or other artful expressions of soulful existence.

In the vignette at the beginning of this chapter, Dori asked: "What if there is no expert in the room? What if the room itself is the expert? What if there is something that wants to emerge in our gathering that can only happen if we pause, sit still for a moment, and invite one another into a time of questions?" She then evoked the memory of "holy ground" through the brief reading from Douglas V. Steere.

FTE regularly gathers diverse young adults from across North America to help them discern their gifts, identities, and purpose as potential leaders of faith communities. To invite these people into a time set aside to discern next steps such as mentoring, interning, or pursuing theological education, we use an audio recording of Howard Thurman to invite self-awakening questions. Slowly, Thurman speaks these words, which we invite you likewise to read slowly:

> There is in every person something that waits and listens for the sound of the genuine . . . There is in you something that waits and listens for the sound of the genuine in yourself. Nobody like you has ever been born and no one like you will ever be born again—you are the only one....
>
> If you cannot hear it, you will never find whatever it is for which you are searching and if you hear it and then do not follow it, it was better that you had never been born. You are the only you that has ever lived; your idiom is the only idiom of its kind in all the existences, and if you cannot hear the sound of the genuine in you, you will all of your life spend your days on the ends of strings that somebody else pulls....
>
> The sound of the genuine is flowing through you. Don't be deceived and thrown off by all the noises that are part even of your dreams and your ambitions that you don't hear the sound of the genuine in you. Because that is the only true guide you will ever have and if you don't have that you don't have a thing....Cultivate the discipline of listening to the sound of the genuine in yourself. [5]

---

[5]Howard Thurman, "The Sound of the Genuine" (Baccalaureate address, Spelman College, Atlanta, May 4, 1980). Speech edited by Jo Moore Stewart for *The Spelman Messenger* 96, no. 4 (Summer 1980): 2–3. The entire speech can be accessed here: www.uindy.edu/eip/files/reflection4.pdf.

In the pause that follows, we pose a question in the form of a story prompt: "Tell a story about a time when you heard the sound of the genuine in you." Eventually, the room fills with the hum of voices, as people turn to one another, share their stories, and begin practicing the art of listening to what surfaces from a self-awakening question.

Parker Palmer writes about introducing a poem or reading as a "third thing," which invites both *intentionality* and *indirection*, focusing intentionally on an important topic, but approaching it indirectly, in a way that invites "creative meandering" rather than a "forced march."[6] Palmer writes:

> I call these embodiments "third things" because they represent neither the voice of the facilitator nor the voice of a participant. They have voices of their own, voices that tell the truth about a topic but, in the manner of metaphors, tell it on the slant. Mediated by a third thing, truth can emerge from, and return to, our awareness at whatever pace and depth we are able to handle—sometimes inwardly in silence, sometimes aloud in community—giving the shy soul the protective cover it needs.[7]

Thurman's writings are a type of third thing and part of an immense treasure chest of resources that help awaken our deepest selves. Using a digital audio recording of his voice—rather than simply reading the piece—connects listeners to Thurman's embodied presence, which is so much a factor in the way we hear, trust, and respond.

Thurman's "Sound of the Genuine" works well for FTE because we are often introducing newcomers to the practice of **Self-Awakening Questions** for the specific purpose of helping them name their own callings or nurture the callings of others. Thurman was a Christian mystic, as well as an activist, scholar, and mentor to many leaders in the civil rights movement. His prose has a rhythm and deep imagery that approaches the poetic. Although the reading is heard together by a group, it may evoke something different in each person. It is a practice of being alone together, which reinforces a communal worldview and evokes a willingness to go inward.

In choosing a muse to invite the practice of **asking self-awakening questions**, sift carefully through your own communal treasure chest. What artists, poets, mystics, pieces of music, or image-rich meditations lie close to the heart of the institution, group, or cause around which you are leading change? Drawing deeply from our own wells holds the potential for individuals and communities to descend into their own

---

[6]Parker Palmer, *A Hidden Wholeness: The Journey Toward and Undivided Life* (San Francisco: Jossey Bass, 2004), 92.

[7]Ibid., 93.

memories and weave more thickly the communal fabric that ties them together. Using familiar metaphors in unfamiliar spaces can liberate new energies or allow a new story to emerge.

For example, in preparing to use the CARE practices to train a national gathering of United Methodist clergy mentors, one of our collaborators suggested we use a famous passage written by John Wesley, the founder of American Methodism. We listened together to the diary entry known as the Aldersgate experience, in which Wesley reflects upon a time when his doubt receded and he felt his "heart strangely warmed." This reading, known by heart by many in and out of the Wesleyan tradition, can be heard anew by listeners as they invite deep wondering about times in their own lives when they experienced doubt. Hearing this familiar reading communally allowed questions to bubble up about current connections to Spirit and living those connections through vocational expressions such as mentor, pastor, activist, and spiritual guide. Drawing from the deep well of United Methodism evoked what participants already "knew by heart," while inviting new possibilities to emerge.

Discerning truly self-awakening questions

We developed the concept of self-awakening questions to help people excavate, uncover, and reveal what they know to be true within themselves in service to vocational discernment and action.

They have a counterpart in the discipline of "open and honest questions" used by the Center of Courage & Renewal (CCR). In CCR's work, open and honest questions are building blocks toward a Clearness Committee, a spiritual practice borrowed from the Society of Friends, commonly known as Quakers. The Clearness Committee is central to The Circle of Trust approach and helps a person become clear about the truth of their lives.[8]

Within CCR's work, open and honest questions are a disciplined invitation to take an inward journey stimulated by a particular kind of inquiry. The *open* aspect suggests that the one who asks the question does not know the answer to the question. What do you care most about? When have you felt most alive? What stokes your anger? The *honest* element requires the one who asks the question to offer the question as a gift—no strings or expectations attached. The hearer uses the question to explore their own truth, not to satisfy the information needs of the one who asks. It is not a leading question used to manipulate a person into arriving at an answer. It trusts another's ability to reckon with their inner life. It does not assume another knows what they need.

---

[8]http://www.couragerenewal.org/approach/.

Self-awakening questions build on the trademarks of open and honest questions and sometimes break its rules. Self-awakening questions may invite investigation of one's story, context, belief, and worldviews. They may have no agenda, such as, What may be possible for you now that was not possible before?

But they may also be purposefully jarring, aimed at uncovering discomfort, such as, the famous inquiry of W.E.B. DuBois, "How does it feel to be a problem?"[9] Gregory Ellison uses this question in *Fearless Dialogues,* leading participants through what he calls "the Five Hardest Questions in Life" they are:

Who am I?

Why am I here?

What is my gift?

How does it feel to be a problem?

What must I do to die a good death?[10]

Self-awakening questions are goal oriented, in service to the larger process of communal discernment, which will lead to individual and collective action. They are a learned skill that can become an ongoing way of being in the world.

Asking self-awakening questions is an art in which leaders discern the most central ideas to which a group or community may need to attend at a particular moment in light of its covenants, context, and collective aims. Ultimately, it is important to remember that this practice does not stand alone. It takes place in space that has been consciously created for heightened interpersonal engagement. It then feeds and informs the practices of reflection, strategic design, and action through which communities enact their next most faithful steps, which we will describe as the last two moves of the CARE approach.

Letting Questions Breathe

In the story that began this chapter, Dori asked: When in the last day and a half have you felt most alive? She then gave participants a few long moments to think about their answers.

Other examples of self-awakening prompts include:

- Tell a story about why you do what you do, why you love what you love.

[9]W. E. B. Du Bois, *The Souls of Black Folk* (1903; CreateSpace, 2013), Kindle ed., loc. 53.

[10]Gregory C. Ellison II, *Fearless Dialogues: A New Movement for Justice* (Louisville: Westminster John Knox Press, 2017), 112–15.

- Tell a story about a time when someone noticed your gifts and you knew it.
- Tell a story about a time when you *could not* hear the sound of the genuine in you.

Story prompts that surface self-awakening questions can help a facilitator move people into small group reflection in ways that begin with their own experience, not a dogma, creed, or belief. This can helpfully disarm both speakers and listeners, allowing people from different backgrounds or life perspectives to connect on a human level, even if they hold diametrically opposed views. Asking someone to "tell a story about a time" almost always causes people to look inward in a way that might turn up a surprise, rather than a rote answer.

We prime the imagination of participants, then trust them to discern self-awakening questions, reminding them that not all questions that pop into our heads will lead others to a place of self-discovery. Indeed, many questions lead only toward our own agendas or our own attempts to fix perceived problems. Because asking questions that create space for self-awakening is a mindful discipline at which people can improve with practice, we offer a few hints:

- Ask questions that are thought-provoking, stimulate deeper self-reflection, touch a deeper meaning, or generate surprise, opening us to worlds within ourselves that we may have forgotten about or didn't know existed.
- Explore questions that invite metaphor and play with image, allowing the speaker to wonder indirectly—questions such as: What color is that story for you?
- Ask questions that help participants explore both inner and outer realities, including values, passions, and longings.
- Ask questions that help the speaker identify themes, patterns, or vivid images that continue to reverberate.
- Ask questions that help the speaker remember risks, challenges, choices, or outcomes in their story.
- Pace questions slowly. Allow silence between the answer and the next question. Time between words can allow for deeper reflection.
- Slow down, pause, and then trust your intuition in asking questions. If you're not sure that it's a self-awakening question, sit with it for a while and wait for more clarity.

- As you listen deeply to the speaker, allow your questions to emerge from a place where your head and heart are open to the presence of something larger than your ego, what some would call Spirit or Source.[11]

Capturing what surfaces

When you ask a self-awakening question, you also take on the responsibility of listening to what surfaces. A listener who is learning to ask self-awakening questions has already made an important turn: this conversation is not about answers, and it's not about proving you are a good listener! Listeners provide the gift of creating the conditions in which the speaker can hear an inner voice, perhaps one that has been long silenced by outer authorities or put on a shelf by life's exigencies. In the mystery of this dialogical exchange, the listener might also be awakened, and often is. Yet the goal remains a disciplined focus on the speaker.

A good way to describe the mystery at work in the dialogue is through a story that returns us to Howard Thurman. Walter Earl Fluker, in the preface to his edited volume of Thurman's private papers, tells a story about their first meeting. Fluker writes:

> Garrett Evangelical Theological Seminary's Church and Black Experience program held a consultation with Thurman in October 1978. I was selected as the student chaperone to pick Thurman up at the airport and deliver him to his hotel. Instead, we spent the entire afternoon discussing my plans for the future. Such was the generous and gracious spirit of this unusual man. He asked again and again in probing interrogatives that I later discovered were his hallmark, "Who are you, really? What are you trying to do with your life?" I answered matter-of-factly, in the forgivable arrogance of naïveté, "I want to change the church into a moral institution for the transformation of society." His silences were gentle and mocking—and then he would ask again, "But who are you? Who do you seek to become?"[12]

Fluker appreciated being the recipient of these careful questions. He also acknowledged that Thurman seemed to awaken in the exchange. He reflected that

[11]For an optional version of this, see Caryl Hurtig Casbon's "Framing Open Questions" at www.minnesotarising.org/2011/08/art-of-hosting-framing-open-questions.html.

[12]Walter Fluker, preface to *The Papers of Howard Washington Thurman*, (Columbia: University of South Carolina, 2012), 1:xiv–xv.

> Thurman realized that the sum of all the details of one's context, work, relationships, thoughts and intentions neither defines an individual nor exhausts one's meaning. Something always remains beyond apprehension and comprehension . . . Something of each person is always elusive—always refusing to be a subject named, defined and analyzed.[13]

Self-awakening questions are in many ways an expression of love and call to mind Rainer Maria Rilke's wisdom: "Be patient toward all that is unsolved in your heart and try to love the questions themselves . . . Live the questions now. Perhaps you will then gradually, without noticing it, live along some distant day into the answer."[14]

Listening with respect and reverence to another can create the conditions for the inner voice to surface. The self-discovery and disclosure that bubbles up often causes an aha moment and perhaps a lingering attentiveness to work that will unfold in the days, weeks, or months ahead. Nelle Morton, a feminist Christian educator who worked for racial justice in the 1930s, describes this kind of listening. She witnessed it in liminal moments occurring when women gathered to accompany one another "into the abyss . . . where sound is born."[15] She writes of a "depth hearing that takes place before speaking—a hearing that is more than acute listening. A hearing that is a direct transitive verb that evokes speech—new speech that has never been spoken before. The woman . . . had indeed been heard to her own speech."[16]

This kind of listening is very different from normal, everyday listening. So, in addition to priming the pump of self-awakening questions, we describe the kind of listening we hope to invoke. In holy/wholly listening, the listener achieves a disciplined posture of care, hospitality, relaxed awareness, and attentiveness that is both spiritual and physical. The listener is *not* thinking about how to respond or connect to the speaker. Rather, the listener is fully present. Even body language conveys this attentiveness. This practice allows the speaker to feel accompanied by a calm, non-anxious presence.

Poet John O'Donohue evokes the memory of this kind of conversation:

> [W]hen is the last time that you had a great conversation, a conversation which wasn't just two intersecting monologues,

[13]Ibid.

[14]Rainer Maria Rilke, *Letters to a Young Poet*, trans. Stephen Mitchell (New York: Random House, 1984), 34–35.

[15]Morton quoted in Christian Scharen, *Fieldwork in Theology: Exploring the Social Context of God's Work in the World* (Grand Rapids, Mich.; Baker Academic, 2015), 47.

[16]Nelle Morton, *The Journey is Home* (Boston: Beacon Press, 1985), 205.

> which is what passes for conversation a lot in this culture. But when had you last a great conversation, in which you overheard yourself saying things that you never knew you knew? That you heard yourself receiving from somebody words that absolutely found places within you that you thought you had lost and a sense of an event of a conversation that brought the two of you on to a different plane . . . a conversation that continued to sing in your mind for weeks afterwards. As we would say at home, they are food and drink for the soul.[17]

And so we learn to ask self-awakening questions. We listen spaciously, allowing time for the questions to breathe. We hold the insights, stories, and silences that emerge. This constitutes the mindful creation of time and space in which leaders receive the nourishment they need to continue acting out their call, purpose, and vocation.

Watching It Again: CARE at Work

The practice of asking and receiving self-awakening questions gives one access to one another in pursuit of a life of integrity. It reminds us that we are not alone, that we can receive support during times of risk and find sojourners on similar paths, and that all of this is part of pursuing one's vocation. People who explore these types of questions discover a sacred invitation to listen for the deep yearnings that move us and make us come alive, yearnings that may never find expression if not mindfully invited.

But there is also an underside to excavations. Digging into our past—whether personal or communal—can dredge up painful memories. This was the case for Romal Tune. Several years ago, he came to an event we designed to help people attend to vocational unfolding. Tune reflected on how his experience of self-awakening questions opened him to a next step in his vocational journey. One of the questions that Tune was prompted to explore was: Why do you do what you do, love what you love, or care about what you care about? He later wrote this in a blog for the *Huffington Post*:

> I have a passion for reaching out to poor and at-risk youth, which seems simple enough, but this time I was asked to explain why through my personal story. After reflecting on my life's experiences, I told a story about when I was eleven years old. It was a cold, foggy morning in San Francisco. My mother had given me bus fare to get to school and home at

[17]John O'Donahue, "The Inner Landscape of Beauty," interview with Krista Tippet, August 6, 2015, The One Being Project, https://onbeing.org/programs/john-odonohue-the-inner-landscape-of-beauty-aug2017/.

> the end of the day. When she handed me my bus fare, she looked at me with sadness in her eyes and said, "We don't have enough for you to eat lunch today." I got to school and went through the routine of the day, attending classes but somewhat distracted by the fact that I was getting hungry and concerned that if other kids saw that I didn't get in the lunch line, they would know I didn't have money and make fun of me. When lunchtime came I had to make a hard choice: use my bus fare to buy lunch, eat, and avoid potential embarrassment, but then have to figure out how I was going to get home, or go hungry but get home without a problem. That day I chose lunch. At the end of the school day I walked as far as I could so that the other kids could not see me. Then I started looking for strangers to ask for bus fare. There were those who cut their eyes at me as if I should be ashamed of myself for asking. There were those who avoided making eye contact with me so that I wouldn't ask. But then there was that one woman who looked me in the eyes, smiled and said, "What do you need to get home?" It was a dollar and twenty-five cents.[18]

Tune describes that, in telling this story from his childhood, he recognized an encounter with God and an experience of grace. The reflections, group discussions, and questions from that day gave Tune the inspiration and courage to start writing the plan for a new organization to engage churches across the country in improving the academic outcome of students living in poverty and attending high-need schools.

Self-awakening questions provide an opportunity to listen intently to one another and to hear one another into fuller expression.

Self-awakening questions provide an opportunity to listen intently to one another and to hear one another into fuller expression. This kind of listening is an act of courage—from the Latin root word *cor*, which means heart. When we listen courageously, we listen with our hearts to the hearts of others.

Self-awakening questions invited Tune, who had enjoyed financial success as an adult, to remember the feeling of hunger in his stomach and the very real fear of not knowing where his next meal was coming from. That pause, while tinged with painful memories, also held the

[18]Romal J. Tune. "What Are You Called to Do? Finding Spiritual Purpose in the Field," *The Blog, HuffPost,* September 24, 2011, https://www.huffingtonpost.com/rev-romal-j-tune/finding-purpose-in-the-fi_b_945786.html. For more of Romal's story, see Romal J. Tune, *God's Graffiti: Inspiring Stories for Teens,* (King of Prussia, PA: Judson Press, 2013).

power of redirecting Tune's energies, not to a new place but back to a place from which his purpose had always been emerging.

This dynamic of retrieval from the past finds expression in the image and proverb of *sankofa*, an *Akan* term meaning "Go back and fetch it." *Sankofa* is imaged as a bird moving forward, with its head turned backward and an egg in its mouth. The egg represents the treasured knowledge of the past, available as a seed of wisdom for the present. The egg also represents the generations to come who may benefit from that wisdom. The symbol is often accompanied by a proverb translated: "It is not wrong to go back and get that which we have forgotten."

Stephen tells of his elders, some of whom do not like to talk about a portion of their stories because it is painful to remember. These stories can trigger trauma all over again, so leaders should take care not to push people further than they are willing to go.

The CARE practices do not provide a panacea against pain, suffering, or trauma. However, they do carve out a space for people in communities to gain access to the wisdom of those experiences for the sake of the future. Learning to ask self-awakening questions and then stay present for what emerges is a communal task that midwives vocation, purpose, and call.

Awakening Together

Oftentimes, we are awakened not only to our own personal yearnings but also to the ways in which those yearnings are called forth by what is happening in the world. We have been present when self-awakening questions led young adults who grew up in privileged, white, middle- and upper-class settings to name the wealth they've inherited as implicating them and creating a sense of responsibility that motivates their actions in the world. We've seen men awaken to the realities of misogyny and come to embody alternative ways of being male in America. We've seen people, already aware of systemic racism, become more deeply aware of the ways privilege and power keep them from working toward racial justices.

The domain of self-awakening questions is not limited to one's interior life. It is also about questions that awaken us to our public life and civic participation in shaping the world we long to see. The interior life is not separate from the outer life; they are intricately linked. This parallel is illuminated in the example of the Black Lives Matters movement.

#Staywoke became the mantra of that movement, which sprung up in the aftermath of the killings of Trayvon Martin, Michael Brown, and others. This mantra literally enacts *Sankofa*—it goes back and fetches the imagery of Martin Luther King's 1968 speech "Remaining Awake Through a Great Revolution."

We move from self-awakening to staying *woke*. The first is personal, internal, and grows out of a theology of incarnation, in which people, made in the image of God, embody holiness in glimpses. The second is a political and public awareness, growing out of a theology of interdependence that sees us as intricately connected to each other and living into a vocation that precedes our arrival on earth and continues after our departure.

In the next chapter, we turn back to the notions of call and purpose. Through dreams and stories from Stephen's life, we explore a deeply communal approach to vocation that understands each individual life's vocation emerging in the midst of a community's life that can span multiple generations. The ability to ask, hold, and respond to self-awakening questions befriends us in this move.

Questions for Reflection

For the individual learner/leader seeking meaning and purpose:

1. Can you recall a time when you could hear the "sound of your genuine"? Can you recall a time when you *could not* hear "the sound of your genuine"? What would you need to live more consistently in connection with the sound of your genuine? How might you go about finding what you need?

2. Self-awakening questions can be intentional parts of learning environments, but they can also become an intentional part of everyday conversations with friends, coworkers, and family members. The authors state, "When you ask a self-awakening question, you also take on the responsibility of listening to what surfaces." Where and with whom might you begin asking self-awakening questions? How might the questioning/listening loop change a relationship, strengthen a community, or lead you into an action?

3. What was one challenging idea you encountered here? What made it so?

4. What was a powerful or helpful idea you encountered here? What made it so?

5. What is one thing you take with you from this chapter that might help you listen more carefully to what is awakening within yourself or among those you lead?

For the guide/facilitator helping others find meaning and purpose:

1. The authors state, "The domain of self-awakening questions is not limited to one's interior life. It is also about questions that awaken us to our public life and civic participation in shaping the world we all long to see. The interior life is not separate from the outer life; they are intricately linked." How would these statements land with the people you accompany? Does your culture/context acknowledge the permeability between the inner and outer life? If so, what ideas or images speak to that permeability? If not, how might you introduce this concept in ways that are specific to your culture/context?
2. You may more often accompany people who are younger than you, the same age as you, or significantly older than you. In any case it is important to stay connected to "the sound of your own genuine." What work have you done in the past two weeks that flowed out of the sound of your genuine? If you can't answer this question, what might you do today to begin moving in the direction of alignment with your inner wisdom?
3. The authors describe using a famous passage from John Wesley to evoke conversation about vocation when working with United Methodists, who come from the Wesleyan tradition. What stories and images does your tradition know by heart that might be a helpful muse for asking self-awakening questions?
4. What was a challenging idea you encountered here? What made it so?
5. What was a powerful or helpful idea you encountered here? What made it so?
6. What is one thing you take with you from this chapter that might help you listen more carefully to what is awakening within yourself or among those you lead?

For those leading organizational change:

1. How might the practice of self-awakening questions help you clarify strategic directions, surface the core values that shape your organizational culture? How might they help you unearth the gifts present or needed now within your community or organization to advance the direction of your mission?

2. How might the practice of self-awakening questions help you see what needs to be discontinued to live more fully into what you are called to do now as an organization or community?
3. How might self-awakening questions surface the ways in which your organization is complicit in the injustices you are seeking to alleviate?
4. What was one challenging idea you encountered here? What made it so?
5. What was a powerful or helpful idea you encountered here? What made it so?
6. What is one thing you take with you from this chapter that might help you listen more carefully to what is awakening within yourself, your organization, or among those you lead?

For all:

1. Review *Another Way Manifesto.* Which sentences stand out to you after reading this chapter?
2. We are building an interactive playlist to accompany each chapter. You can find it on Spotify at **Another Way: The Book.** The songs we recommend for this chapter are "Mirror" (Live) by Lalah Hathaway and "Wake Up Everybody" by Harold Melvin & The Blue Notes. Please add to the playlist as you are inspired.

CHAPTER 4

Doing the Work Our Souls Must Have

Do the work your soul must have.

—Katie G. Cannon

In this chapter—for good reason wedged between the CARE practices of A: Asking Self-Awakening Questions and R: Reflecting Theologically Together—we explore again the questions of vocation, meaning, and purpose. Here, through dreams and stories from Stephen's life, we explore a deeply communal approach to vocation. By imagining vocation as the work our souls must have, we see that vocation takes shape across the long arc of *one* life spent searching for purpose and acting out call. Yet we will see that each individual life's vocation emerges in the midst of a community's life and can even span generations.

Wisdom from an Ancestral Teacher

Stephen shares a dream:

Ancient. Courageous. Embodied wisdom. The teacher came in the form of a long-feathered, royal blue bird that soared in circles outside the back of my deceased paternal grandparents' porch. I gave the bird my undivided attention and was unaware of two bats hanging in the shadowy corner of the porch. It was only when one of the two bats fell from the dark corner that I shifted my gaze in that direction. The keeper of bats appeared from a threshold to retrieve the bat. In a low whisper to the bat, the keeper said, "Not yet. The lesson must unfold," and returned the winged carrier of lessons to its resting post in the corner of the porch ceiling.

While I was distracted by the bat keeper and his enigmatic message, the beautiful bird took advantage of the moment and descended. She glided past the two of us and into the house, which became a makeshift classroom. Unfamiliar with the teacher who had come to tutor us in the wisdom of the ancestors, the students in the room—my startled family members—began making a commotion. Some of them were scared because they recognized the rare bird and her associated taboos. Others believed the bird was dangerous and could kill if she gripped you with her poisonous talons. I had never seen anything like this beautiful bird and the rich royal blue color of her coat. Unaware of the teacher in our midst, my family members shooed away the bird and the lessons she carried like an unwelcome guest.

Hurriedly, I grabbed my camera to take a few pictures of the bird as she flew through different rooms of the house. Click. Click. I was only able to get two shots as the bird made her way toward me and glided inches above my head with her outstretched wings. Quickly, I made my way into the foyer and toward the front door, following the bird while family members yelled "Be careful!" As I opened the door, the bird glided out of the house. I followed in full pursuit of this teacher's wisdom, until we were standing outside, where most of life's lessons surface.

As this mysterious, winged creature circled above my head, we connected on a deeper level, eye to eye. The teacher flew toward me and perched on my left arm. Her blue-feathered coat was so vibrant that I could barely see her large, soul-piercing eyes. I was uneasy, due to warnings about her poisonous talons. She could sense my fear. I stood very still as she gripped my shaking arm with her talons to balance her weight. Knowing the folklore that preceded her and the taboos associated with her kind, the bird imparted her lesson by scratching my arm with her sharp talons, but intentionally not breaking my skin.

I lifted my arm, and as she took flight into the vast world of the unknown, I looked down to see if her talons had penetrated my skin—or worse, poisoned me.

Reflection Upon the Dream

When Stephen awoke, and in the days since, he pondered the meaning of this dream. For him, the teacher in the form of this rare bird represents the transcendent wisdom and sacred practices of his ancestors. The bats symbolize the fear that many African Americans have internalized around accessing that ancestral wisdom and those practices. These ways of knowing and practicing typically go to the grave with the dead, remaining forever lost to the living. The bird emblematizes the beautiful and sacred wisdom and practices of our ancestors that are present and at home within many of us and our families. But because of misinformation and fear, most people are scared of or don't know how to retrieve and embrace the lost wisdom and practices of our pasts.

The dream's lesson took root in Stephen. It said to him: Fear less. Retrieve the ancestral gifts entombed in the graves of your community. Share this healing wisdom to create a more hopeful future for others.

In sacred literature, dreams often contain instructions that help set the path for people and communities. Here, Stephen's dream and its interpretation provide a biopsy—a living extract—of the larger body of his vocational journey.

Stephen's dream guides us into a rhythm of **story** and **reflection** that is woven throughout this chapter. Through that rhythm, we invite you to explore your own sources of wisdom that detoxify and revise the limiting worldviews that shape you. Listen for where "deep calls to deep," uncovering the connections between grief and joy, while also acknowledging the importance of mystery that is part of the quest for certainty and meaning. This quest can deepen, thicken, and broaden the way you might imagine "the work our souls must have," particularly in relation to memory, time, and leadership for the future.

As we do this exploration, listening, and broadening, it is helpful to recall the definitions of purpose, call, and vocation introduced in chapter 2:

- **Purpose** is the *telos* or the ends toward which a life aims. Purpose is the answer to the question "Why am I here? Toward what end is my life pointing?"
- **Call** is the time-bound, episodic expression of purpose, as it bubbles up repeatedly over the course of a lifetime.
- **Vocation** is the long arc of a life spent searching for purpose and acting out callings, and it applies both to communities and to their individual members. While vocation often appears more clearly as we look back on our lives, trying to figure out our next steps toward lives of meaning and purpose is the ongoing work of vocational discernment.

When we at FTE introduce vocational discernment to young people, we ask them to explore communally three questions: (1) Who am I? (2) What are my gifts? (3) How am I to use my gifts for good in the world? These three questions point to *identity, gifts,* and *purpose.*

Thinking together about Stephen's life journey, we see his gifts and experiences weaving a pattern that is inextricable from his community and the way he lives into his purpose every day. We see:

- a child, formed by the Black Baptist church in the South, who was curious at a young age about myth, folklore, and the stories that helped him make meaning of difficult experiences, particularly related to mental illness of family members,
- a young person with a deep knowledge of Scripture encountering a series of traumatic losses for which his Christian upbringing gave insufficient answers and which sent him on an ongoing quest to make sense of God in light of these losses, and
- a pastoral leader, organizational executive, parent, and spiritual innovator who ceaselessly hunts and gathers, exploring by any means necessary the multiple experiences, sacred texts, and wise sages that might shed light on the questions: What are we here for? What is our purpose?

In the stories that follow, Stephen illustrates how his primary vocational concern centers around finding better answers to the questions: What are we here for? What is our purpose? A central thread of *his* vocation is to explore the theological sources of vocation ever more deeply and broadly, inviting others to step into a future that will mourn if we do not complete "the work [each of] our souls must have."

Ritual in Community

Stephen shares:

"This child comes from heaven with challenges awaiting," the priest offered. My wife and I took our baby girl Nya to the priest to learn more about both the purpose for which she was born and how we might assist her in her growth and development. The priest pulled a few ritual elements from the weather-worn bag he carried. He would use these items to pray, discern clues about Nya's purpose, and bless her. When he was ready, he took Nya into his arms. She played with sacred elements draped around his neck. He prayed over Nya and began a ritual process of discerning her larger purpose and gifts in service to the broader community.

He discerned that she has spiritual and intuitive gifts that will be a blessing to others and that some form of service she offers will be healing to others. As we began our new journey as parents, these initial clues reminded us of Nya's larger purpose, affirmed by a larger community of family and friends.

The same priest returned to our home to perform the same ritual after the birth of our second child, Kai. After his spiritual practice of prayer, discernment, and blessing, the priest said, "She comes to bring joy." It will take years to unpack the full meaning of this statement, but once again it serves as a reminder to us during challenging times of parenting.

Eleven years later, a different priest came for a visit. With no prior knowledge of the initial priest's words, he, too, prayed and blessed our two daughters who were now eleven and nine years old. The priest said to Nya, "You struggled to put your feet on the earth but your ancestors are strong and were with you. Your life started off hard but has gotten sweeter. You have a lot of gratitude. You have a deep understanding about humanity and as you get older you will be able to share deep insights with people. Your path needs to be aligned with the spiritual work that is your destiny."

Concerning Kai, he said, "You will bring a lot of blessings to your family. Part of your destiny is to be as good as you can be. You have a sweet side, but you are very, very strong. You are a good mediator. You like to solve problems, and make sure things are equal and fair. You need to be involved in charity work to appreciate your blessings. You are very blessed and came here with that."

Today, I'm still surprised how the two priests verified each other words and connected dots that continue to ring true in the lives of our two daughters. I'm even more amazed about how a larger community of friends, family, and strangers have affirmed the girls' gifts and their lives' evolving journeys toward meaning and purpose. It will be interesting to see how the inner and outer tug of their worlds align and shape what they decide to do with their lives with regard to the broader community.

Reflection on the Story

These stories of discernment and blessing are strikingly similar to the story of Jesus's birth in the Gospel of Luke. Jesus's parents took him to the religious elders in Jerusalem, as was customary. Simeon, an elder in the community, took Jesus into his arms and pronounced that the child was "destined for the falling and the rising of many in Israel, and to be a sign that will be opposed so that the inner thoughts of many will be revealed."[1] While it would take several years for Simeon's pronouncement over Jesus to unfold, in the telling of this story his parents and his community glimpsed Jesus's larger purpose and contribution to the world.

Perhaps that glimpse actually helped Jesus to live into his purpose. Perhaps the community held that vision of his life as they watched, cherished, and nurtured the very characteristics that allowed him

---

[1]Luke 2:34–35.

to live out a story about the future that was foretold by an elder's blessing. The community surrounding Stephen's daughters is doing likewise.

When seen as part of a community's story, individual leadership looks like people stepping into and out of moments of preparation, listening, remembering, imagining, risking, reflecting, acting, and reflecting again. What if Jesus's story is exemplary and instructive for other children? What if every child embodies particular gifts to be nurtured and honed in community, for the sake of the child's own soul and for the sake of the world? What if communities embraced the task of forming, shaping, and nurturing call, purpose, and vocation *in each person* with this in mind?

> *What if communities embraced the task of forming, shaping, and nurturing call, purpose, and vocation in each person?*

An example of this kind of nurture occurred in Stephen's young life. He belonged to Friendship Missionary Baptist Church, a large, traditional middle-class church in Charlotte, North Carolina, known for its teaching ministry and service to the wider community. That church stoked Stephen's curiosity in the sacred arts of the Spirit and nurtured questions he had about God, community, and the African American experience. That church catalyzed his call to ministry. Specifically, Mother Mary Pearson, one of the saints of the church, embodied Friendship's characteristic way of noticing the gifts in young people long before they recognized these gifts in themselves.

Stephen remembers, "Mother Pearson was an astute observer of the Spirit's movement in the lives of those with whom she sought to conspire. She was known to work herself into a frenzy on Sundays and say, "Preaching got good today!" One evening, Mother Pearson grabbed me by the hand and said, "God has his hand on you. God is working on you. Don't get discouraged. Keep your hand in God's." I was struck by her certainty about my place in God's work as she shared these words. Yet I wondered, "If God has his hand on me, doesn't God have God's hand on everyone?" I was even more curious about how Mother Pearson knew God's hand was on me, because certainly I did not always feel that way. Like sprouting seeds, her words would take root in my subconscious. My curiosity and nagging questions would water and bring them to bloom."

The idea of community that is central to Jesus's birth narrative grounds the biblical perspective of vocation in the deeply communal worldview[2] of its North African cultural context. This worldview informed fundamental beliefs about what it means to be human, where children come from, what they bring with them, and how they have been equipped to fulfill a particular purpose in the community into which they are born.

What we do with our days, how we focus our intellectual, social, and spiritual gifts, how we go about creating a rhythm of life—all of this has a ripple effect in our families, our communities, and the world. The idea that our lives might have meaning and purpose beyond our own personal ambitions expands conventional notions of vocation and calling that grow out of Western individualism.

As we saw in chapter 2, African American and African people's communal worldviews provide rich sources for developing a broader understanding of meaning, purpose, and vocation.

Within such a communal worldview, each person arrives in time and space with at least one purpose. This purpose is connected to the past and points toward the future but is in service to the larger community and world. One perspective that is central to this idea is that before a child is born, the child made an agreement with God concerning the child's life purpose. When the child is born, the elders of the community work to discern clues regarding the purpose for which the child was born. Clues revealed in the child's personality, family history, ancestral line, and the broader community offer a trail of breadcrumbs that points to the larger purpose at work in the child. If the community is attentive and nurturing, helping the child to connect the dots between the clues, the gifts and purpose of the child will emerge in due time.[3] As Jeremiah suggests, God knew us before God formed us in our mother's womb.[4] Before we were born, God set each of us apart and appointed us as God's servants, seers, and healers to various communities around the world.

---

[2]Marimba Ani, *Let the Circle Be Unbroken: The Implications of African Spirituality in the Diaspora* (Baltimore: Nkonimfo Publications, 1997), 3–4. The author provides a framework for understanding a worldview. She says that a worldview refers to the way in which a people make sense of their surroundings and make sense of life's circumstances and vicissitudes, ideas for which we sometimes turn to "religion." The term *worldview* is related to "religion," but not necessarily in its institutionalized form. A worldview results from a shared cultural experience, just as it helps to form that experience. It presents us with a systematic set of ideas about many things. Its significance is profound, and it has far reaching effects on those who share it. It affects our perceptions of nature, ourselves as human beings, of each other and our relationship to all being. According to Ani, a worldview helps to inject "meaning into life; to determine which are meaningful experiences and events and which are not." A people's worldview affects and tends to determine their behavior.

[3]Malidoma Patrice Somé, *The Healing Wisdom of Africa: Finding Life Purpose Through Nature, Ritual, and Community* (New York: Penguin Putnam, 1998), 33.

[4]Jeremiah 1:5. See also Psalm 139:13–16.

Stephen's friend and mentor, Alton Pollard III, illustrated this biblical and African worldview with powerful, soul-stirring words at Stephen's ordination. Mirroring back to the gathered community the best of Trinity African Baptist Church's self-understanding as an African American religious community called to serve God, Pollard said:

> The call is not relegated to the pages and personages of ancient history. As African American griot scholar Vincent Harding so eloquently writes, "The mystery and wonderment of the call, the voice of the holy comes to us in this day and time also often and especially through the dark daughters and shining sons of Africa in this country. It comes through the proud testimony of a people, of a Black people whom God has never left without a witness, whom God has never left alone." I hear my people calling me through and across generations.
>
> I speak of callings today. Because whether you know it or not, my sisters and brothers, whether you believe it or not, all of us in one way or another somehow have been called. Now, by the call I'm not talking so much about a profound epiphany. I'm not simply talking about a singular, spectacular, exceptional, special, or extraordinary spiritual experience—as real and important as those are. I'm talking rather about the quiet gathering up of the substance of one's life. The gentle nudge that more often than not occurs somewhere down in the depth of the human spirit and is birthed within the summoning community, awaiting community, expectant community, Beloved Community. And its hopes and dreams culminate in our capacity to hear and respond.[5]

In that moment, Pollard was reminding Stephen and his community that there exists a collective vocation that is generational, intergenerational, and ancestral. He was acknowledging that Trinity itself and Stephen as a member of Trinity's community are called to take their respective places in an ancient stream alongside a community of freedom fighters, peacemakers, warrior-healers, and builders of the Beloved Community for the sake of a better world.

Suffering and Vocation: Three Vignettes

It can take a lifetime for a person to discover their purpose and even longer for a community's purpose to unfold. Often in the case

[5] Alton Pollard III, (sermon at the ordination of Stephen Lewis, Atlanta April 27, 2003.)

of individuals and communities, life's biggest questions arise through tragedies and disappointments. This was the case in Stephen's life.

Stephen writes:

It's difficult to understand my unfolding vocational journey and decisions outside of traumatic experience including a rare birth defect, the mental illness of my mother, and the death of a close friend. These and other experiences became wise guides on my journey toward becoming who I am today. I invite you to ponder your own vocational autobiography as you journey with me through these stories and the meanings that arose through them.

Vignette 1

"It looks like he has a problem," Dad shared with my mother over the phone. Mom said, "I need to know." Dad responded, "I don't want you to worry and will tell you what the doctor said when I get there. Wrap up really good and put on your boots. I'm coming to get you."

It was a snowy, winter day in January and he had just learned from my pediatrician that I had a rare birth defect. One of my kidneys had not developed properly. One week earlier, my mother—a twenty-one-year-old, first-generation college graduate—had given birth to me. One week later, she learned that that her firstborn needed surgery. Multiple factors made surgery risky: the doctors were concerned that at less than ten days old I was too young to withstand surgery, I would be one of the youngest patients at the time to be put under anesthesia, and I was the specialist's youngest patient ever. To improve my chances of surviving, the doctors and my parents had decided to wait another week for my immune system to develop. On the day of the surgery, the pediatrician shared with my mother that I would be fine but advised that she draw on her faith to get through this moment. After several hours of surgery and another week in the hospital, I returned home—to a community of family and friends who had encircled us in prayer as my parents navigated the frightening first weeks of parenthood.

Twenty-nine years later I married my life partner, who suffered from an excruciating debilitating medical condition: endometriosis. She was one of a few patients treated by a renowned specialist who drew medical residents from across the world to train in the treatment of this condition. Only after nine surgeries did she find relief and a quality of life she had never known before in her adulthood.

The sheer randomness of these serious life-altering medical conditions never fails to catch me off guard. There is no theological reason for the pain and suffering my wife and her family had to endure, nor was there for me and my family when I was an infant. In both cases, we survived and thrived, while others did not.

Why?

These experiences lead me to feel acutely the inequity of life's sufferings and to search for meaning amid the randomness.

Vignette 2

"Don't take my baby away from me," my mother yelled as tears streamed down her befuddled face. "Don't take my baby away from me!"

The morning breeze carried these words through the air. To my fourth-grade mind, they sounded like an activist's bullhorn drawing attention to me, my mom, and the scene at the front entrance of Briarwood Elementary school. As my grandfather sought to console my mother and put her back into the car, I made my way down the concrete pathway to the front door of the school, as if I were walking through a tunnel of intruding eyes of snickering schoolmates.

This was the first time I remembered recalling that a larger community was now aware of what my family and I privately had known for some time—that something was wrong with Mom. As early as six years of age, I remembered many nights praying, talking, and negotiating with God to help her. As a family, we had to face the fact that Mom's bout with depression was not a passing phase, but a doorway to a lifelong journey and struggle with bipolar disorder. This was deeply unsettling, because the person who is supposed to protect and guide my little brother and me was confronted with the fight of her life, a fight for her own mental health and emotional well-being.

Later in life I discovered that Mom would not be the only one in our family to fight mental illness. This dreaded disease and its many manifestations would rain havoc on other immediate and close family members as well, including my wife's younger brother, who lost his life fighting mental illness.

Vignette 3

"She's gone," the strained voice amid the veil of grief and tears whispered on the other end of the phone. "What do you mean she's gone?" I responded, as my heart pounded through my chest. "You need to come home quickly," said the voice on the other end of the phone.

I was entering the last year of graduate school in my preparation for ministry. I had just learned that my girlfriend had died in a tragic parasail accident while vacationing with a friend. Some bad weather had rolled in. The parasail fell out of the sky, and she was trapped underwater. The friend harnessed to her survived, but my girlfriend did not. I was stunned, in a daze of disbelief. As I traveled with her family to retrieve her body, I remember thinking: "This is not supposed to happen to people, especially young adults in their twenties, who are trying to be faithful to a call, preparing to serve others on behalf of God."

At the morgue, I placed one hand on her body and the other one on the shoulder of my girlfriend's mother to console her. In the silence of our tears, I prayed, "Lord, everyone speaks and preaches about your power and goodness. Scripture bears witnesses that we can do all things in Christ . . . The gospel conveys stories of you raising people from the dead or awakening them from their sleep. This moment is as good of a time as any to demonstrate the goodness and power that others attribute to you. Will you in this moment return this child to her mother?"

No such luck. It felt as if my prayer to God fell on deaf ears.

This was not the first time I had encountered a traumatic death of someone so young and close to me, nor would it be the last. Death violently claimed the life of a close childhood friend and his brother when I was in my early twenties, and then claimed the life of my brother-in-law when I was in my early forties.

Stephen's Reflections on the Vignettes

These defining moments of my life lie at the core of my vocational trajectory because they forced me to pursue questions such as:

- How do those called to ministry learn to speak and work on behalf of the divine if God cannot always be trusted to provide the basic needs of one's family?
- What is the call and vocation of skeptics?
- Why does divine favor, grace, and blessing seem to be meted out inequitably regarding both the quality of life and life itself?
- Are there concepts of God that can hold up to the hard questions about life and death and divine action in human affairs?
- Why is the church too often silent or just plain wrong on issues pertaining to mental illness?
- Where can people turn to be tutored in the sacred arts that might aid people amid life's real, heartbreaking situations?

The dominant perception of my Christian upbringing that there is an all-knowing, all-powerful, sovereign, loving God makes no sense given that traumatic experiences rain down on some people and not on others. I found the forms of Christianity represented by my church and seminary experiences incapable of helping me to wrestle with the deeper questions that such tragedies raised in me. Normative Christian ideas about grace, mental illness, evil, and suffering are insufficient. Trite answers such as "God's ways are not our ways" and "We are born into sin because of the fall" no longer worked for me. I needed a more expansive library of spiritual narratives beyond the go-to tale of Job in order to wrap my head and heart around why innocent people—particularly young people—suffer at the hands of a supposedly all-powerful, all-knowing, and loving God. I needed to detox from normative conceptions, theologies, and interpretations of God in search of better answers.

Perhaps you can understand that I pursue these questions not as a mere academic exercise but as a quest for my very survival. I'm no quitter, but there were long stretches when I was exhausted and felt like giving up. I knew that if I did not find something more, these life-smoldering, heart-crushing experiences would snuff me out.

And I am not alone! Others like me long for alternative frameworks to those that their church upbringings provide to make sense of suffering. What became clear for me is this: we cannot control the volatile tides that life brings, but maybe we can learn to build better boats.

I needed a better vessel—a sacred vessel, crafted from the indigenous materials of my heritage. I would do this for myself and for my people—my daughters, my mother, and my extended community—so that we could navigate the harsh conditions of life without being torn asunder.

And so I went in search of ancestral understandings of God to combat the dominant conceptions that had shaped me heretofore. I went underground looking for sources that could help me bring the faith of my upbringing out of captivity to traditions that had domesticated it. I spent time exploring the mystic traditions of Christianity, Islam, Hinduism, Buddhism, and African-derived religious traditions in particular to widen the aperture of my understanding of God, especially as it relates to suffering, death, mental illness, and calling.

What I discovered is this: Suffering comes with the experience of being human, and one's perspective can determine how one experiences and works with it. Suffering is psycho-somatic pain, meaning that it impacts the mind, body, and spirit of a person. Sometimes suffering is multigenerational, genetically coded, or situational. It sometimes hides out in the subconscious realms of our psyche and muscle memory, like a kid's game of hide-and-seek. Life experiences, painful encounters, and anxiety can trigger and awaken moments of trauma or suffering.

I have come to realize that there is no logic when it comes to suffering. Because it is a type of pain, we try to make sense of the pain. We ask: Is there a reason for the pain? What does the pain mean? Is there a cause for my suffering? Is it the result of a choice I have made? While there may be answers for simple forms of temporary suffering, when it comes to more complex forms, adequate answers are more elusive. In these instances, a person and loved ones must come to terms with suffering as a permanent resident in their lives. In these instances, suffering persistently nudges the sufferer and/or loved ones to ask heart-wrenching questions about the meaning and purpose of life.

While not all do so, some choose to wrestle with suffering rather than retreat into denial or bitterness. These sojourners follow a rabbit hole into the dark tunnels of life's mystery, where only questions illuminate the path in front of them. It is a lonely and isolating inward journey, because only they alone can fully experience their suffering. Encounters with the ultimate source of suffering, however, can lead to transformation, new insights, wisdom, and healing to share with those who might face similar encounters.

For me this journey was intimate and private, but at the same time I found wise guides, teachers, and counselors to accompany me as I descended into the luminous darkness of my own emotional memories. Howard Thurman was one of those guides:

> The individual enters a fellowship of suffering and the community of sufferers. The only point to be held steadily in mind is that, despite the personal character of suffering, the sufferer can work his way through to community. This does not make his pain less, but it can make it inclusive of many other people. Sometimes he discovers through the ministry of his own burden a larger comprehension of his fellows, of whose presence he becomes aware of in his darkness. They are companions along the way.[6]

Wrestling with my suffering was necessary in order for me to reckon with the gut-wrenching pain of my own experience in hopes of discovering an illumined path of healing and transformation to share with others. Again, Thurman's words resonate:

---

[6]Howard Thurman, *Disciplines of the Spirit* (Richmond, IN: Friends United Press, 1963), 77.

> This is why we very often see people as profoundly changed by their suffering. Into their faces has come a subtle radiance and a settled serenity; into their relationships [comes] a vital generosity that opens the sealed doors of the heart in all who are encountered along the way. Such people look out upon life with quiet eyes. Openings are made in a life by suffering that are not made in any other way. Serious questions are raised and primary answers come forth. Insights are reached concerning aspects of life that are hidden and obscure before the assault.[7]

I discovered an ancient, underground river of truth that rises up in all of these traditions. This river helped sharpen my understanding of what being a follower of Jesus means in a way that church could not because of the limitations of its language, dogma, and institution-building project. I discovered that faith and certainty are not the same. Too much certainty about what, why, and how God works gets in God's way.

As a Black man, I needed to reclaim the spiritual giftedness of my own twoness—being both African and American. I needed to acknowledge that I am here because of enslaved ancestors, who came to this country as stewards and inheritors of spiritual worldviews, traditions, and practices. I needed to excavate the African spiritual inheritance that runs through my blood and veins. Why? Because this is the soil that birthed the soul of the Black church and its syncretized[8] expressions of spirituality, and that in turn made possible the survival of Black people in this country. These sources nourished a communal sense of purpose, steeped in the multi-generational resistance and resilience of freedom fighters, warrior-healers, and dream defenders working to create a better life for future generations.

These sources nourished a communal sense of purpose, steeped in the multigenerational resistance and resilience of freedom fighters, warrior-healers, and dream defenders.

An essential aspect of my purpose in life is to excavate the indigenous, spiritual technology and wisdom of African diasporic people. These are gifts to be shared with the world and are essential in

[7] Ibid., 76.

[8] Syncretism is an often-maligned process. Colonialism would have us believe that syncretism is the "dangerous" inclusion of non-European, non-white, non-colonized ways of knowing in our (white Western) interpretation of ancient texts, history, and worldviews. In fact, there is no pure non-syncretized form, tradition, or expression of Christianity. All religions involve mixing, adapting, and integrating diverse worldviews. Considered in this light, syncretism is a creative way people make meaning of their lives, culture, practices, and surroundings in a new context and can lead to the invention of a new form or container, such as the Black church.

building the kind of sacred compass necessary to navigate the turbulent seas of our lives in order to avoid shipwrecks on the journey toward a life of purpose and wholeness.

The Widening Work of Retrieval

Through our work at FTE, we meet young adults who yearn to make sense of the strong tailwinds in their lives. They yearn for ancient wisdom that can withstand the big questions, worthy dreams, and severe tests of resilience and perseverance that greet or confront them daily.[9] As Barbara Brown Taylor once said at an FTE gathering:

> Strong winds really do blow through people's lives. Those winds don't come with maps explaining where they came from or where they're going. What you're supposed to do about them and how everything is going to turn out in the end you do not know, and so it is with everyone who is born of the Spirit.[10]

Life's experiences may include an involuntary crisis brought on by tragedy, poverty, or some form or loss (mental and physical disease and death, in Stephen's case). Or they may be the "shipwreck" that occurs when a person voluntarily ventures beyond his known world to empathize with those from a vastly different economic, racial, or societal home.[11] This is particularly important for many of the young people we meet who are seeking to find lives of meaning and purpose beyond "me, myself and mine" but whose church communities do not consistently provide the quality of engagement and interaction to nourish their ongoing search.

In Stephen's autobiography, we see a young adult searching for answers beyond the confines of his church community and mainstream Christianity. We see him searching for clarity and wisdom about his experiences and the questions and wonderings stirring deep within him. As he found, removing ourselves temporarily from the life-ways and practices that typically surround and shape us can help us to listen more clearly to ancestral urges that can guide us. In many ways, Stephen's search is like that of an astronaut who travels outside the earth's atmosphere and returns with a larger perspective of the earth. He moved far enough beyond the atmosphere of the Christianity in which he had been steeped to be able to see his experiences from a

---

[9]Sharon Daloz Parks, *Big Questions, Worthy Dreams: Mentoring Emerging Adults in Their Search for Meaning, Purpose, and Faith* (San Francisco: Jossey-Bass, 2011).

[10]Barbara Brown Taylor (sermon at FTE's Calling Congregations Conference, Atlanta, October 9, 2010). The entire speech can be heard here: https://soundcloud.com/fteleaders/bbt-sermon-ftecc See also Barbara Brown Taylor, *Learning to Walk in The Dark* (San Francisco: Harper Collins, 2014).

[11]Sharon Parks, *The Critical Years: Young Adults and the Search for Meaning, Faith and Community* (New York: Harper Collins, 1986), 24–25.

different vantage point. Wisdom traditions widened the aperture of his understanding beyond his own habitat. This is particularly important because it's nearly impossible to understand the Christian Bible from a western European cultural perspective given that it was written in such a different Middle Eastern/North African/Mediterranean context. Engaging other perspectives is a way of gaining a broader perspective on the normative ways of understanding one's own context.

"Widening the aperture" describes what it was like for Stephen to gain a broader perspective on his life. This image of aperture from the field of photography refers to the opening in a camera lens through which light passes. The wider the aperture, the greater the light exposure, and it is used particularly in environments where there is less light. A wider aperture also offers a sharper focus on the photographer's subject, resulting in less depth of field and a blurrier background. In darker periods of Stephen's journey, perspectives from different wisdom traditions—especially from African-derived religious perspectives and practices—provided him with essential light, widened his understanding, and brought his situation into sharper focus. He says, "Life would happen and then the wisdom and practice from other perspectives would come along to open up my world. This either broadened my perspective or focused my attention on what was before me. Oftentimes, I ended up reconstructing my perspective by looking at my experience through another window and in so doing enlarging my worldview."

In adapting and adopting a worldview not immediately our own, there is always a danger of misappropriation. In reality, all of Christian history describes a collaborative process between Spirit and humanity, a process of syncretism—improvising, adapting innovating, and appropriating. In Stephen's vocational journey, the instinct of survival eventually summoned him to spend time examining the spiritual worldviews and practices of African-descended people.

Again it is Thurman who affirms this instinctive summoning and shows the value in doing so. In his 1979 autobiography, he wrote:

> I longed to discover the sources of indigenous African religions, to explore the underground spiritual springs that ran deep long before the coming of Islam or early Christianity. I hoped to find a common ground between Christian religious experience and the religious experience in the background and in the heart of the African people. If such a common ground could be located and defined, it seemed to me that the finest insights in Christianity could be energized by the cumulative

boundless energy of hundreds of years of the brooding Spirit of God as it expressed itself in many forms in the life of a great people.[12]

Thurman, along with numerous storytellers and scholars of the African diaspora, shows how some African people found in Christianity themes and ways of understanding the world that resonated with their own inherent ways of being. He encourages the work of engaging in the interplay between inherited worldviews and the worldview exemplified in Stephen's dream at the beginning of this chapter.

People of European ancestry have always drawn upon their Celtic, Nordic, Iberian, and Roman roots to make sense of their own Christian understandings and daily realities in the changing landscapes of history. Unfortunately, people of other racial/ethnic ancestries are too often shamed, or worse, demonized, when they do likewise. However, they should be encouraged to continue drawing upon the myths and wisdom of their ancient histories in order to embody faithful expressions of Christianity that reflect their own particularity and authenticity. Why must they do this? Because this work of retrieval beats back the ways in which colonial Christianity seeks to erase non-European ways and artificially props up a version of Christianity that undermines the dignity and humanity of non-European cultures. Beating back such ways of erasure is especially important because historically African diasporic people and other communities of color have been required to accept white cultural captivity in American and European traditions as synonymous with the Christian story. This cultural bondage limits our imaginations about the sources and practices that nurture our sense of vocation.

Concerns about appropriation and misappropriation are ultimately about power and who controls the narratives.

Fortunately, many African-descended Christians have long resisted colonized versions of Christianity and have reclaimed the value of their own cultural traditions as central to the practice of Christianity in its many forms. Mark Lomax argues that African theological frameworks, traditions, and practices are as useful to African people as European ones are to people of European descent. He suggests that while European Americans taught African Americans to avoid incorporating the wisdom, practices, and symbols of indigenous cultures into their

[12]Howard Thurman, *With Head and Heart: The Autobiography of Howard Thurman* (Orlando: Harcourt Brace,1979), 197.

spirituality, they commonly incorporated "symbols of Christmas trees, bunny rabbits and Easter eggs derived from various pre-Christian Germanic, Nordic and Anglo-Saxon tribal practices."[13] In other words, there is no such thing as a "pure" Christianity. Concerns about appropriation and misappropriation are ultimately about power and who controls the narratives that shape us and our imagination, particularly the marginalized and dispossessed among us.

Marginalized and dispossessed people must author their own narratives. Like people of European descent, they must retrieve the best from the past to shape the biographies of the present and future.

The Deepening Work of Excavation

Marginalized and dispossessed people must author their own narratives. Like people of European descent, they must retrieve the best from the past to shape the biographies of the present and future. The beautiful bird in Stephen's dream reflects this practice and is reminiscent of the aforementioned Akan principle of *sankofa*, also represented as a bird. Recall that the *sankofa* bird looks back, holding an egg in its beak. The egg symbolizes the wisdom of the past, which is needed for the future. The proverb accompanying the bird is "We must go back and fetch that which we need to move forward."

Actress Viola Davis echoed the vocational practice of *sankofa* when she paid homage to the late playwright August Wilson in her 2017 Academy Award acceptance speech.[14] She said:

> You know, there's one place that all the people with the greatest potential are gathered. One place and that's the graveyard. People ask me all the time, what kind of stories do you want to tell, Viola? And I say, exhume those bodies. Exhume those stories. The stories of the people who dreamed big and never saw those dreams to fruition. People who fell in love and lost. I became an artist—and thank God I did—because we are the only profession that celebrates what it means to live a life. So, here's to August Wilson, who exhumed and exalted ordinary people.

---

[13]Mark Ogunwalè Lomax, respondent to Will Coleman, "Christianity as African Religion: Exegeting and Reconsidering its Biblical and Theological Origins," Copher Lecture at the Interdenominational Theological Center, Atlanta, March 20, 2018.

[14]Maddie Crum, "Viola Davis's Best Supporting Actress Oscar Speech Totally Steals the Show," *HuffPost,* February 26, 2017, www.huffingtonpost.com/entry/viola-davis-oscars-speech-totally-steals-the-show_us_58b05ae5e4b060480e073b3b.

Remembering and reclaiming the ancient knowledge, power, pride, authority, and legacy of his people fueled [Jesus's] public service on behalf of the dispossessed.

We invite not just artists, but everyone to join in the work of exhuming and exalting that from our past that chooses to live through us. Davis's words are a provocative metaphor for what we find in Luke's narrative about Jesus's baptism: "Now when all the people were baptized, and when Jesus also had been baptized and was praying, the heaven was opened, and the Holy Spirit descended upon him in bodily form like a dove. And a voice came from heaven, 'You are my Son, the Beloved; with you I am well pleased.' Jesus was about thirty years old when he began his work." [15] Luke then traces Jesus's genealogy in what amounts to an ancestral tree.[16]

What was the work that Jesus began? The work began with Jesus exhuming and retrieving fragmented, genealogical stories of his ancestors. The genealogy is a list of names that may not mean much to the reader of Scripture other than to authenticate Jesus's messianic role. Similar to the list of names of our own family trees, names signify so much more to the descendants and family historian. They represent stories of our ancestors and memories about who they were, their faith, and how they overcame in the face of struggle and uncertainty. Our family genealogies reveal to us stories about our people—from whom and where we come, their hopes and dreams and their contributions. More importantly, genealogies remind us that we were born into an ancestral lineage and we take our rightful place alongside heroes and

[15]Luke 3:21–23.

[16]Mark Ogunwalè Lomax offers three important observations about Jesus's genealogy: (1) "As a preacher who is a son out of the African diaspora and a member of an oppressed people; as a believer in God and a follower of Christ, I cannot afford to ignore the fact that the divine and human drama recorded in the pages of our Bible has its origin in Africa. Nor should anyone else. Geography matters especially when it is occupied territory. Those whom we call "the Jews" did not exit Egypt tabula rasa, with an empty consciousness. They were in fact Egyptians (the word Hebrew/Habiru-foreigners/wanderers perhaps obscures who they really were) who had been thoroughly baptized in Egyptian religious practice and culture on Egyptian/African soil. Further, it is clear that the writers of the gospels of Matthew and Luke believed the historic and genetic connection to Egypt important enough to mention in their narratives." (2) [I]f "Jesus is a Son out of Egypt then he is African . . . It means, in part, that God chose an Afrikan as God's son, anointed him, and used him to fulfill divine purposes in the world." (3) "The identification of Jesus with Africa and by extension, with Africans, allows . . . [us to] see and acknowledge those without privilege and pedigree in the text and . . . observe and declare ways in which God is surely as present with the underprivileged, the outcasts, and the poor as God may be with the privileged and the prosperous." In "Christian Theology And AfroCultures: Toward an Afrikan Centered Hermeneutic," Black Theology Project, February 27, 2018, www://btpbase.org/christian-theology-and-afrocultures-toward-an-afrikan-centered-hermeneutic.

heroines, queens and kings, freedom fighters and warrior-healers, god-bearers and prophets, dispossessed and possessed mothers and fathers who came before us and on whose shoulders we stand. If you want to understand Jesus and his purpose, you must understand the lineage from which he emerged. Black preachers often speak of Jesus as the one who "came down through forty and two generations" to celebrate his coming as a harbinger of the hope of the ancestors and the disinherited.

We imagine that as Jesus began his public ministry, he began with exhuming and retrieving the stories of his people. Remembering and reclaiming the ancient knowledge, power, pride, authority, and legacy of his people fueled his public service on behalf of the dispossessed. It fueled his resolve and resiliency in moments of temptation and tribulation.

This is an instructive reminder for young leaders as they begin their public ministry: You do not stand alone. You step into an ancestral legacy. Stephen was lucky enough to be reminded of this at the moment of his ordination.

Stephen writes:

In the midst of the dense, emotional fog of the experience, my attention was attuned toward the rhythmic, congregational responses of "Umm hmm," "yes sir," and "say it," as the sacred artist offered:

> Yes, it is true that your life has not been a bed of roses. Life ain't been no crystal stair. God didn't promise that. Yes, it's true. Like Langston Hughes, you've seen rivers. You've known the downside of life, disappointment, deception and defeat . . . But the call is so fiercely gripping, encompassing and pervasive . . . It is deep calling unto deep. A love that will not let you go. The divine imperative. The soul's hunger. Something within that you cannot explain . . . But you will understand it better by and by and so shall we all, as you come to live out more clearly your calling . . . As fantastic and impossible and preposterous as it may seem, God has called you! You are called to tell the story of how we overcome. You are called to carry forth the struggle. You are called. And even greater things than these shall you do. You will press across new borders. And become the very means of change that you wish to see in the world. In spite of yourself, beyond yourself, you must go into this new calling. Stephen, no turning back. No turning back. *Asé*.[17]

[17]Pollard, sermon at ordination of Stephen Lewis.

These were the concluding words spoken to me in my initiation rite of becoming an ordained minister. It would take years for me to metabolize the profound truths of Pollard's words poured into my heart and soul. But this experience continues to stir something deep within me. It shapes my ongoing vocational journey and serves as a reminder during the endarkened passages of time.

This work is life-giving work when done with a community of good companions and wise guides.

Recurring Themes

Stephen has always felt an abiding sense of being born in this moment in time to get something done—to fulfill a purpose for the sake of the greater good of the community. He writes: "Deep within me, curiosity and questions have always been my inner world companions on life's journey. This is how I'm wired." These companions tutored him to accept nothing at face value and helped shape a healthy skeptic. As a result, he tends to color outside the dominant, status quo lines of life. As frustrating as it can be, he embraces the grey areas of life's journey, those areas chock full of uncertainty, paradoxes, and inexplicable experiences that raise huge questions about our understanding of God, our relationship to the divine, and our agency to create a more hopeful future.

In this chapter, we encountered the ways in which trauma, shipwreck, and heartbreak change the course of a person's life and can deepen the ways a person moves in the world. What helps people move through life-altering experiences and retrieve the wisdom from them? The freedom to pursue answers to life's most fundamental questions unencumbered by a limiting worldview. This work is life-giving work when done with a community of good companions and wise guides, and a deep passion for finding alternatives within confining and defining circumstances.

From Stephen's stories and our reflection on them, we see a deeply communal understanding of vocation emerging. This moves us beyond static definitions of call, purpose, and vocation to hear interwoven, recurring themes.

This "work our souls must have":

- **Is primal and sometimes is simply about staying alive.**[18] Sometimes the best we can do is just to hold on . . . in hopes

[18]Patrick Reyes, *Nobody Cries When We Die: God, Community, and Surviving to Adulthood* (St. Louis: Chalice Press, 2016), 3.

that we're not torn asunder. The first call is to steward the breath (*ruah* or *pneuma*) entrusted to us for as long as we can.

- **Is ancestral and calls us to remember, reclaim, and reconnect.** It is not restricted to a single lifetime but connects us to a lineage of people who have come before us and conspired with God to create a better world for their children and future generations. We drink from wells that we did not dig. We sit under the shade of trees we did not plant. We stand on the shoulders of and are shaped by those who went before us, even those we cannot see. Remembering, reconnecting, and honoring the blood, sweat, tears, hope, and toil of our ancestors is deeply tied to "ripening into ripening" that is vocation.[19]

- **Is revealed in the mystery of life.** We must search the face of uncertainty that ripples across the oceans of our lives. Only after being lured and encountering uncertainty through the crucible of life does it reveal something deep within us—an indigenous wisdom and truth about ourselves and our community. We gain greater perspective into what animates the deepest expressions of our soul and role and our agency to choose how we will spend the remainder of our days.

- **Is heartbreaking.** It is this urge for survival that draws us outside of easy normative, clean and sanitized categories we have inherited into thickly imagined and embodied vision of what it means to follow "the way of Jesus."

- **Is resilient.** We cannot control the volatile tides of change, but we *can* learn to build better vessels to navigate the harsh conditions of life and community, without being torn apart. We can learn to increase our capacity to maintain our core purpose and integrity in the face of dramatically changed circumstances.

- **Is communal.** Scripture reminds us that there is a great cloud of witnesses[20] surrounding us. This metaphor and expanded sense of community includes our ancestors—those who have come before us—and our progeny—those who will come after us. One's purpose does not derive solely from the whims of one's own ambition, gifts, and aspirations. Instead, it evolves

[19]emilie townes, "womanist understanding of vocation," speech given on April 13, 2015 at an FTE event in Nashville. It is archived at www.leadanotherway.com.
[20]Hebrews 12:1.

out of the community's web of mutuality—where people are in relationship with each other, living together, and learning what it means to be human and humane toward others. One's purpose is concerned with one's whole life including one's roles as a partner, spouse, parent, friend, family member, business owner, or caregiver; one's career, concerns, and contributions to the larger community. In community, we acknowledge our inheritance of the past and the promise of the future. We discern the needs, hopes, and dreams for our common life together in community and the broader world. We affirm that each person has a role to play. And we anticipate that the gifts and purpose of each person will be made known, nurtured, and celebrated.

- **Is a practice of *sankofa*.** Our vocation is not always limited to our own occupation of time and space. It reflects also the hopes and dreams of those who've come before us, including the unanswered dreams of previous generations. Thus, vocation is an ongoing act of retrieval—retrieving the best of the past to nourish the seeds of the future.

Vocation is doing the work our souls must have.

Vocational discernment is a central task of leadership. Widening our sources for vocational imagination helps create and sustain the kind of leaders for which the world is crying out. A communal worldview reminds us all that vocation is not just about our career ambition, mission statements, or what we plan to do for the rest of our lives. Echoing a signature axiom of the late Katie Cannon, a pioneer in womanist theology, emilie m. townes reminds us that vocation is:

> rooted in justice-making [and] is an important way we gain strength for the journey so that we learn to live creatively in the tight circle of choices that are given to us by this social order we all live in but also plot, scheme, and realize ways to craft that tight circle into a spiral of possibilities for this generation and serve as the standing ground for the generation and the next generation and beyond.

simply put, vocation is doing the work our souls must have[21]

[21]townes, 2015.

Questions for Reflection

For the individual learner/leader seeking meaning and purpose:

1. This chapter returns to the importance of community in the task of discerning meaning and purpose in life. Community is defined broadly, with examples including immediate family, extended family, neighbors, church or faith community members, and ancestors who've gone before. How do you define community? What aspects of community are available to you in your search for meaning and purpose? If a sense of supportive community is lacking for you now, how might you go about finding or building it?

2. Stephen's story surfaces multiple encounters with trauma, loss, and suffering. Each of these occasions caused him to ask questions about the images of God that shaped him. These occasions also set his life on a journey to retrieve wisdom from sources beyond his upbringing, to include an ever-widening circle of ancient spiritual wisdom. He writes: "I needed to detox from normative conceptions, theologies, and interpretations of God in search of better answers." What are the traumas or losses in your life that give rise to deep questioning? How is your image of God changed in the midst or aftermath of them? What does your "search for better answers" look like?

3. What was one challenging idea you encountered here? What made it so?

4. What was one of the most powerful or helpful ideas you encountered here? What made it so?

5. What is one thing you take with you from this chapter that might help you tend more carefully to "the work your soul must have?" If this language does not resonate with you, what poem, song lyric, or phrase from your life's journey better describes your search for meaning and purpose?

For the guide/facilitator helping others find meaning and purpose:

1. The authors compare the ritual enacted around Stephen's young daughters to the rituals described around the birth

of Jesus and ask: "What if every child embodies particular gifts to be nurtured and honed in community, for the sake of the child's own soul and for the sake of the world? What if communities embraced the task of forming, shaping, and nurturing call, purpose, and vocation in each person with this in mind?" Have you experienced a community that lives out this ideal? How would you begin to cultivate such a sense of shared responsibility for nurturing call where it does not yet exist?

2. In working with people who've experienced multiple traumas, it is important to create spaces in which people are not re-traumatized. What stories come to mind of people (in history or in your own life) whose purpose seems to emerge out of their unique experience, trauma, or pain point? How might you help people lean into their trauma as a source for vocational discernment?
3. What was one challenging idea you encountered here? What made it so?
4. What was one of the most powerful or helpful ideas you encountered here? What made it so?
5. What is one thing you take with you from this chapter that might help the people you accompany exhume and excavate the gifts, stories, or rituals of their heritage and communities so that they may flourish?

For those leading organizational change:

1. How do the stories of your own vocational journey—your traumas, sufferings, dreams, or visions—inform your vocation as a leader? What practices might help you become more self-aware about them so as to engage them more mindfully?
2. How does your organization reckon with its own ancestral history? Is there historical trauma in the wake of previous leaders that still shapes the organization's story? How might you lead efforts to unearth organizational stories from the past in order to reclaim the deep wisdom and gifts your organization needs to flourish in its mission now?
3. What was one challenging idea you encountered here? What made it so?

4. What was one of the most powerful or helpful ideas you encountered here? What made it so?
5. What is one thing you take with you from this chapter that might help deepen your understanding of "the work your soul must have?"

For all:

1. Review *Another Way Manifesto.* Which sentences stand out to you after reading this chapter?
2. We are building an interactive playlist to accompany each chapter. You can find it on Spotify at **Another Way: The Book.** The songs we recommend for this chapter are *"Sankofa"* by Cassandra Wilson and "Rollcall For Those Absent" by Ambrose Akinmusire. Please add to the playlist as you are inspired.

CHAPTER 5

R: Reflecting Theologically Together

Do not be conformed to this world, but be transformed by the renewing of your minds, so that you may discern what is the will of God—what is good and acceptable and perfect.
—Romans 12:2

In this chapter we turn to the third practice in CARE: Reflecting Theologically Together. Here we explore theological reflection as an indispensable discipline for leaders and communities that seek to lead change on purpose. Within the CARE approach, theological reflection engages and critiques inherited ways of reading sacred literature and social life, enabling us to glimpse alternatives to the status quo. This approach, driven by focused dialogue and careful attention to our embodied experiences, also stimulates imagination and insight into particular next steps leaders can take to build experimental alternatives or to help change ineffective and unjust systems.

Effective and sustainable change in systems relies on corresponding shifts in our collective awareness, assumptions, and actions in relationship to that system. Through theological reflection together, we can scrutinize and shift ideas about ourselves and the world that undergird the very realities we hope to change.

Living and Leading Vignette

During a visit to Cape Town, South Africa, Stephen and Matthew walked with a delegation of U.S.-based faith and justice leaders through Robben Island, the infamous site of the prison where Nelson Mandela spent twenty-seven years as a political prisoner before his release in

February 1990. Robben Island is more than a prison. Just west of the coast of Cape Town, it is a two-mile misted shore landscape with rich stone and mineral quarries overlooking the cape and an imposing line of lifeless gray stone prison buildings from shore to shore. Home to a colony of penguins and occasional seals, this island's subdued beauty is hauntingly permeated by the stench of the bloody memory that saturates the soil.

René August, the Anglican priest and veteran of the South African anti-apartheid struggle we mentioned in chapter 2, led us to a limestone quarry where she stopped to share the history of that place. That quarry was one of the sites on the island where Mandela and other political prisoners were forced to work without pay to produce minerals from which the apartheid government would profit. Their punishment for the pursuit of freedom was unpaid labor in harsh conditions, including the grueling work of harvesting minerals from the ground under the heat of the South African sun. Over time, the fine dust from the limestone settled in the eyes of the imprisoned men, causing some of them to lose their vision. In defiance of the indignity of imprisonment and the oppression of apartheid, Mandela and his fellow prisoners together turned that quarry into an academic department of what they called "Robben University." While they labored in groups, they would hold Socratic seminars around subjects that developed their political acumen, historical knowledge, and leadership skills.

Standing at the mouth of the quarry, August invited our group to reflect on our lives and leadership in light of the history of this island and the sacred stories of Scripture. "Remember the story of the talents in Matthew 25?" she asked us. Most of us were Christian leaders familiar with the New Testament. So we nodded in the affirmative. This parable refers to talents—which were a form of currency—and is often cited to encourage "good stewardship" among churchgoers.

She retold the story. "The landowner was going on a trip and called three of his slaves (from the Greek word *doulos*) before he left. In a feudal or slave economy those who own the land do not work the land. They extract income from the labor of others who, in turn, gain little or nothing from their efforts. So, to one slave he gave five talents, to the next he gave two talents, and to the third he gave one. Two of them traded for more money, which would further enrich the landowner. They returned the money, with interest, to the landowner. They were good slaves who managed the little resources the landowner had assigned to them and they were both rewarded with greater responsibility in the landowner's estate.

"But one of the enslaved men chose a different way, he simply buried the money. So, when the landowner returned to collect his unearned income, he gave the landowner back exactly what he was given. We have been taught to call the last slave the *un*faithful one. But what did the so-called unfaithful slave say to the landowner? 'We know that you are a harsh man. You reap where you have not sown, and you gather where you have not scattered seed. The enslaved man's resistance speaks. It says: 'You are an unjust person and I refuse to participate in this exploitative game even if you will throw me crumbs for my efforts.'"

August then reoriented those of us steeped in traditional ways of reading this story, "We have been taught to read this passage as though this landowner is a metaphorical stand-in for God. But this landowner is described as the *opposite* of what we say about the nature and character of God. God is not unjust. God does not reap where God has not sown. So how have we come to see God in support of this arrangement of injustice?"

She reminded us, "How you read a text is determined by from where you're reading and with whom you're reading." She then asked us a series of poignant questions that invited us to link Mandela's story to the story of this sacred text, as a way of reading the stories of our own lives:

- To whom was this slave unfaithful: God or this unjust landowner?
- Who was the unjust landowner in Mandela's experience?
- Who are the unjust landowners in our communities?
- Where are the systems of economic exploitation in your community?
- In what ways are we participating in furthering or disrupting those systems?
- Are we called merely to be good slaves who help manage an unjust system?
- How might God be calling us to stand alongside this "unfaithful" slave, to stand alongside Mandela, to interrupt the exploitative business-as-usual in our communities?

Afterward, we walked a few paces from the quarry to a former prison building where we reflected further in group dialogue around the significance of this site and this story for our lives and our leadership going forward.

Creating Conditions for Theological Reflection

The time-honored process that August led on Robben Island is commonly called theological reflection. Robert Kinast describes this process as a communal undertaking "that begins with an actual, pastoral situation; correlates theological resources with this situation; and aims at an informed course of action."[1] Theological reflection is a process of making sacred meaning out of human experience. It is one of many forms of reflection in which individuals, communities, and organizations attempt to locate their experiences in a larger story that helps form a robust sense of personhood and purpose.

Reflecting together theologically on meaning and purpose is the third practice of the CARE approach.

Metanoia and Critical Theological Reflection

As understood in the CARE approach, theological reflection is a process that, when repeated over time, fosters deep change in our shared awareness, self-understanding, and collective action. Done well, it facilitates *metanoia*, a Greek word commonly translated as "repentance" that literally means a "change of mind." *Metanoia* suggests being "transformed by the renewing of your mind,"[2] a shift in our consciousness and way of being in the world that directs our action toward the embodiment of empowering alternatives. This inner "change of mind" is a necessary element of transformative change in systems and communities.

[T]heological reflection is a process that, when repeated over time, fosters deep change in our shared awareness, self-understanding, and collective action.

While theological reflection can be done individually, the CARE approach does theological reflection as a communal leadership discipline. The meanings we make and the purposes we discern in this form of theological reflection seek to locate the "me" in the "we." They invite a shift in how we see, think, and act collectively. Dialogue is the core process of such theological reflection, which is a "stream of meaning flowing among and through us and between us."[3]

---

[1] Robert L. Kinast, "Pastoral Theology, Roman Catholic," in *Dictionary of Pastoral Care and Counseling*, ed. Robert J. Hunter and Nancy J. Ramsay, expanded ed. (Nashville: Abingdon Press, 2005), 873.

[2] Romans 12:1–2.

[3] http://sprott.physics.wisc.edu/Chaos-Complexity/dialogue.pdf, 2

The CARE approach to theological reflection operates within a tradition of *critical* theological reflection that requires an explicit reckoning with the impact of systems, power, and agency on our understanding of self, community, relationship to the sacred, God-sense, and faithful work in the world. Systematic theologian Willie Jennings correctly asserts that all "theological reflection is quintessentially a traditioned enterprise."[4] While multiple traditions coexist, we are making a distinction here between conventional modes of theological reflection and a tradition of *critical* theological reflection. Conventional theological reflection tacitly reinforces systems of oppression by focusing solely on personal piety and spirituality while ignoring power, privilege, and systems. This is theological negligence that leaves the status quo intact and unscrutinized. Critical theological reflection, on the other hand, scrutinizes the flesh and blood realities of social life. Using the lens of sacred ideals, it is a tool for reimagining our world.

Theological reflection can alter the ways we imagine ourselves in relationship to the Creator, other living beings, the sacred universe, and all that dwells therein.

The personal and social work of theological reflection draws its symbols, images, and language from the social worlds we inhabit. In turn, it can alter the ways we imagine ourselves in relationship to the Creator, other living beings, the sacred universe, and all that dwells therein. In fact, the interpersonal and institutional realities that we have inherited and desire to change are themselves the fruit of our shared mental models about the relationship between humans, the divine, and creation.

The CARE approach develops faith-rooted change-making leadership. If faith-rooted leaders who seek to make a positive difference in the world are not reflecting on the theological dimensions of systems, power, and agency, they're not adequately doing theological reflection. Our failure to cultivate robust reflective practices that frame the social within the scope of the sacred produces ever-deepening ruptures between the claims of Christian faith and the flesh and blood impact of Christian communities on the lives of people and the planet. The CARE approach embraces a time-honored practice of critical theological reflection that sparks a renewed faith-rooted imagination toward just action. Critical theological reflection makes God-sense of our lives in light of the ways in which power, social/economic systems, and human agency shape the "stuff of life." Through it, we activate

[4]Willie Jennings, *The Christian Imagination: Theology and the Origins of Race* (New Haven: Yale University, 2010), 69.

often-neglected empire-resisting traditions of Christian faith to create change in the world.

This practice assumes that theology is something people do, not merely what we think. So theological reflection in this mode is reflection *on* action *for* action. It is a rhythm of acting, seeing, thinking, and acting again. This process calls leaders to intermittent pauses in activity that, when in conversation with context, community, heritage, and tradition, provide critical insight and perspective to refine our thinking and guide our efforts. For leaders seeking change in communities and systems, this clarifying rhythm is essential to fostering right relationship, deep wisdom, and group intelligence toward collective action.

We are doing theology with our spirits, brains, and bodies.

The power of this practice draws from its engagement with multiple ways of knowing. Doing theological reflection means not merely articulating ideas and rational concepts, but also engaging feeling, bodily sensation, and nonrational modes of knowing such as dreams, meditations, visions, and intuition. As Audre Lorde writes, "We recognize that all knowledge is mediated through the body and that feeling is a profound source of information about our lives."[5] In critical theological reflection, we invite attention to all of these means through which eternal meaning may be made of our temporal moments. We are doing theology with our spirits, brains, and bodies.

A Storied Example

As the young adults walk into the room the first voice they heard was Nina Simone's, singing "Old Jim Crow, what's wrong with you? It ain't your name, it's the things you do" through the speakers.[6] Matthew was facilitating a workshop in 2010 on "The New Jim Crow" mostly for white young adults participating in year-of-service programs through faith-based volunteer organizations, the same year of the publication of Michelle Alexander's landmark book on mass incarceration. Most of these young leaders would be spending their year of service in communities that had been affected by the meteoric rise of mass incarceration in the United States during the latter quarter of the twentieth century. This workshop explored the emergence of the system of mass incarceration in the United States and invited the participants to consider how they may be called to respond to the

[5]Audre Lorde, *Sister Outsider* (Berkeley, CA: Crossing Press, 2007), 53.

[6]"Old Jim Crow" songwriters: Jackie Alper, Nina Simone, Ron Vander Groef; lyrics © Warner/Chappell Music, Inc. See www.metrolyrics.com/old-jim-crow-lyrics-nina-simone.html for complete song lyrics.

impact of this system on the communities they would serve. While some of them had read and heard reports and stories about the prison industry, and others had been involved in the growing efforts to disrupt and dismantle the system, most of them had not connected this social problem to a theological framework.

Matthew writes:

With Ms. Simone's searing psalm setting the tone, we begin with a "Living Likert." We arrange the room in five sections that correspond to the five levels of the Likert scale;[7] strongly agree, agree, neither agree nor disagree, disagree, strongly disagree.

To begin surfacing their assumptions about the issue, I invite the young leaders to respond to a set of carefully crafted statements. The instruction is this: "Place yourself in the section that best represents your response to six statements." I place the first statement on the screen.

The thirteenth amendment to the U.S. constitution abolished legal slavery in the U.S..

The response is unanimous. Everyone in the room shifts to the "strongly agree" section. There's hardly enough room for all of them to fit. Then I ask one of the participants to pull out a smartphone and "look up the thirteenth amendment. Read section 1 out loud." A woman proceeds to read,

"Neither slavery nor involuntary servitude, except as a punishment for crime whereof the party shall have been duly convicted, shall exist within the United States, or any place subject to their jurisdiction."

She looks at the phone as though she has seen a ghost.

"What did you notice?" I ask.

"Except!" she exclaims. Incredulous, she reiterates, "It says slavery is illegal . . . EXCEPT! So it allows for slavery as punishment for a crime? I never knew this was in the Constitution. I just thought this abolished slavery in the United States!"

This review of the wording of the thirteenth amendment reveals a consequential constitutional nuance clouded by the widely held notion that this sacred text of American civil religion ended legal enslavement in the United States unequivocally, once and for all. Then in a state of shared shock, the living scale shifts in recognition of this new awareness. They slowly change their position until the whole group

---

[7]The Likert scale is a rating scale measuring how people feel about something, developed by American psychologist Rensis Likert in 1932.

drifts in a stunned stupor to the other side of the scale. It's unanimous again. *Strongly disagree.*

As a group, we work through five more statements this way.

- Legal discrimination against people of color ended with legislative landmarks such as Brown vs. Board (1954), the Civil Rights Acts of 1964, and the Voting Rights Act of 1965
- Mass incarceration would end if the government spent more money on education and less money on prisons
- The most effective way for people of faith to address the rise of mass incarceration is through ministry and service to at-risk individuals whose behavior is likely to lead to incarceration
- The sharp increase in the U.S. prison population is due to drug policies that were enacted to respond to rising crime rates
- Citizens who have served prison sentences for felonies can reenter society and fully participate as citizens

With each new statement, they move more tentatively to the positions they would have to explain and defend in dialogue. They are no longer so sure about what they were sure about. Disorientation has begun to set in. The discussion that follows immediately jars them out of their sense of certainty about an array of sacred cows about which they were holding unscrutinized assumptions: the role and function of the faith community in society, the facts of U.S. history, the fairness of the U.S. legal system, and the foundation upon which that system rests, the U.S. Constitution.

"So before we talk about the *New* Jim Crow, let's talk about the *Old* Jim Crow. Who and what was Jim Crow?" I ask.

"A set of laws used to discriminate against Black people after slavery?" a young man ventures sheepishly.

"Good. Yes, it reestablished the racial caste system of slavery even after slavery was legally ended. Okay, that's *what.* Now for the *who.* Who was Jim Crow?" A cartoonish depiction of a white man in blackface appears on the screen. I briefly explain the genesis of "Jim Crow."

Thomas Dartmouth "Daddy" Rice was the early nineteenth-century white actor who made his fame and fortune playing and posing as a lazy, slow-witted, fumbling slave. His character was named Jim Crow. Rice's theatrics popularized a dehumanizing caricature of Black men as intellectually inferior brutes that require white dominance for their own well-being. Rice's Jim Crow gave moral cover to the white supremacist worldview of American slavocracy and served as an artistic pretext for the establishment and justification of Jim Crow laws that would reinforce the social, political, and economic dominance of whites in the United States (not just the South) for decades after slavery had been legally abolished . . . *except*.

We then turn to the New Jim Crow. We listen to a talk given by *New Jim Crow* author and legal scholar Michelle Alexander. Alexander's research demonstrates how the current system of mass incarceration functions as a renewed system of exploitation that mimics its legal and socio-political ancestor, Jim Crow. She reads this passage from the introduction to her landmark book:

> In the era of colorblindness, it is no longer socially permissible to use race, explicitly, as a justification for discrimination, exclusion, and social contempt. So we don't. Rather than rely on race, we use our criminal justice system to label people of color "criminals" and then engage in all the practices we supposedly left behind. Today it is perfectly legal to discriminate against criminals in nearly all the ways that it was once legal to discriminate against African Americans. Once you're labeled a felon, the old forms of discrimination—employment discrimination, housing discrimination, denial of the right to vote, denial of educational opportunity, denial of food stamps and other public benefits, and exclusion from jury service—are suddenly legal. As a criminal, you have scarcely more rights, and arguably less respect, than a black man living in Alabama at the height of Jim Crow. We have not ended racial caste in America; we have merely redesigned it.[8]

We watch and listen as Alexander reveals how Jim Crow, both old and renewed, leverages social labels and the "exceptional" thirteenth amendment to the Constitution to legitimize social caste based on racism. She documents and discusses the strategies of political figures such as Richard Nixon, Ronald Reagan, and Bill Clinton, who used drug policy as a tool that criminalized and disproportionately punished Black and Brown communities in order to gain and sustain political power. From convict leasing to the War on Drugs, Alexander demonstrates how laws follow culture and custom to bake into our common life the evil of oppression and exploitation.

Her powerful lecture hits these unknowing young leaders like a ton of bricks. I invite them to acknowledge and investigate their emerging ideas, irritations, and sensations with a series of questions, pausing for dialogue around each line of inquiry.

---

[8]Michelle Alexander, *The New Jim Crow: Mass Incarceration in the Age of Colorblindness* (New York: New Press, 2010), 2.

- What facts did you discover about mass incarceration?
- What feelings did you experience as you discovered these facts?
- What does this have to do with your *faith*? What implications does Alexander's argument have for your life of faith and your work in service and ministry?

For these young leaders motivated by their faith to pursue a life of service, this final question is where the rubber meets the road. Some of them suffer from passion burnout and are overwhelmed by being introduced to yet another expression of evil. Others are blissfully unaware of the systemic forces that have shaped their lives and the experiences of the people they feel called to serve. I'm asking them to consider for themselves: Is this just another one of the endless items on the list of social ills that I passively acknowledge and attribute to the evil of the world? Or is there something in this that calls to the core of who I am, what I believe, and what I may be called to do?

The stakes rise as we approach a story from Scripture. Together we read Acts 16:16–24 (Message):

> One day, on our way to the place of prayer, a slave girl ran into us. She was a psychic and, with her fortunetelling, made a lot of money for the people who owned her. She started following Paul around, calling everyone's attention to us by yelling out, "These men are working for the Most High God. They're laying out the road of salvation for you!" She did this for a number of days until Paul, finally fed up with her, turned and commanded the spirit that possessed her, "Out! In the name of Jesus Christ, get out of her!" And it was gone, just like that.
>
> When her owners saw that their lucrative little business was suddenly bankrupt, they went after Paul and Silas, roughed them up and dragged them into the market square. Then the police arrested them and pulled them into a court with the accusation, "These men are disturbing the peace—dangerous Jewish agitators subverting our Roman law and order." By this time the crowd had turned into a restless mob out for blood.
>
> The judges went along with the mob, had Paul and Silas's clothes ripped off and ordered a public beating. After beating them black-and-blue, they threw them into jail, telling the jailkeeper to put them under heavy guard so there would be

no chance of escape. He did just that—threw them into the maximum security cell in the jail and clamped leg irons on them.

Standing near a whiteboard in that conference room, I then invite our group to reflect on their lives and leadership in light of the history of mass incarceration and this sacred story from Scripture. "How many of you are familiar with this story?" I ask. Only a few hands rise in response. "Well, how many of you have heard of the story that follows in Acts about what Paul and Silas did in jail?" The majority of hands in the room go up: many of these young leaders are children of the church; the Sunday school lessons seem to have stuck.

I observe, "Like you, when I was in Sunday school, I was always taught about the part of the story that comes after this. Paul and Silas are in jail praying and God comes along and breaks open the jail to set Paul and Silas free. But I rarely looked to see how they came to be incarcerated in the first place and what God was breaking them out of. So let's look again at the prequel to the jail episode."

I begin to retell the story:

Paul makes an intervention here. Interestingly enough, he had been bypassing this girl for days on his way to the house of prayer. Only out of frustration, he focuses on this girl and performs an exorcism. Then all hell breaks loose.

All of a sudden a series of characters begin to show up, all of whom have a problem with Paul and Silas. Apparently Paul's frustrated intervention has interrupted an economic arrangement that depends on this girl's enslavement. First the slave owners appear. Then the police come to serve and protect the slavers. The cops come to take Paul and Silas before the judge in that first-century criminal justice system. Then the mob beats them down. Everyone who appears in the story sides with the social order that enslaved the girl.

Paul and Silas land in jail because they accidentally disturb a beehive of actors who take issue with their disruption of this girl's exploitation. Let's call it an act of frustrated service that arouses owners, police, the judge, and a mob all of whom take violent issue with the way that Paul and Silas have "disturbed the peace."

This leads us to the story of Paul and Silas's imprisonment later in Acts 16.While every character in the story sides with the slavers and exploiters of this woman, notice that God's activity in this story is not neutral. As Paul and Silas pray and sing in that jail, an earthquake erupts and "shakes the foundations of the prison." While this beehive of characters take action in support of the social order, creation organizes itself to disrupt the system of punishment used to keep the status quo in place.

I go on to share that the church often takes its stand with the biblical mob. It tends to sanction theologically the legal system's definitions of crime as sin. The church and its notions of "service" and "prison ministry" ultimately aim not to disrupt unjust systems, but to appear to be charitable while not "disturbing the peace." Michelle Alexander observes that when we conflate crime, deviance, and sin, it lends theological legitimacy to the New Jim Crow. It does to folks who are deemed criminal what Jim Crow did to Black folk: it puts them in a category that makes them even more vulnerable to exploitation and violence. She argues that a theology that gives sacred sanction to the criminalization of people and communities generates a wicked morality. It allows us to dismiss "those people" as objects who are unworthy of our care, compassion, and concern. Disrupting and dismantling mass incarceration requires not just political reform, but theological revolution.

Disrupting and dismantling mass incarceration requires not just political reform, but theological revolution.

I then lead the group into a dialogue punctuated by questions crafted to "disturb the peace" of our deeply held notions of Christian service and charity. These young leaders painfully reckon with their own privilege and work as young adult volunteers in faith-based service organizations.

I use the following questions to invite these well-intentioned young people to come to grips with the insufficiency of "service" alone to address the systemic issues that plague the communities that shaped them and the communities they serve.

- Paul's act of faith-rooted service stokes the response of an unjust complex system upheld by multiple actors. You are going into communities to engage in "service." What are the unjust systems into which you are likely to stumble? What are the larger forces that that make your service necessary?
- Remember Archbishop Oscar Romero's wise observation: "When I give food to the poor, they call me a saint. When I ask why the poor have no food, they call me a communist." What is the "why" behind the need you seek to serve?
- What are the systems of reward and punishment that either encourage or discourage you to disrupt and dismantle the systems you stumble into through service work?

- What does it mean for you to participate with God and creation in "shaking the foundations" of the social order that exploits and enslaves?

Critical theological reflection is a reflection *on* action *for* action. This study and theological reflection on the problem of mass incarceration creates an instance for these participants to reckon with the significance of their work in faith-based volunteer service. At the close of this session, many participants are eager to figure out how they can contribute to the movement to end mass incarceration. I offer resources, organizations, and opportunities that they can support and engage to further their understanding of the complex constellation of social, political, economic, and theological forces that undergird the New Jim Crow.

After one workshop, a young white man spoke up for another subset of these emerging leaders. His first words were a statement of identity. "I am a young Republican." Visibly disturbed, he took me (and Michelle Alexander) to task for suggesting that white male Republicans that he admired, namely Ronald Reagan and Richard Nixon, would knowingly implement policies and strategies designed to harm people of color.

After the session ended, I lingered with him for a few moments, paying close attention to his argument and his affect. He turned red as he approached and confronted me near the whiteboard. "How dare you! And how dare Michelle Alexander malign these men and suggest they used race to win elections!"

Critical theological reflection is disruptive. *Metanoia* disorients. Shifts in consciousness are seismic, often experienced as earthquakes. It can cause some of us to feel as if our very world—the basic ideas upon which we ground our identity—is falling apart. I recognized quickly that this experience disturbed this young man at the core of his unexamined identity: white, male, Republican, Christian, good.

I responded, "You're upset with me about verifiable facts that, if you accept are true, will begin to unravel the myths and stories that have shaped your understanding of who you are. The fact that Nixon and Reagan employed political tactics to criminalize Black and Brown people to gain political power is neither a secret, nor a disputed fact. Google Lee Atwater. Google the Southern Strategy. Look up Dog Whistle Politics. It's all right there."

"Now here's my challenge to you," I continued. "Will you channel your anger into study of the issue? Or will you go away from here insisting on being angry and refusing to examine the basic facts of this history? Your choice will reveal to you what you really care about."

Sacred and Social Dimensions

In the two examples in this chapter, theological reflection does not pretend to be the neutral act of passive bystanders. Rather, it is a process that requires reckoning with three interrelated lines of critical theological inquiry; systems, power, and agency. On Robben Island, August used the parable and the quarry as mirrors through which we could more clearly view the systemic arrangements, power dynamics, and collective choices that have shaped the situations in which we live and lead. She then invited us to interrogate God-concepts through which we tend to interpret the parable, the quarry, and our work in the world. In this mode of critical theological reflection, the "God question" is not only, "How is God at work in our experience?" It is also, "What are the dominant notions of God at work here and how are they shaping our thinking and action?" A final question points us forward, asking, "What is our next most faithful step, if we are to align our ongoing actions with this renewed view of who God is and how God is at work?"

Matthew's workshop with the young adult volunteers used a dialogue-driven process to scrutinize unexamined assumptions about sacred texts and social systems. In that New Jim Crow session, Matthew carefully led the group in rereading and reinterpreting the revered social text of the U.S. Constitution, the sacred biblical text, and the subtle social scripts of Christian service that shape our imagination about how we may be called to live and lead as an expression of our faith. His encounter with the angry young man is an example of how such a process may rattle the unexamined myths around which we have constructed our identities.

Both August and Matthew demonstrate that theological reflection is not limited to reflection on the Bible. Theology is an expression of our understanding of our relationship to ourselves, God, human communities, and creation. That understanding is shaped more by written and unwritten "texts" than the Bible alone. Critical theological reflection excavates all aspects of history, culture, and faith that have, perhaps invisibly, informed our understandings of who we are and what we are called to do in the world.

The meaning we make in this process is sacred and social. It comes to life at the intersection of our personal, contextual, historical, and scriptural narratives. It invites us to explore these narratives as they reveal forces at work in us and among us. More importantly, these new meanings provoke us to alter our ways of thinking, being, and acting that open a way for liberating alternatives to stifling systems of oppression and exploitation. Critical theological reflection is a dialogical process that assumes that *metanoia* emerges "when the day-to-day thinking of community members has altered their day-to-day decisions and actions, which leads to a change in the culture of the community that entrenches those new ways of thinking. Their thinking is changed when the language, stories, and narratives the community uses is altered in a profound way."[9]

A Leadership Practice

Practiced leaders learn to turn to critical theological reflection regularly, as a way of constantly aligning and realigning their actions with God's hope for the world. The conversation at Robben Island came midway through a pilgrimage in which formally and informally, within our minds and in conversation with others, we engaged in meaning-making on various occasions.

Getting into the habit of asking theological questions in conversation with systems of power and privilege is like exercising a muscle. The more we exercise that muscle, the stronger it becomes. We notice its presence and use it more readily, sometimes arriving alone at insights around which we later invite the reflections of others, and sometimes as an explicit group process in which we literally reflect *together* about a situation around which we need to lead change.

Theology done this way is deeply connected to what's happening inside us. This work is not just happening in our heads. We feel it in our bodies. It flares up in conflict with others as we go about this way of leading. Disorientation is not gentle. It disrupts, because we don't like change, loss, or the difficult work of renegotiating new identities. And this work is a corrective to the malformed ways in which we've practiced theology as if it happens in a neutral environment, unaffected by long histories of exploitation and oppression.

What situation calls for theological reflection? When do we look at the history, context, and lived experience of a particular community in light of our emerging understandings of God and Scripture? We do this every time we enact a ritual, perform a liturgy, or preach a sermon, but our communities benefit if we also do this when we prepare to protest an injustice, organize an action, engage in service, run for public office, or start an enterprise for social good. This is a leadership practice not limited to "church" moments, but best applied to the social, economic, and political dimensions of our lives and our leadership.

---

[9]Gervase R. Bush, "Dialogic OD: A Theory of Practice," *OD Practitioner* 45, no. 1 (2013): 12.

Questions for Reflection

For the individual learner/leader seeking meaning and purpose:

1. The authors define theological reflection as "a process of making sacred meaning out of human experience." They describe it as one of many forms of reflection in which individuals, communities, and organizations "attempt to locate their experiences in a larger story that helps form a robust sense of personhood and purpose." What is the larger story within which you locate your experience? Is that story religious, geographical, generational? Is that story static or shifting?
2. Critical theological reflection is disruptive. "Shifts in consciousness are seismic, often experienced as earthquakes." Can you think of a time in your life when you experienced theological reflection as disruptive, seismic, or like an earthquake? What was that experience like for you? What do you need to do to ground yourself in the wake of such a disruption?
3. What was one challenging idea you encountered here? What made it so?
4. What was one of the most powerful or helpful ideas you encountered here? What made it so?
5. What is one thing you take with you from this chapter that might help you think more critically and more theologically about the ways in which your context forms or deforms you?

For the guide/facilitator helping others find meaning and purpose:

1. In the story at the beginning of this chapter, René August turns a common interpretation of Christian scripture on its head through a dialogical, place-based educational experience. Such critical theological reflection "does not pretend to be the neutral act of passive bystanders. Rather, it is a process that requires reckoning with the three interrelated lines of critical theological inquiry: systems, power, and agency." How do you use your position as a guide/facilitator to lead people into

examining their assumptions about sacred texts and social systems?

2. What historical narratives grounded in your geographical proximity might be generative for such a process? What stories from your community's sacred text might need to be reinterpreted in light of current justice issues such as mass incarceration, immigration reform, environmental racism, or emerging definitions of sexual consent?

3. What was one challenging idea you encountered here? What made it so?

4. What was one of the most powerful or helpful ideas you encountered here? What made it so?

5. What is one thing you take with you from this chapter to inspire you in the work of inviting others into a rhythm of acting, seeing, thinking critically, and acting again?

For those leading organizational change:

1. The authors describe *metanoia* as an inner change of mind that is a necessary element of transformative change in systems and communities. They describe it as "disruptive ... seismic ... often experienced as earthquakes." Can you recall a time in your own journey into leadership that such a shift occurred in your thinking? What were the conditions that allowed this to happen?

2. How do you foster critical reflection on actions that your organization has taken or will take that may be in the best interests of its mission but are harmful to other people or communities?

3. What was one challenging idea you encountered here? What made it so?

4. What was a powerful or helpful idea you encountered here? What made it so?

5. What is one thing you take with you from this chapter that might help you be more critical about your organization's norms, strategies, and day-to-day actions in light of your organization's values?

For all:

1. Review *Another Way Manifesto*. Which sentences stand out to you after reading this chapter?
2. We are building an interactive playlist to accompany each chapter. You can find it on Spotify at **Another Way: The Book.** The songs we recommend for this chapter are "Doxology (I Remember)" by Derrick Hodge and "Take Me to the Alley" by Gregory Porter. Please add to the playlist as you are inspired.

CHAPTER 6

Liberating Leadership

There's power in healing work. But it isn't personal power.
It cannot satisfy an individual's craving for self-importance.
It's a real power that has nothing to do with our small,
selfish dreams. It's the power to help life create itself.
—*The Healers,* Ayi Kwei Armah[1]

The Hero's Cape

Matthew writes:

A brisk April morning released pale shafts of sunlight through a row of windows running along the roofline, illuminating the packed sanctuary. In the pulpit and pews, the warmth of the gathered saints had knocked off the early morning chill of this Chicago spring day. The cumulative heat generated by standing room only, shoulder-to-shoulder Black bodies in worship and praise formed an energetic embrace around all who entered that sacred space.

"Amen," I mumbled into the microphone. Standing in the pulpit at the sacred desk, I awkwardly gathered my Bible and the long yellow pages of legal paper on which I had scribbled my first sermon. It was over and I was relieved. As I fumbled with my papers the congregation shouted and praised the God of our ancestors. At the age of fifteen, I had preached my "trial" sermon, my first since I had discerned a call to ministry a few months earlier. It was entitled "Lions, Bears, and Giants." Drawn from the story of David and Goliath, it was a ten-minute message about the power of faith in overcoming seemingly insurmountable challenges. On this youth Sunday, when the young people got to "run the service," my church family praised God, celebrating the evidence that the faith had taken root in another generation.

[1]Ayi Kwei Armah, *The Healers* (Nairobi, Kenya: East African Publishing House, 2012), 120.

The order of service typically left little to be done after the sermon. Usually, after the pastor finished the sermon and extended the invitation to discipleship, he and the pulpit guests would gather their Bibles and ceremoniously float down the blood-red carpet in the center aisle to the double doors at the sanctuary entrance and wait to give the benediction. Meanwhile the Hammond B-3 would whine and wail, inviting us to participate in a sweet moment of meditation before the final good word. After giving the benediction at the door, the pastor would greet exiting worshipers as they crossed the threshold from the humid sanctuary to the chilly rigors of Black life on the Southside of Chicago.

But this time, before I could gather my things and take the ceremonial walk down the aisle, my pastor put his hand on my shoulder. "Hold on, Matt," he said. With his left hand on my left shoulder he looked to the usher and motioned with his right hand as if to say, "Come here." I was puzzled. Why are we stopping? Is something wrong? Nothing ever happens between the sermon, invitation, and benediction. The head usher walked briskly down the middle of the sanctuary with a black garment in her hand. With a smile she handed the pastor a cape she had gone to retrieve from his study.

He took the sacred vestment from her and placed it on my shoulders. I didn't expect it to be so heavy. The cape felt at once like both a weight and a warm blanket. "Rev" presented me in his cape to the congregation. Upon the sight of this teenaged preacher in the pastor's vestments, the congregation erupted in praise. Pastor, the ushers, and the congregation seemed to have conspired to claim and charge me. I had been simultaneously blessed and burdened with responsibility for helping to carry on a sacred leadership tradition of Black faith. In this sacramental moment, the community and the context assigned public meaning to my personal sense of call.

Healers help living systems reconnect to their wholeness.

That mantle landed like a ton of bricks on my shoulders and my psyche. In retrospect I am aware that since that moment I have been negotiating the relationship between the calling that had taken root in me and the tradition that had been placed on me.

From Warrior-Hero to Warrior-Healer

Heroes rescue folks in danger and fix what's broken; healers help living systems reconnect to their wholeness. The CARE practices assume a leadership ethos that is tied to the well-being of communities and their leaders. In this chapter, I share a way of reenvisioning leadership that moves us from heroes to healers. It evolved from my experiences within the prophetic Black church tradition and the broader Black freedom struggle. This evolving vision I call "liberating leadership." Liberating leadership seeks to dismantle the dominant forms of living and leading that reinforce the oppressive norms of empire. It helps to create alternative ways of being that open new, expansive possibilities for communities to flourish. Liberating leadership undergirds CARE, and simultaneously, the CARE practices help to create conditions in which "liberating leadership" can emerge.

The story that begins this chapter illustrates the beginning of my initiation into the work of a warrior in a distinct leadership tradition, often called the prophetic Black church. Each Communion Sunday my home congregation would profess: "There is no task more sacred than the liberation of Black people. God has called us to this task." In this mission-driven faith community, the pastor was a warrior-hero, an icon whose inimitable powers and charisma led the church's charge to live up to its call.

Liberating leadership is a way of working within and beyond current structures of reality to explore and enact life-giving alternatives to the death-dealing systems of empire.

This chapter builds from that time-honored tradition, imagining an alternative ethos that widens our perspective and practice of leadership to acknowledge the complexity of contemporary needs and realities. This emerging ethos, called *liberating leadership*, shifts the focus from an out-front warrior-*hero* who leads the charge to a warrior-*healer*[2] who cocreates the conditions for the community to discover its power and address its complex challenges.

In light of rampant gun violence in the United States and escalating military engagement globally, "warrior" language can be troublesome, especially for those who embrace nonviolence as a philosophy and way of being the world, but both the hero and healer are types of warriors. As warriors, both the hero and healer are called to work that requires militancy, not necessarily militarization. These models both include nonviolent approaches to social change. They are freedom fighters acting in the interests of their communities, and ultimately in the interest of humanity itself. However they do so out of different worldviews and with different weaponry.

Liberating leadership is a way of working within and beyond current structures of reality to explore and enact life-giving alternatives to the

[2]I first encountered the term *warrior-healer* through the work of Wekesa Madzimoyo at the Aya Educational Institute in Atlanta. Madzimoyo's *warrior-healer-builder* is an archetype of whole personhood that employs "balance, depth, self correction, and protection against oppressor-injected scripts that misdirect our thoughts, feelings, and actions away from protecting and nurturing our families and our community" (http://www.ayaed.com/bml/).

death-dealing systems of empire. Before envisioning the leadership of a warrior-*healer,* let's explore the characteristics and the limits of the warrior-*hero.*

The Warrior-Hero

The warrior-hero tends to stand as a proxy for *his* people. The warrior-hero shows up nobly on the battlefield on behalf of *his* community. *He* answers the call to service knowing that self-sacrifice is a job requirement. *He* faces down known enemies that would annihilate *his* people. *He* fights on behalf of *his* village against the forces of oppression and thereby attempts to protect the community from the bloody brutality of the war that has been waged against it. In exchange the people celebrate *him,* often deferring to *his* leadership, positioning *him* as a special member of the species.

The male pronoun predominates here because this is most often a male-centered leadership model. It privileges men and reserves legitimacy for those who approximate the dominant styles and perspectives most often exhibited by individual male leaders. It therefore negates the experiences and wisdom of women, non-heterosexual men, and those who identify as transgender.[3]

Warrior-heroes are lionized for their possession of special qualities and their ability to overcome great challenges. Exalted as an exemplar of an ideal, the warrior-hero embodies a paradoxical message to ordinary people—here is an extraordinary figure to whose stature and example we should all aspire. Yet, this hero is extraordinary precisely because of unusual qualities that most of us do not possess.

At once inspiring and discouraging, the warrior-hero model of leadership contains a self-sabotaging glitch that can undermine the very aims it seeks to achieve. In my experience, the cape felt at once like both a weight and a warm blanket. The cape was both traditional sacred vestment of a clergyperson and the costume of a superhero. The garment brought with it the comfort of a community that had embraced me and my calling. It also came with a heavy expectation—the burden of embodying the community's heroic ideals. It is an image that may feed the ego but can so easily set one up for failure.

Limitations of the Warrior-Hero

My trial sermon was a moment that evidenced God at work in my life in a particular way. In response, the congregation enthusiastically embraced my calling to ministry. This call to ministry was interpreted

[3]Erica R. Edwards describes this erasure of the knowledge and experiences of marginalized peoples as epistemological violence in *Charisma and the Fictions of Black Leadership* (Minneapolis: University of Minnesota Press, 2012), 19–22.

first by the community as a call to *preach*. In this warrior-hero tradition, the typical weapon of choice is the word.

The word, when well used, has the power to envision new worlds, spark imagination, and inspire movements. Public communication, be it written or spoken, has long been a key tool for social change in Black religious leadership. The iconic figure in whom this tradition found its most well-known expression was Martin Luther King Jr. Following King's assassination and the naming of a national holiday in his honor, his example grew to mythic proportions. It created a sort of template that was used to shape—and often limit—the ways aspiring young, mostly male, faith-rooted leaders imagined themselves in the public square.

Unfortunately, dominant contemporary expressions of the warrior-hero tradition are largely the product of myths about King and the role of faith-rooted leadership in the Black freedom movement.[4] While recognizing the usefulness of sacred public rhetoric in social change, our mis-memory of the role of faith leadership in pivotal movements for social change and liberation limits our imagination about what faith-rooted liberating leadership looks like. Impulses toward liberating leadership can be warped by these misinformed models, thereby generating practices that reproduce some of the most destructive and oppressive legacies in our history, such as the marginalization of women and persons with disabilities in leadership.

Mental models determine the reflexes out of which we lead. If we don't broaden our imagination, we will attempt to use a word-wielding warrior-hero model to address every episode of oppression and injustice, when in fact liberating leadership can draw inspiration and guidance from an array of forms and traditions.

Reflecting on her experience as an activist-minister in the civil rights and Black power movements, Barbara Holmes observes,

> One problematic aspect of the movement was its commitment to unending struggle and ongoing battle readiness. This is a noble commitment to free a people from hangings, apartheid, and genocide, but one that engenders a particular stance toward the world. When struggle becomes the main construct of human life, reality tends to be saturated with tension—a guarded awareness, limited communications, overachieving and an inability to connect to other realities.[5]

---

[4]In *Charisma and the Fictions of Black Leadership,* Erica R. Edwards locates the roots of this leadership tradition in the post-Reconstruction era. She argues that Black charismatic leadership functioned as a strategic device to sustain Black political agency and respectability in an era of white American terrorism against Black communities.

[5]Barbara Holmes, *Race and the Cosmos: An Invitation to View the World Differently* (Harrisburg, PA: Trinity Press International, 2002), 31.

What Holmes names here is the way in which the practice of the warrior-hero role shapes one's approach to life. War can become calcified as a way of being in the world, a particular practice of citizenship and leadership that makes of God a cosmic commander, the self a driven soldier, and all others potential enemies and targets in the theater of endless battle.

For leaders interested in liberation, the warrior-hero model both empowers and stifles our ability to initiate alternatives to the status quo. It is a tradition as noble as it is troublesome. It is a tradition whose laudable aims are undercut by its assumptions and practices.

An Alternative Way: Liberating Leadership

The warrior-healer is an alternative to the warrior-hero. The warrior-healer model embodies *liberating leadership,* which encompasses two interdependent meanings. Here *liberating* is both a verb and an adjective. In its verb form, this *liberating* points to leadership that liberates. It is the "relational and collective process" that builds the capacity of a community to envision and enact a future distinct from its past.[6] That collective capacity then finds expression in individuals who play leadership roles that, in the best cases, respond to the felt and expressed needs of the community. Leadership that liberates involves both an inner and outer process that flows from what the late Miles Jerome Jones calls "a people's new self-understanding in relationship to the Eternal."[7] It transforms complex living systems that dehumanize people and oppress communities into realities that more closely approximate what King called the Beloved Community, or what many Christians call the kin(g)dom of God. Liberating leadership is the work of warrior-healers who seek to create conditions in which all creation flourishes and is uninhibited in its ability to live fully into its sacred worth, identity, and potential.

In its adjectival form, *liberating* involves liberating or freeing the concept of leadership from its conventional use and practice. Public imagination around leadership tends to be limited to individual leaders granted authority and credibility by the power of their public performances and proclamations, as was symbolized in the story of my trial sermon and moment of affirmation by the congregation and its leadership. But what does leadership look like when it doesn't depend on a special individual? How might our capacity for dismantling

[6]Stephen Preskill and Stephen D. Brookfield, *Learning as a Way of Leading: Lessons from the Struggle for Social Justice* (San Francisco: Jossey-Bass, 2009), 3.

[7]This exploration of liberating leadership draws heavily from the late Miles Jones's idea of liberation of oppressed peoples as "a new self-understanding in relationship to the Eternal." "Digging Deeper Wells" (unpublished lecture, Trinity United Church of Christ, Chicago, 1994).

domination and cocreating systems that foster right relationship be enhanced when our notions of leadership are set free in ways that privilege the life force and wisdom of the community itself? How does our imagination around leadership then become liberated from narrow meanings when the community itself is the agent?

Leah Gunning Francis's book *Ferguson and Faith: Sparking Leadership and Awakening Community* recounts an example that hints toward this shift. Gunning Francis relates the story of Traci Blackmon, pastor of Christ the King United Church of Christ in Florissant, Missouri. She responded to the shooting of Michael Brown by a police officer in Ferguson, Missouri in August 2014 by inviting folks to gather and pray at the police station after church the Sunday following the shooting.

Blackmon observed that clergy did most of the talking at the first few community gatherings. She watched the young people's anger grow as it remained unspoken and they went unacknowledged. It slowly dawned on her that the young people needed the opportunity to speak their pain, share their perspective, and be a key part of strategizing a plan: "So I said, 'We're having a town hall meeting tomorrow.' Then I knew it had to happen. I didn't have to have the answers. We, collectively as clergy, didn't have to have the answers, but we did need to have a way that people could plug in."[8]

Recognizing that she and other recognized leaders didn't "have to have the answers," Blackmon pivoted from being the one holding the microphone to the one creating a space for others to speak and strategize. Her shift in awareness and action is an example of liberating leadership at work. Other clergy similarly enacted liberating leadership in the movement that followed by mobilizing others to work for collective liberation of people of color experiencing police brutality. They left behind a notion of leadership as a single messianic figure whose greatest weapon was inspiring public speech. They embraced a model of leadership that creates space: for *others* to speak their truths, listen deeply to one another, and determine the strategic direction that can best guide a community's collective action.

What Liberating Leadership Is *Not*

Deeply ingrained leadership reflexes often stymie the emancipatory efforts of communities seeking alternatives to systems of domination and oppression. If Blackmon had not taken the time to reflect on what was going wrong, she may never have realized her mistake, and her leadership reflexes may have gone unchallenged. Such reflexes are so deeply embedded that they need to be surfaced

[8]Leah Gunning Francis, *Ferguson and Faith: Sparking Leadership and Awakening Community* (St. Louis: Chalice Press, 2015), 26–28.

and deconstructed one at a time, so that we can choose alternative practices that call an alternative reality into being. These deeply embedded leadership reflexes derive from unscrutinized social scripts that liberating leadership aims to disrupt.

Liberating leadership is *not* synonymous with public speaking

In traditional leadership models, the power to lead tends to be reserved for people who have the ability to speak. While oration may be an important skill for leaders who inspire and organize communities to pursue Beloved Community, it does not stand proxy for leadership. The ability to conceive, write, and deliver ideas is a critical skill set that communities need in order to make meaning. But speeches, sermons, and other public statements are not the sole source of that meaning-making, nor should they be. Alone, they fail to help communities develop practices and enact strategies that turn ideas into tangible alternative systems.

Ella Baker embodied and championed a collective, distributed leadership model that called for meaning-making to be the work of a whole community, including the least lettered among us. She urged freedom-seeking folk to move meaning-making into strategic organized activity, building communities that together pursue questions, experiment with answers, analyze situations, and use iterative collective action as a resource from which to learn over time.

In a thinly-veiled critique of Martin Luther King Jr. and the warrior-hero model he represented, Ella Baker declared:

> I have always felt it was a handicap for oppressed people to depend so heavily on a leader, because unfortunately in our culture the charismatic leader usually becomes a leader because he has found a spot in the limelight. There is also the danger in our culture that, because a person is called upon to give public statements, such a person gets to the point of believing he is the movement. Such people get so involved with playing the game of being important that they exhaust themselves and their time and they don't do the work of actually organizing people.[9]

Ella Baker modeled an approach to leadership that suggests *public listening* rather than public speaking may be the most important skill in

[9]Ella Baker, "Developing Community Leadership," in *Black Women in White America: A Documentary History*, ed. Gerda Lerner (New York: Pantheon Books, 1972), 351. Resources for further research on Ella Baker include: Barbara Ransby, *Ella Baker and the Black Freedom Movement* (Chapel Hill: University of North Carolina Press, 2003) and Charles Payne, "Ella Baker: Models of Social Change," *Signs* 14, no. 4 (Summer, 1989): 885–99.

a community when facing complex and systemic ills. Deep listening to the embedded knowledges, concerns, questions, and emerging answers within a community opens and sustains its access to its own wisdom and ability. "Give light and the people will find a way," she advised. This vital process of discovering and illuminating the community's collective wisdom and capacity for self-determination is precisely what tends to be eclipsed when public performance casts itself as leadership. In this way, Baker exemplifies a compelling alternative of liberating leadership.

Liberating leadership *is not* about lone rangers

The lone ranger is a conventional model of leadership that assumes that there is only room for one leader at a time. When new leadership emerges, the baton or torch must be passed to a new leader. Leadership here is a personal possession, not a communal practice. It is a talisman of personal power, not to be shared or distributed, except to the next one in line.

Our dominant notions of leadership arise from the Western intellectual tradition that privileges the individual as the source and end of all useful endeavors. The "Great Man" theory[10] of history suggests that pivotal shifts and advances in human history are the result of the extraordinary genius and strength of a single great (usually male) leader. All of our hopes reside in a messianic figure, a warrior-hero, who is uniquely endowed with extraordinary power and unusual personal qualities. This tends to be how we read sacred literature. It's also how we read social life.

Drawn from the fictional twentieth-century character, the lone ranger metaphor signifies a peculiarly American myth drawn from the wells of Western colonial individualism. This mythical model is the Lone Ranger, a white male cowboy who alone is the arbiter of justice, embodiment of virtue, and violent conqueror of the frontier and its Indian inhabitants. Lest we forget, an indigenous sidekick, Tonto, whose name to Spanish speakers means "moron," accompanied this character. Ironically, the dominant forms of faith-rooted justice-seeking leadership, which often rail against the effects of colonialism and white supremacy, are frequently infected with the lone ranger ideology.

The limitations of lone ranger leadership are painfully well known. Lone rangers are quite effective in calling attention to issues that require remedies by also calling attention to their own personality and activity.

---

[10]One of the progenitors of this theory in historiography was Thomas Carlyle. See Thomas Carlyle, *On Heroes, Hero-Worship and the Heroic in History* (New York: Fredrick A. Stokes & Brother, 1888).

Charismatic individuals are often highly influential and typically most effective in pointing back to themselves, sometimes motivating people to follow their personal example. One of the problems with this form of leadership is its conflation of a personality with a cause, which thereby dooms the cause to death in tandem with the leader's own decline. More important, lone ranger leadership rarely succeeds at solving complex challenges and creating sustainable change. It tends to operate in episodic activity that focuses on achievable wins, rarely taking on the strategic, systemic dimensions of communal challenges, where wins are not as readily identifiable or achievable. Such an approach reflects well in the short term on the lone ranger's ability to address the ostensible symptoms of an issue, but fails to touch its less visible root causes.

When we unlearn and release lone ranger leadership as a toxic reflex, we gain access to a replenishing well of inspiration, integrity, and support.

While the most harmful long-term effects of lone ranger leadership impact the larger community, this model also wreaks havoc on the integrity and well-being of the lone ranger as an individual. Martyr myths serve as excuses for the personal costs of living and leading as a lone ranger, but behind the public veil of charismatic leaders often lie painfully fragmented people whose brokenness is exacerbated by the ways they learned to lead.

Even those of us who critique this model often default to it. Who we are is often sharply disconnected from what we do. This is what Parker Palmer calls the divided life.[11] In service to propping up a persona, without which we believe the cause will falter or even fail, we hide or repress the dreams that enliven us, the visions that inspire us, and the fears that shake us. Burnout and the myriad of maladies that afflict people in organizations and movements attempting to do good in the world are the result of a set of cynical assumptions about what necessary evils we have to accept in order to accomplish change in the world.

When we unlearn and release lone ranger leadership as a toxic reflex, we gain access to a replenishing well of inspiration, integrity, and support. We discover renewed congruence between our inner and outer architecture. Rather than seeking to accrue personal power, we form sustainable collaborations with trusted partners who share in a collective vision.

---

[11]Parker Palmer, *A Hidden Wholeness: The Journey Toward an Undivided Life* (San Francisco: Jossey Bass, 2004) ,5.

In the novel *The Healers*, writer Ayi Kwei Armah tells the story of Densu, a young apprentice to a master healer in a West African town named Esuano. During the early days of Densu's training, the master, Damfo, grounded him in the ethics and values that guide the leadership role to which Densu aspired. In one lesson Damfo emphasized the nature of a healer's true power: "There's power in healing work. But it isn't personal power. It cannot satisfy an individual's craving for self-importance. It's a real power that has nothing to do with our small, selfish dreams. It's the power to help life create itself."[12]

Damfo's wise counsel provides a perspective that enables leaders to reckon honestly and humbly with some of the most complex challenges within us and within our communities. Even in the face of difficult circumstances, we experience a greater potential to work out of a sense of purpose, passion, and even joy. We liberate *ourselves* into greater flourishing as we shed the oppressive idea that we have to go it alone, and thereby give ourselves access to wider and deeper well of wisdom and power.

Liberating leadership does not use people as means to achieve an end

In *The Healers*, Densu, the healer in training, was faced with a choice between two paths. One of his mentors offered him the opportunity to join a cadre of leaders whose power was derived from the magic of manipulation. Meanwhile Densu sat at the feet of another mentor who gradually invited him to the path that drew its strength from authenticity and connection to himself, others, the earth, and life itself. Densu chose the latter. His healing aspirations were rooted in a desire for "a life lived with people who did not see other human beings as only material they could use and handle."[13] Even the most well-intentioned efforts to dismantle oppression and inaugurate eternal alternatives can fall into the habitual flaw of using people to achieve change. Borrowing logic from the industrial-age innovation of interchangeable parts, this leadership reflex uses people in congregations, organizations, and movements as incidental replaceable assets in the machine of the mission. This model pays very little attention to the quality of our relatedness to one another, but overemphasizes our value to the bottom line, be it financial, social, or environmental. This buys into the basic idea that is the bedrock of all oppression, injustice, and inequity: there are some people who are not

[12]Armah, *The Healers*, 120.
[13]Ibid., 61.

worthy of our care, compassion, and concern.[14] Then, "those people" become expendable tools to be exploited for the benefit of another person, an organization, or a cause.

While this flawed logic often informs our beliefs and practices, the contrary is true. Human beings are the ends, not the mere means, of liberation. Rightly construed, experiences and resources are the means we use to meet the ends of holistic human flourishing. Causes and programs are the means: people's development toward full humanity is the end. The sacred stories of pilgrimage, be it the biblical Exodus or the march for civil rights from Selma to Montgomery, remind us that the journey itself forms us and transforms us in preparation for the destination. Without this awareness, we tend to march into a new land holding onto the mind-set of the bygone world. The slogan for the 1968 Memphis sanitation workers' strike (the work stoppage that King went to support when he was murdered) was not, "I want fair wages." The slogan of that campaign revealed that they were engaged in a more fundamental fight. Their signs read "I Am a Man." In the fight for fair wages and work practices, they shook off the fear of Southern terrorism and affirmed their humanity in the face of brutal repression and dehumanization. The struggle for justice emboldened their sense of humanity. Even if the movement fails to meet its stated goals, that inner treasure becomes a lasting resource by which the community experiences re-humanization. It generates the sustainable capacity to continue fighting to affirm our humanity, a necessary precondition for Beloved Community.

In the early 2000s a broad coalition in the State of Georgia built a statewide movement to repeal a piece of legislation named GA SB440. Passed in 1994, amid the racism-laden "Tough on Crime" movement, this bill automatically tried and imprisoned youth and children as adults and mandated extraordinarily punitive sentences for juvenile offenders convicted of "seven deadly sins" including murder, armed robbery, and rape. Predictably, nearly 80 percent of the teenagers convicted and sentenced under this law in Georgia were Black boys.

When I served as associate pastor for youth and children at First African Presbyterian Church in a suburb of Atlanta, the youth ministry

[14]Michelle Alexander, *The New Jim Crow: Mass Incarceration in the Age of Colorblindness* (New York: New Press, 2010), 18: "If the movement that emerges to challenge mass incarceration fails to confront squarely the critical role of race in the basic structure of our society, and if it fails to cultivate an ethic of genuine care, compassion, and concern for every human being—of every class, race, and nationality—within our nation's borders (including poor whites, who are often pitted against poor people of color), the collapse of mass incarceration will not mean the death of racial caste in America. Inevitably a new system of racialized social control will emerge—one that we cannot foresee, just as the current system of mass incarceration was not predicted by anyone thirty years ago."

took up this policy struggle as a ministry priority. On one notable occasion, the youth testified at a public hearing about the harmful effects of the law. Nate,[15] a bright but relatively mild-mannered and quiet thirteen-year-old high school freshman, prepared and delivered a formal statement at the hearing. He openly challenged the legislators to fight for the lives of Black boys as though they were fighting for their own lives. One of the legislators curtly interrupted his challenge, "Wait, give us a break! We weren't the ones that started this." Nate sharply replied, "Yeah I know, but you are the ones who can stop this!" The folks in that crowded hall gasped and applauded the surprising courage and quick wit of this young man. Years later, Nate and his mother shared that the impact of that experience on Nate's self-image and confidence was immeasurable. In that moment, in the face of those powerful policymakers, Nate found something in himself he didn't know he had.

In the short term, we lost this painful legislative battle, but the legislative outcome was not the only thing at stake. Through the process of organizing and mobilizing, our community won a bolder and more confident young man who knew then more than ever before that he could stand in the face of power and speak his truth. In the years following that fight, SB440 was slowly dismantled and replaced by less punitive laws for youth offenders. However, Nate's newly discovered courage and power was a gift that would continue to benefit him and his community.

Liberating leadership is not best known for its products, but by its processes

The common approach to determining the quality of leadership has to do with the products of leaders. Speeches, budgets, achievements, acquisitions, awards, and honors are markers of product-focused leadership. We tend to determine whether a leader is effective solely by what he acquires or what she achieves. To be sure, achieving goals and objectives is important, but if that is the sole measure by which we assess leadership, we are likely to miss an all-too-common pattern in product-focused leadership. Leadership products may be obtained by way of processes that themselves create a toxic, inhumane environment that snuff out the life force of all who dare participate in the production.

Wendell Berry's poem "Questionnaire" asks questions that illuminate the costs of the all-too-frequent dissonance between product and process:

---

[15]This young person's name has been changed.

1. How much poison are you willing to eat for the success of the free market and global trade? . . .

2. For the sake of goodness, how much evil are you willing to do? . . .[16]

What if instead of focusing on the products of leaders, we paid more attention to the processes of leadership? This would mean focusing not on "what we achieve" but on "how we achieve it." A focus on process considers both how we're doing and how we're being.

A movement within the food industry provides a helpful analogy. Growing sectors of the food industry have begun to tie the quality of their products to the processes by which they arrive at grocery stores, farmers' markets, and restaurants. Consumers are increasingly aware that a piece of chicken or a stalk of celery is more likely to contribute to health if its producers use methods that do not harm the earth, avoid the use of hormones to increase bulk and profitability, and do not neutralize nutritional value with poisonous pesticides and genetic modifications.

When our goal for food is based on taste alone, these considerations don't matter. The end product's impact on our taste buds' desire for salt and sugar is most important. But when our goal for food is based on health for self, community, and creation, the sustainability and ecological impact of the processes shift to being of the utmost importance. Unsustainable processes result in unhealthy products.

The same is true for leadership. If our goals amount merely to "sweet" wins that we may achieve in the short term, the outcomes alone may be our chief consideration. We are likely to pursue those outcomes, and do so by any means necessary. But if liberating leadership is concerned with the flourishing of communities and creation itself, we must work with heightened awareness of the long-term impact of our leadership processes on the very humans and communities we seek to serve. Means matter.

Attention to process—*how* we listen, *how* we engage in dialogue, *how* we organize time, *how* we receive and integrate feedback, *how* we convene and connect people, *how we* manage organizations, *how* we build leadership in others, *how* we design organizational experience, *how* we motivate and mobilize collective action, *how* we tend our inner lives—all this reveals key markers of liberating leadership. Attention to process is central to the design and implementation of the CARE practices.

---

[16]Wendell Berry, "Questionnaire," in *Leavings: Poems* (Berkeley, CA: Counterpoint: 2010), 12.

Creating Conditions for Liberating Leadership to Emerge

Liberating leadership is a process of creating alternative spaces—classrooms, homes, sanctuaries, neighborhoods, offices, community centers—in which we experience a glimpse of the world for which we long. It is where we come to know in our cells how liberation looks, feels, and sounds. These alternatives to dehumanizing hierarchies are experiments, not yet solutions. They are prototypes in which we may invite the village to dive into the dissonances between the world as it is and the world as it might be. This is a space of active collective inquiry through which we open ourselves to the emergence of new knowledge and awareness derived from iterative risk, failure, and learning.

By actually living and leading in such spaces, even for brief clarifying moments, we learn to desire them, require them, and prioritize the regular creation of them.

At a national gathering of justice-focused clergy, organizers, students, and activists, Stephen and I used the CARE process to organize a series of intergenerational circles in which venerable veterans of movements for freedom, justice, and equality sat and talked with young leaders who aspired to carry on the liberating legacy of their forebears. The normal arrangements in these kinds of meetings tend to involve inspiring speeches and sermons with an engaged audience that listens and cocreates the experience in the classic call-and-response pattern of African-derived oratory. But this time, to create conditions for a different kind of interpersonal engagement, we removed lecterns from the rooms and reorganized these spaces as small intimate circles. No speeches, no sermons, no talking heads, and no large audience. In a facilitated process, we invited young faith-rooted activists and veteran leaders to suspend the tendency to position themselves on leadership pedestals. We created space within which they could slow down and simply tell stories to one another, eye-to-eye, in intimate circles that had been preconditioned by silence and Spirit.

In a CARE-based process we gave them prompts such as:

- Tell a story from your experience that expresses what you care about most.
- Tell a story about a time when what you cared about was at risk, challenged, or threatened in some way.
- What choice did you make when what you cared about was at risk? What did you do?

With each generous round of storytelling and listening, we spiraled into deeper attention and sacred stillness. Being held in the unusual embrace of holy attention, faith-rooted freedom fighters let down their guard and shared their grief, hopes, and rarely confessed anxieties. As facilitators, we began to feel as though the floor of the room had just dropped a few inches. We had moved to a new depth together. A presence emerged among us, and we were aware that the room had been transformed from a hotel ballroom to an ancient mountainside with a burning bush. We could almost hear the words of God to Moses: Take off your shoes, for you are standing on holy ground.[17]

Afterwards, a young activist-pastor reflected on the sacred experience of this intergenerational circle in CARE-conditioned space: "Listening to these stories in that way transformed me. I decided in my heart that I want to be really free, and not just talk about it, and I really want my people to be free. This is what I'm called to."

What in this gathering led to this transformative affirmation? How do we create the conditions for such spaces to emerge? We do this by reminding ourselves and one another to:

- Create hospitable space for our whole selves to show up,
- Slow down and listen to one another with reverence, as though we are hearing the words of a sacred text,
- Redesign relationships from top down hierarchies to cocreative communities,
- Explore shared passion and purpose, forming collaborations and partnerships around common vision,
- Hold each person's full humanity as indeed the highest end, insisting that no other end justifies the treatment of people as a means,
- Know that what matters most is the process—not the mere product—of leadership; if we pay attention to *how* we lead, *what* we achieve tends to unfold in powerful and unexpected ways.

Liberating leadership requires that we set conditions for the transformation of spaces, individuals, relationships, and our future. In its wake, we can see that another way and another world is possible. With attention to the ways we gather, connect, and mobilize people, we can help to cocreate that world, one room at a time. To do so will require us to revise our old models of leadership.

---

[17]Exodus 3:5

Beyond the Warrior-Hero

Liberating leadership does not require abandoning the warrior altogether. It means retooling this archetype, imagining a bit more broadly who the warrior is and how that person operates in service to the village.

The warrior-hero is the representative who operates on behalf of the community and stands between the community and whatever threatens it. The warrior-hero puts him or herself in the way of danger to take up that noble task. The function of this singled-out leader is always to fight and that fight is focused on a very clearly defined enemy or goal. While that approach may be honorable, it is ultimately insufficient in situations where complexity is at work, especially when the so-called threat is an aspect of our very selves, an inner enemy.

Complex Challenges: Out There and In Here

The effectiveness of the warrior's role as a fighter who faces down threats as a representative of the village depends on clarity about what the threat is and from where it comes. But what if the threat is both external and internal? What if we are wrestling with a constellation of complex threatening factors—environmental, spiritual, interpersonal, political, and social? If all you have is a bow and arrow, every challenge begins to look like a target, and we may fail to recognize that our weapons are ill suited to the complexity that threatens our communities.

Author Adam Kahane describes complexity as a situation that has three characteristics. Complex challenges are:

- dynamic
- generative
- social

Dynamic characteristics refer to situations in which it is difficult to tie single causes in a linear fashion to single effects. Most often we're dealing with multiple causes that interact with one another to create multiple effects that are difficult to track. These effects crop up over time, sometimes months, years, or even centuries later.

Generative characteristics arise out of the interplay of multiple factors, producing new offshoots that we could never have anticipated. Complexity necessarily involves the element of surprise. Leading in complexity necessarily involves leading into mystery, operating in a seemingly endless "not knowing" space. Here, the only certainty available is the presence of the unknown.

Social characteristics refer to ways in which people experience the realities that emerge from these situations, all from their own dearly held viewpoints. As stakeholders who see the situation from particular angles, we often dig into our own perspectives at the very moment we should be loosening our grip and looking for other viewpoints. Complexity calls for practices that place multiple perspectives in conversation to tell the most complete story possible of the ever-evolving challenges the community is facing.[18]

Kahane's description of complexity, while helpful, lacks a fourth characteristic that may be the most difficult to address. The challenges we face, with all of their dynamism, generativity, and social difficulty, are also multidimensional: they reside in both the inner and outer life.

Whether we are seeking to initiate change around poverty, food insecurity, or domestic violence, we must inevitably confront problems that don't just reside *out there*. We must also reckon with the problematic ways of seeing and being in the world that are deeply ingrained *in here*, where the mental models that drive our activity lurk just beneath conscious awareness and often go unnoticed and unscrutinized. For both the village and the warrior, the outer world is a reflection of our inner world, and vice versa. This ancient principle, known as the law of correspondence, reminds us "as above, so below, as within, so without, as the universe, so the soul"[19]

Reckoning with the unknown, and surviving in a constantly shifting landscape like the ones Kahane describes, requires leaders to adopt a curious, humble posture that is grounded in self-awareness yet open to wisdom from elsewhere. This can only happen if leaders are doing their own inner work, constantly reflecting, befriending their shadow, and acknowledging the ways in which they are implicated in the very evil and suffering they seek to alleviate.

An Inner Shift

In 2013 the Forum for Theological Exploration hosted a national consultation of key academic executives leaders to address the racial and ethnic diversity deficit in graduate theological education. After three days of intense and endless analysis of our entangled system, one program director looked in wonder at the gathered group and announced a sudden awareness. She exclaimed, "It occurs to me that everyone who can do something about this problem is in the room!"

---

[18]Adam Kahane, *Solving Tough Problems* (San Francisco: Berrett Koehler, 2007), 1–2.

[19]For study on this principle, see Roger L. Cole, *The Kybalion: A Study of The Hermetic Philosophy of Ancient Egypt and Greece* at http://www.yogebooks.com/english/atkinson/1908kybalion.pdf.

It would have been easy to respond sarcastically to her awakening, "Duh! Of course we are! That's why we brought you here." Despite her discovery of the obvious, she gave the gathered leaders an important gift: she spoke out loud and surfaced a shared belief that had not been named. Part of what inhibits change, even when we have the "right people" in the room, is the belief that the institutions we lead and the challenging situations we face are "out there." We imagine them as the ogre who lives on the distant hillside and occasionally comes down the hill to frighten the townspeople. In turn, we imagine ourselves as passive observers of an inevitably unfolding future over which we have little power.

Her aha moment was the ripple effect of an inner shift, at once subtle and tectonic. Because she was doing this work in a space set up to support liberating leadership, she was able to recognize that neither the problems we were lamenting nor the solutions we hoped to create were "out there." They were both also "in here." In an instant, the way she imagined her relationship to the issues changed. She experienced a flash of perspective that opened a shaft of light through which she could glimpse a new possibility for how "we" might lead differently. Her insight called the room into accountability. She helped us recognize that current conditions and their root causes are not permanent fixtures of our field—at least they do not have to be. The systems we inherited were designed and reinforced over time by people in the roles we now occupy, to produce the outcomes that we say we want to change.

Systems that bring evil to bear on flesh and blood are only effective and sustainable to the extent that they set up shop in our souls.

In that moment, she offered the room a choice. Will we leave to our heirs in the church, academy, and broader society a system that we passively inherited and did nothing to transform, or will we leave a system that we actively construct out of values that meet the needs of our time, thereby repairing the legacies of injustice left to us by our forebears?

Theological education is but one example. In education, health and medicine, food, religion, business, law, and criminal justice, we recognize that we are living and leading in systems that consistently produce undesirable results. Health disparities, mass incarceration, income inequality, miseducation, and failing schools are just a few of the "products" of these systems.

Systems that bring evil to bear on flesh and blood are only effective and sustainable to the extent that they set up shop in our souls. They

Healers form the necessary conditions for life to create itself.

become as fundamental to our reality as gravity, and limit our imagination of what might be. We reproduce results we say we don't want by internalizing the unconscious assumptions about ourselves and the world upon which these systems are built. Then we reproduce the symptoms in our thinking, feeling, relating, and doing. If systems could not find a home in our thinking (head), feeling (heart), and instincts (gut), they would not persist. Further, if leadership for systemic change does not recognize and ground its efforts in the unseen inner dimensions of our common life, its efforts are likely to involve unsustainable episodes of activity that merely tinker with (and reinforce) the current social order.

The systems that recycle trauma, dis-ease, and disparity are as much "in here" as they are "out there." Likewise, the liberating alternatives we long for reside in the subtle, often unseen dimensions of our collective and individual inner lives.

Glimpsing the Warrior-Healer at Work

Heroes rescue folks in danger and fix what's broken. In contrast, healers help living systems—people, communities, ecologies—that have been fragmented to reconnect to their wholeness. Healers form the necessary conditions for life to create itself. The work of the hero tends toward visibility, while the work of the healer most often goes unseen, unrecognized, underground.

The primary task of liberating leadership is to create alternative spaces for a different future to emerge. Liberating leadership cultivates conditions in which people may actually experience another way. In this other way, the Eternal incarnates a holy alternative to the stifling status quo. In our cells, we experience enough creative dissonance to anchor the idea that the status quo is not a given, but a choice. Another world is possible. We glimpse it coming to birth through numerous partners around the world.[20]

In Toni Morrison's novel *Beloved*, we catch a glimpse of the warrior-healer at work in the person of Baby Suggs, a holy woman who lives at a house called 124 in a community of formerly enslaved people:

> When warm weather came, Baby Suggs, holy, followed by every Black man, woman, and child who could make it through, took

[20]We name here a few contemporary warrior-healers and their communities: Emily McGinley at www.urbanvillagechurch.com; Rich Havard at https://www.letsgetinclusiveuic.org, Kit Ford at https://argrowshouse.org, Jen Bailey at https://www.faithmattersnetwork.org, René August at https://freedomroad.us, Starsky Wilson at https://deaconess.org/starsky-wilson, Gregory Ellison at www.fearlessdialogues, and Ruth Padilla DeBoorst at https://www.resonateglobalmission.org.

> her great heart to the Clearing—a wide-open place cut deep in the woods . . . In the heat of every Saturday afternoon, she sat in the clearing while the people waited among the trees.
>
> In the silence that followed, Baby Suggs, holy, offered up to them her great big heart . . . "Here", she said, "In this here place, we flesh; flesh that weeps, laughs, flesh that dances on bare feet in the grass. Love it. Love it hard. Yonder they do not love your flesh. They despise it . . .
>
> More than eyes or feet . . . More than your life holding womb and your life giving private parts, hear me now, love your heart. For this is the prize."[21]

Baby Suggs, *holy*, gathers in the Clearing a community of emancipated Africans attempting to live free in the North. To reduce Baby Suggs to the role of preacher would be to shroud her gift as a warrior-healer. She doesn't merely preach to a listening audience; she leads her community in a participatory process through which they reconnect to themselves and one another. The tree stump in the Clearing is the place from which she loves and calls the community to love with her "great big heart." Here in the Clearing, Baby Suggs, *holy*, operates as so much more—she is a facilitator, a choreographer, a designer of movement and process.

> "Let your mothers hear you laugh," she told [the children]. . . . "Let your wives and children see you dance," she told [the men].. . . "Cry," she told [the women]. . . . "For the living and the dead."[22]

Even in "free" territory, white terrorism and economic subjugation lock in the imagination and life chances of Black folk. The root structure of this system *was* and *is* a way of seeing and being in the world that fragments minds from bodies, flesh from spirit, feminine from masculine, sacred from secular, and matter from immaterial. From these roots sprout the deep sense that Black flesh embodies evil and by the very vice of its being deserves punishment. These weeds grow first and most perniciously in the inner world.

In the Clearing, Baby Suggs, *holy*, channels and designs ways for the children, men and women to be with each other so that they enjoy an incarnational experience of themselves prized, new, different, free, beloved. She invites her community to immerse themselves in the full flow of emotions available to the human family: joy (laughter), power (dance), and grief (weeping). She calls them to stand in the very place

[21]Toni Morrison, *Beloved* (New York: Vintage, 2004), 104.
[22]Ibid., 103.

where "yonder" had established a regime of power that relied on the lie of their inhumanity and fully be. "We flesh. . . Yonder they do not love your flesh."[23]

Warrior-healers do their work in the inner world, ever aware of the outer world, ever aware of yonder. Warrior-healers cocreate and facilitate communal spaces in which yonder's norms and values no longer dominate the inner lives of the community. Baby Suggs, *holy*, leads this community, with its despised flesh into the Clearing to feel the "groundlife" under its feet, stemming from an alternative root system; to participate in laughter, dance, weeping and loving that grounds their inner life in "a new self-understanding in relationship to the Eternal."[24] Her leadership organizes underground public space and participatory practices that reconnected the community to itself, its Life Force, its inner resources. "Love it. Love it hard," Baby Suggs says.

Baby Suggs, *holy*, cocreates with this community a space where her daughter-in-law, Sethe, would later testify, "Bit by bit, at 124 and in the Clearing, along with the others, she had claimed herself. Freeing yourself was one thing; claiming ownership of that freed self was another."[25]

Sethe's testimony is the boon that the warrior-healer pursues. More than being "unslaved," the warrior-healer facilitates a reconnection with what Thomas Merton calls a hidden wholeness,[26] out of which Sethe is able to repossess herself and "claim ownership" of her freed self.

Herein lies the root of revolution. All tyrannies, oppressions, and domination systems lose their footing on the necks of subjugated peoples when the unslaved—after emancipation—reconnect to and own their whole selves. This is the work of the warrior-healer. This is the beginning of the end of empire.

Questions for Reflection

For the individual learner/leader seeking meaning and purpose:

1. When you reflect on the communities and/or leaders that formed you, do you see aspects of the warrior-hero model, the warrior-healer model, or something altogether different?

[23]Ibid.

[24]Jones, 1994.

[25]Ibid.,111–12.

[26]Thomas Merton, "Hagia Sophia," in *A Thomas Merton Reader,* ed. Thomas P. McDonnell (New York: Image/Doubleday, 1974, 1989), 506.

How would you describe the leadership models that you saw as a child, teenager, or young adult? What portions of those models do you see living themselves out in you? How might you become more intentional about living and leading in ways that embody your deepest values?

2. Liberating leadership creates alternative spaces in which to glimpse the world we wish to see. "By actually living and leading in such spaces, even for brief clarifying moments, we learn to desire them, require them, and prioritize the regular creation of them." Can you remember a time when you glimpsed a way of living that tended to the souls of leaders or that embodied concern for the flourishing of communities and creation itself? What created the conditions for liberation in that moment?
3. What was one challenging idea you encountered here? What made it so?
4. What was a powerful or helpful idea you encountered here? What made it so?
5. What is one thing you take with you from this chapter that might help you be more intentional about the leadership models you seek to embody?

For the guide/facilitator helping others find meaning and purpose:

1. "Liberating leadership seeks to dismantle the dominant forms of living and leading that reinforce the oppressive norms of empire. It helps to create alternative ways of being that open new, expansive possibilities for communities to flourish." How do you see liberating leadership undergirding the CARE practices? How do the CARE practices help create the conditions in which liberating leadership can emerge?
2. In mentoring the next generation of leaders, mentors often default to the leadership models by which they were formed. How do you reinforce ways of mentoring that explicitly embody the values you hold? Who are the leaders you see modeling liberating leadership? What are the characteristics you see in them?
3. What was one challenging idea you encountered here? What made it so?

4. What was one of the most powerful or helpful ideas you encountered here? What made it so?

5. What is one thing you take with you from this chapter that might help you foster liberating leadership in your own context?

For those leading organizational change:

1. This chapter asserts: "When we unlearn and release lone-ranger leadership as a toxic reflex, we gain access to a replenishing well of inspiration, integrity, and support." Can you think of a story from your own leadership journey when you learned that the "lone ranger" model was limited, insufficient, harmful, or toxic? Can you think of a time when you were able to "shed the oppressive idea that we have to go it alone?" What made that possible?

2. This chapter argues that leaders are often measured by sweet wins and short-term outcomes achieved "by any means necessary," while liberating leadership is concerned with the flourishing of communities and creation itself. What would it take in your organization to change a "by any means necessary" mentality? Can you think of a time when the flourishing of community was a celebrated outcome?

3. What was one challenging idea you encountered here? What made it so?

4. What was one of the most powerful or helpful ideas you encountered here? What made it so?

5. What is one thing you take with you from this chapter that inspires you to try on or live more deeply into the role of the warrior-healer?

For all:

1. Review *Another Way Manifesto*. Which sentences stand out to you after reading this chapter?

2. We are building an interactive playlist to accompany each chapter. You can find it on Spotify at **Another Way: The Book.** The songs we recommend for this chapter are "Who" by Mayyadda and "Ella's Song" by Sweet Honey in the Rock. Please add to the playlist as you are inspired.

CHAPTER 7

Enacting the Next Most Faithful Step

A system cannot fail those it was never meant to protect.
—W. E. B. Du Bois

You never change things by fighting against the existing reality. To change something, build a new model that makes the old model obsolete.
—Buckminster Fuller

In previous chapters we have discussed three of the four CARE practices; (C)reating space, (A)sking self-awakening questions, and (R)eflecting together theologically on meaning and purpose. In this chapter, we describe the fourth practice: (E)nacting our next most faithful step.

The CARE practices are building blocks in a process of discernment. Each discipline is communally oriented, shaped by culture and context, and driven toward alternative life-giving possibilities for individuals and communities. (E)nacting our next most faithful step is a practice of transforming insight into reflective action. Here we emphasize immediate action that enables us to unearth, test, and reflect on our assumptions and actions in pursuit of a new heaven and new earth. Each word used to describe this practice suggests a set of critical questions that should inform our action.

Enacting. How do we increase the likelihood that the inspiration and information we derive from discernment and learning experiences will be applied in some meaningful way when we return to our places of service and leadership? People need a physical opportunity to practice the possibility that they have begun to envision in dialogue, inquiry, and reflection with others. Otherwise, exposure to new possibilities becomes stuck in the world of ideas. Our bodies are the sites where we make the world anew. We need practices that give our bodies a chance to make ideas tangible.

Next. New possibilities often arrive in grand visions. We imagine alternatives as expansive portraits of a desirable future. Yet bringing colorful worlds into being takes place one brushstroke at a time. Grand alternatives require attention to granular details. Visions call us forward into unknown territory. While we are entranced by possibility, the path to the new contains unexpected barriers and hazards. Reflective attention to our *next* immediate action releases us from the paralysis of analysis and helps us learn step by step about the terrain into which we are moving. We are often overwhelmed in our attempts to facilitate change because we fail to shrink the task. Failure to attend to the next proximal action can lead to burnout, if our passion overwhelms our capacity to enact the vision of the change we seek.

Most Faithful Step. A core set of values and commitments drives our pursuit of alternatives. How do we keep our grounding principles front and center as we try to create something new? When we incarnate our imagination, we are honoring those values by testing them against the terrain of our common life. To seek what is *most* faithful is to recognize that our efforts don't get it right every time. *Most* faithful means pursuing our best approximation of the embodiment of our ideals. To what and to whom must we remain faithful as we attempt to bring into being a new heaven and a new earth? If our efforts toward alternative realities are not anchored in deep values, we run the risk of reproducing the very conditions we say we want to change.

If our efforts toward alternative realities are not anchored in deep values, we run the risk of reproducing the very conditions we say we want to change.

Living and Leading Vignette

In late May 2018, we convened two hundred emerging and established Christian leaders from the United States and Canada for a four-day leadership forum entitled, "Courage to Build Beloved Communities." Fifty years after the assassination of Martin Luther King Jr., we wanted to explore with these leaders how we might enact King's notion of Beloved Community in our diverse local and regional spaces of ministry, leadership, and service.

We wanted to stimulate the imagination and memory of the gathered community toward a particular end. We wanted folks to leave this gathering disoriented to the world as it is as a result of having glimpsed the world as it could be. But disorientation alone is not enough: we also wanted to give these leaders a process to take home, one they could adapt to address the seemingly intractable problems in their communities.

Matthew frames the experience

Matthew framed the experience into which we were inviting the gathered leaders by saying:

> In the Western Christian liturgical calendar, we are gathering in "ordinary time" or post-Pentecost. In the sacred story of Scripture, this is a moment after the followers of Jesus witness his public lynching by crucifixion at the hands of the Roman Empire.
>
> This is after they witness God nullifying that lynching by raising Jesus to life and emptying that borrowed tomb.
>
> This is after the folk who followed in the Way of Jesus experience the promise of the Spirit of God at Pentecost, empowering them to bear witness to Jesus's victory over the forces of death.
>
> This is after the Spirit of God fell on them like fire and they spoke in multiple languages, bearing public witness to the power of God over the forces of death.
>
> And now, post-Pentecost, in the second and third chapters of the book of Acts, the followers of Jesus are exploring and experimenting with a difficult question:
>
> How do we *be* the body of Christ while navigating the very empire that executed him?
>
> Their question is also our question. This is what we mean when we talk about "Courage to Build Beloved Communities." Their question is our question because in many ways our context is an echo of their context. In this empire, we are seeking to reckon with the evils that pervade our world, repair the harm that disproportionately affects the most vulnerable among us, and foment a revolution that cultivates alternative ways of being community in the Way of Jesus.
>
> Over the next few days we will explore and experiment with this question via a process of communal discernment through dialogue and shared design.

In the room of nearly two hundred leaders, we then begin to cocreate the container that will hold the journey we are undertaking. With attention to pace, cadence, and rhythm, together we revisit the Covenants of Presence that will enable us to show up together whole, courageous, and humane:

We come as equals,

- Slow down, so we have time to think together,
- Listen deeply,
- Stay curious about each other,
- Embrace constructive conflict to enhance your learning.

Designing for the Beloved Community

During the next two days in worship, idea labs, large group reflection, and small group dialogue, we explored local models of ministry and case studies. They stimulated our imaginations about how organizations and ministries are already trying to cultivate diverse expressions of Beloved Community in specific contexts.

Then we committed the final two days to an in-depth design process that captures what we mean by (E)nacting next most faithful steps. We called it "Designing for Beloved Communities."

We invited twenty courageous leaders to share prepared stories about a specific pain point in their communities. These stories served as the basis from which the rest of the process would unfold. Accompanied by a supportive team of listening leaders, these storytellers mined their stories to clarify values and craft a vision of an alternative future for their communities. Through facilitated dialogue, guided imagery, personal reflection, and group ideation, they then translated grand visions of alternative futures into actionable tasks, prototypes, and projects that would test the viability of their ideas on the ground in their home places of service and leadership.

Each of these storytellers left the gathering with a next most faithful step, one that was ready to be enacted with individual communities. But each one also left with a process to take home, to use in discerning the future together with their own communities. In what follows, we lead you through the process we used to facilitate communal discernment to transform an idea into actionable step toward change.

Enacting the Next Most Faithful Step

This process is built on the principles of human-centered design (HCD). Human-centered design is based on the adage, "Nothing about us without us." It grounds any design process with the people for whom a solution is being designed and generates solutions with them that are customized to their needs and desires. The HCD approach consists of three phases: inspiration, ideation, and experimentation. The inspiration phase consists of listening deeply and empathically to a situation and the people most affected by the problem. The ideation phase involves making sense of the data derived from deep listening and generating ideas that may address the problem. In the experimentation phase, problem solvers build prototypes to test and evaluate iteratively in pursuit of a viable solution.

Guided by these principles, we walked through each of the following steps in our process of "Designing for Beloved Communities." The entire day was designed as a facilitated process that would lead storytellers and the people who chose to accompany them in an exploration. From the starting point of their stories, they mined their values and visions to determine specific actions to which they were called in their communities. The process looked like this:

1. **Listen:** Get into close proximity with the folks most directly affected.
2. **Ideate:** Imagine alternatives to the status quo that help create a future you wish to inhabit.
3. **Try something:** Experiment by bringing your ideas/ideations to life and testing them in your context.

Two additional steps of Reflect and Begin Again happen when people return to test their ideas in communities.

4. **Reflect:** Think and learn what happened with your experiment, whether it gained any traction, and what needs to happen in the next iteration of your experiment.
5. **Begin again:** Take the next step toward listening again to the people who will be most affected by the solution, ideate with them, and try something to move closer to a viable solution that addresses the problem.

Listen

We began with a story. On a Thursday morning in a large group plenary, we invited on-the-spot volunteers to name pain points in their communities that they hoped to address. About twenty people came forward and named an example of communal suffering, brokenness, and possibility deeply embedded in their contexts.

We then invited embodiment. We asked the nearly two hundred remaining participants to move toward a speaker whose pain point resonated with them. Once they were gathered in small clusters, our colleague Patrick Reyes led the room theological reflection around women in leadership, using the biblical story of Miriam as a muse. He then led an image theater exercise adapted from the Theatre of the Oppressed methodology.[1] After hearing more detail about each specific pain point, the groups worked together, using their bodies to construct human sculptures that depicted each story.

Slowly from the ground of that room began to sprout embodied sculptures of diverse communities who are reckoning with harrowing and complex challenges. These included rights and voice denied to Palestinian Christians, racial disparities in mental health access, lack of acknowledgment and accessibility for people with disabilities, and hunger and food deserts in the American South. In turn, each half of the room then temporarily broke out of their bodily sculptures, taking time to walk to the other half of the room as if it were a living museum, observing the other living statues.

Next we invited change. Patrick asked the groups who were witnessing a statue to insert themselves as leaders, by joining a statue, and offer a response to the particular pain point. "With consent from each member of the group, use your bodies together to choose how to respond to this situation as a leadership task," Patrick invited. Group deliberations began to build to a low rumble as individuals negotiated with their teams and their own imaginations. In one pocket of the room an image of an impenetrable wall of intolerance shape-shifted: a table of community and acceptance emerged. In another corner, a scene of violent strife and contention softened into a space in which trauma was lovingly held by a healing community. Bodies began to try on new forms, new shapes, new relationships, new ways of being.

Following this simulation, we extended an invitation:

> In this session, you reflected with your group on the pain point you hope to address in your community. Tomorrow, your group will design a vision of what Beloved Community might look like in that context. We are inviting you to prepare by bringing the story of your community's pain point to begin that group discernment process.

---

[1]Theatre of the Oppressed (T.O.) is an approach to community-based education that uses theatre as a tool for social transformation. The methodology was created by Augusto Boal, a Brazilian practitioner in theater and education strongly influenced by Paulo Freire.

> Storytellers, a word of caution: these will be stories of a community. We cannot presume to tell the community's story without involving the community in the storytelling. Call, text, or email your folks back home to help you tell as nuanced and full a story as possible of the situation you feel called to address. Remember the wisdom from the disability rights movement: "If it's about us, don't do it without us."

Storytellers did their homework. On Friday morning the room of two hundred again became clusters of ten to twelve surrounding a focus person prepared by the witness of their memory and community to tell a story.

Storytelling and deep listening are the basis of this process. To set a strong foundation for the experience that would unfold we spent a seemingly disproportionate amount of time preparing both the storytellers and the listeners for their shared work.

We coached storytellers to share a vivid and detailed ten-minute story they had prepared in advance. This story would describe the problem they felt called to address in their home community. We invited them to tell stories with attention to plot, setting, characters, and context.

- Who are the primary characters (groups) and individuals in this story?
- What is the history and cultural context of this problem?
- Who has the power to make decisions about how resources are distributed here?
- Where do you see abundance and where do you see scarcity in this story?
- How have people and groups learned to relate to one another over time in the community?

We coached the participants accompanying the storytellers in holy listening, asking them to listen as though they were hearing the words of a sacred text. After all, they were. Their job was to cocreate and hold space for this story to unfold.

We instructed them:

> Listeners, give the storyteller your undivided attention. Pay sacred attention to the storyteller's body language, emotions, and imagery throughout the story. When the story is finished, take a deep pause to honor the story and the community. After the group has paused and gathered its thoughts:

- Mirror back to the storyteller what you witnessed.
- Ask clarifying questions that may help bring the pain point into further focus.
- Ask the storyteller self-awakening questions that invite that person to deeper reflection on the story and the community issue.
- Only now, after these intentional moves, are we ready to move to the next step of design.

Ideate

We began ideating by defining the scope of the alternatives we hope to bring into being. For us on this day, that meant defining Beloved Community in context. As people gathered again in clusters after a break. Matthew offered the following:

> In light of the story you just told and heard, what is your working definition of Beloved Community here? Don't go after a general definition. Specifically articulate a definition that responds to this particular pain point in this particular community. For example, if the problem you describe in your story is gentrification in the West End community of Atlanta, a definition of Beloved Community there might be: "Beloved Community in the West End means anchoring and sustaining the presence and community wealth of long-time residents."

Specific definitions began to emerge in response to local situations that surfaced in the room. People spoke into the room that Beloved Community is:

- Building an intergenerational community focused on movements, not moments
- Honoring the narratives of diasporic communities around clean water issues
- Creating an inclusive table of grace fulfilling the needs of hungry people

Creativity without boundaries is chaotic. This step in the process enables us to identify the parameters in which we will work together. Defining the scope of our shared work helps us find the focus necessary to translate a good idea into effective action.

The next step in ideating involves naming our embedded values. These are the implicit norms that guide us, whether we are aware of them or not. Becoming aware and articulate about them helps us understand what matters, what's at stake, and why we care. Values provide a compass by which we make choices about what actions we will take, what adjustments we will make, and what matters enough to measure. At this point in Designing for Beloved Community, Stephen asked, "So what are the theological values embedded in your definitions? What deeply held commitments and beliefs about right relationships does your localized definition of Beloved Community assume?"

In dialogue, each group began to articulate the biblical, theological, and cultural values that had been lurking just below the surface of their stories. They lifted up these words and phrases: love your neighbor, holiness, *shalom,* communal ownership, *imago dei,* community connection, justice, righteous anger, *metanoia.*

After a spacious three-hour respite for lunch and renewal, we returned to the room, to our stories, and to each other.

A third step in the ideation work took us on a meditative journey called a Walk into the Future. Dori invited everyone to identify one or two people with whom they each would feel comfortable sharing at the close of the exercise. Then she began:

> Throughout the Christian story, we find ordinary people who have done extraordinary things because of their encounter with the Holy.
>
> If we are to lead into a future that we cannot yet see, we must tap into the deepest sources of wisdom and guidance available to us. Can you imagine having access to the wisdom of your ancestors? Can we rest in an awareness that all we need is in the room and we can summon resources we don't know we have?
>
> Close your eyes. Take a few deep breaths. Release. Free your mind of worry, concern, questions, excitement, or enthusiasm. Now journey down from your head into your heart and try to become in tune with your feelings, here in these surroundings.
>
> Now, stand up. Close your eyes. Imagine that you are at a doorway, the doorway of our collective future, a more hopeful future, one in which you and your community are actively building Beloved Community in ways that God desires for you . . .
>
> a. Move across the threshold of that doorway. What do you see/hear/feel/experience on the other side of the door?

b. Move more fully into the space on the other side of the threshold. Turn around slowly. Notice what you see. What are you and the people around you doing? What does it look like here? Who is here? What's different? What are people doing? What are you doing? How are people relating to each other? What is the mood of the community? How are you feeling? What sounds do you hear?

c. Now, look back at your past self on the other side of the door. What advice would you give to your past self to help it move forward toward its future self? Imagine a sentence or two that you don't want to forget.

d. Before you leave, name one concrete step you can take—something over which you have power and agency—to make this hopeful future become a reality.

e. Walk back through the doorway *a* to the present.[2]

At the close of the guided meditation, Dori invited everyone to spend more time in their journals, writing down what they saw, felt, and heard, reminding them to be as specific as possible about the images, feelings, and other important qualities of the experience, and to note the sentence or two of advice they had given their "past" self. After a few moments of journaling, she invited folks into dyads or triads to take turns sharing what they had seen, and then a few people offered what they saw into the room. One woman expressed envisioning her ancestral home and receiving words of sustenance from her maternal grandmother. Others expressed gratitude for the mystery of moving into their own quiet space but coming back up into the community. This meditative interlude functioned as an embodied moment of experiencing self-in-community.

Try Something

In the final move of the day, we invited each group to support each storyteller in turn in describing in as detailed a manner as possible the key features of the future they envisioned. Then together they worked to shrink this detailed future or change to identify a single *next most faithful step or task* the storyteller could take to make tangible some element of the vision they saw. That task would be a way to incarnate and test some aspect of their collectively inspired vision in real time and real terms upon returning home.

---

[2]This exercise is an adaptation of guided journaling from The Presencing Institute. For examples of similar exercises, see www.presencing.org/resource/tools/guided-journaling-desc.

For some, the next most faithful step or task was a set of conversations that they could immediately put on the calendar with people in their communities. For others, it was an organizational design and vision they needed to put on paper. Still others named revising and implementing a course of action that procrastination and fear had halted. Through this process they found the necessary courage and inspiration to put these next steps into action.

We reminded those who had identified their next step or task that it is a guess-in-action. It is not a quick fix. We reiterated that as their solution takes shape and hits the ground in their community, they should use it as a means to surface their assumptions and work with others to refine their thinking and their action. This is the practice of building to think. We use the initial sketch of newly imagined spaces, programs, organizations and resources as prototypes. Through reflection and assessment of what works, what matters, and what doesn't, these prototypes become our teachers. From them we learn how best to take another (and another and another) faithful step toward solving the complex challenges our communities face.

Any design is born of a story. If we change the story we tell, we are better positioned to change the systems we inhabit.

In the case study just described, we engaged people in prolonged encounter with each other. We used dialogue, questions, storytelling, and holy listening to move people into a place of shared wisdom and collective creativity. This two-day process provided a rare opportunity for leaders to see their situations from an unusual angle with a little help from some friends. This process is an adaptable template. We and others use it within the work of organizational and community life to stimulate reflective design that roots collective action in shared values and vision. It works for organizations seeking to live into new ways of being and it works for individuals seeking to discern their unfolding vocations. It is a process through which people and groups become co-authors of the futures they hope to see.

Storytelling, dialogue, and collective imagination create an experience that ingrains in the bones of the gathered community a simple truth that can drive our work forward.

Everyday Design

Any design is born of a story. If we change the story we tell, we are better positioned to change the systems we inhabit. Each process, each program, each neighborhood, each economy, each organization in which we participate is the product of design. And each system over time will generate the very outcomes it is designed to produce.

Examples of this theory abound across sectors and testify to the power of change that can occur when we choose to redesign for the outcomes we desire, instead of holding fast to systems that no longer achieve the desired effect or were never designed with our flourishing in mind.

The assumptions embedded in our stories generate the design that we put together as a result and the outcome that occurs. Here are three examples of the relationship between the stories, design, and results.

An ecclesial story:

Story: Pastors are primarily responsible for interpreting tradition, giving care to needy parishioners, and proclaiming the gospel through preaching and teaching.

Design: Schools that train pastors are largely organized in academic disciplines that future ministers are expected to master. Their education for ministry emphasizes their facility with tools and traditions of thought, interpretation of Scripture, and public communication.

Result: Pastors frequently report that theological education does not prepare them for the actual work of pastoral ministry, which calls for skills in organizational leadership, community organizing, and creative problem solving.

A medical story:

Story: The human body is essentially a collection of parts that operate in predictable, mechanistic ways. When this animated machine with fragmented parts malfunctions, it can be replaced or repaired without much thought for other parts. The aim of medical interventions is to manage disease and alleviate the symptoms of illness that show up in these parts, whether they are tumors, sores, or sniffles.

Design: Medical care is organized in siloed specializations. Medical centers are expressions of this disaggregated design. Cardiology (heart) is located on the fifth floor, neurology (brain) is on the ninth floor, and gastroenterology (gut and digestive system) is on the third floor. To tend to the whole of one's body is to engage a maze of specialists, who rarely communicate with one another, let alone generate shared knowledge about the patient leading to disconnections between the head (cognition), heart (emotion), and gut (intuition).

Result: Health is deemed as synonymous with "not sick," "not broken," "no symptoms." When the symptom is gone, there's not much to be offered to people to cultivate healing and wellness.

A theological story:

Story: The almighty Creator of heaven and earth channels the *Creator's* will and vision through the gifts of special individuals who in turn are destined to provide divinely sanctioned direction to the rest of us. As some church folks say, "Vision for the people is given to the pastor first!"

Design: Congregations and cause-driven organizations are hierarchically arranged to concentrate power and decision-making authority in the hands of a special, inspired few who are believed to possess an unusual connection to the Creator.

Often, the "new" stories that can enable us to cocreate a new reality are right under our noses.

Result: The gifts and talents of people in churches and cause-driven organizations lie dormant and underutilized for the mission in deference to the assumed experts and authorities at the top of the hierarchical food chain. More important, most people at lower rungs of the chain of command internalize a diminished sense of their ability to effect the very change they hope to see.

These three examples illustrate the often unseen connection between the story, the design, and the result. What are the stories embedded in the design of your spaces and systems you know best? For whom are they designed? What was the narrative plot the designers had in mind as they crafted the innards and contours of those spaces and systems? How might a different story make possible the design of a different way of being in the world? Pursuit of alternatives to the status quo requires that we uncover these embedded assumptions in existing systems and in the alternatives. Pursuit of alternatives systems must begin with a new story. Often, the "new" stories that can enable us to cocreate a new reality are right under our noses.

We invite you to take the process of enacting in your own context the next most faithful step we explored here. Play with it, experiment with it to uncover the new stories out of which your community might consciously design the solutions that they need now.

Questions for Reflection

For the individual learner/leader seeking meaning and purpose:

1. The authors write that "Our bodies are the sites where we make the world anew" and "We need practices that give our

bodies a chance to make ideas tangible." The chapter describes an exercise of statue building from Theatre of the Oppressed. What other practices do you know that enable us to make ideas tangible in our bodies? Can you think of a time when you glimpsed the possibility of a better world through embodied actions with others?

2. Now that you have walked through the entire CARE process, think about the next challenge or decision you face in your life. How might you use the CARE process to help you gain clarity? How might you incorporate elements of it into a group or community in which you take part or lead?
3. What was one challenging idea you encountered here? What made it so?
4. What was one of the most powerful or helpful ideas you encountered here? What made it so?
5. What is one thing you take with you from this chapter that might help you enact your next most faithful step as you seek to live and lead change on purpose?

For the guide/facilitator helping others find meaning and purpose:

1. Now that you have walked through the entire CARE process, think about the next meeting, retreat, or learning journey you need to create or adapt to accompany others. How might you use the CARE process to help people in your context explore and pursue their own meaning and purpose?
2. The authors note that "bringing colorful worlds into being takes place one brushstroke at a time." How might this idea be helpful to people who are overwhelmed when thinking about the future?
3. What was one challenging idea you encountered here? What made it so?
4. What was a powerful or helpful idea you encountered here? What made it so?
5. What is one thing you take with you from this chapter that might help you invite others to move from ideas to actions in pursuit of their meaning and purpose?

For those leading organizational change:

1. Human-centered design rests on the assumptions that engaging the life-stories, emotions, and contexts of the people with whom you are creating change gives shape to a better design. What are the stories embedded in the design of the organization you lead or the spaces and systems you inhabit? For whom are they designed?
2. How might you engage deeply with the stories of the people most directly affected by your organization's actions? How might you develop accountability to the people most directly affected by the decisions you are making?
3. What was one challenging idea you encountered here? What made it so?
4. What was one of the most powerful or helpful ideas you encountered here? What made it so?
5. What is one thing you take with you from this chapter that helps you and others move from ideating to experimenting and learning from failures?

For all:

1. Review *Another Way Manifesto*. Which sentences stand out to you after reading this chapter?
2. We are building an interactive playlist to accompany each chapter. You can find it on Spotify at **Another Way: The Book.** The songs we recommend for this chapter are "Step by Step" by Sweet Honey in the Rock, "Alright" by Kendrick Lamar, "New World Coming" by Nina Simone. Please add to the playlist as you are inspired.

CHAPTER 8

Embodying CARE

Another world is not only possible, she is on her way. On a quiet day, I can hear her breathing.
—Arundhati Roy

The practices you've experienced in this book grow out of a collective pain point the three of us repeatedly felt in our professional journeys. Again and again we found ourselves muttering. "There's gotta be another way . . . "

- Another way to thrive in life-giving leadership, rather than feel our life's energies draining away amid exhaustion and burnout
- Another way to mentor young leaders into vocations as change agents who can turn their hopes for common good into action
- Another way to lead that affirms and feeds our soul's deep longings
- Another way to imagine and enact the future that wants to emerge through us

We discovered through leading workshops on the CARE practices that there is indeed a better way. This stuff really works!

While we were trying out these practices with our external partners, we began using them within our own organization. At this point, we've been living and leading with these practices so regularly that they've become almost second nature. One result is the ongoing evolution of our workplace culture. It is a culture that values the inner and outer tug of each individual's call and vocation. It is a culture that values slowing down, pausing to acknowledge that our best work is done collectively, when we make time to catch up with one another. It is a culture that continues to change, as our individual and collective vocations evolve to meet the challenging issues arising in the changing landscape in which we live and work. We have built into the culture a practice of reflection that gives us the opportunity to name when we fall short and figure out how to move forward. Yes, we miss the mark on each of these aspirations. By keeping before us the disciplined intention to align who we are and who we want to be with what we do and how we do it, we come closer and closer to our ideals. This work is never done.

In what follows, we recap the CARE practices, showing how they changed our organization. You will see here how the practices come into play not as universal, linear steps, but rather as context-specific iterative moves that weave into and around what we do again and again. The practices become more familiar each time we do them, and missing the mark only fuels our desire to try again to improve next time around. The ensuing stories are snapshots of us trying on these practices and returning to them regularly in our organizational life.

Exploring an Alternative Future

In 2012, the Fund for Theological Education saw a crisis coming as it inched towards its sixtieth anniversary. In our own sphere, we recognized a drastic misalignment between our stated values and where our resources were deployed.

We became aware of a yawning gap between what we said we valued and some of the outcomes we noticed in our work. For example, one of our core programs involved fellowships for young people exploring calls to pastoral ministry. This program consistently attracted an applicant pool that was 80 percent white, middle-class, mainline Protestants. As recruiter for the fellowship programs, part of Matthew's mandate was to attract a more racially, ethnically, and theologically diverse pool of applicants. After a few seasons of unsuccessful attempts, he became frustrated with the seemingly intractable problem. None of the creative recruitment strategies he attempted moved the needle. And yet, promising young leaders of color were out there. We knew them!

The solution did not appear until Matthew and other colleagues began to ask a different set of questions. Instead of asking, What do we need to *do* differently to include others, he began asking, How do we need to *be* differently. In conversation with others, he began to look closely at the program design, assumptions, and criteria that governed the fellowship. Our design assumed that certain markers of individual academic achievement were the key predictors of readiness for success in Christian leadership and pastoral ministry. Our fellowship criteria defined the "best and brightest" as those with high GPAs and well-written essays. It required nomination by seminary deans and presidents. In short, it centered on those who were already achieving success in academia within a very particular set of cultural norms. While those markers may be the normative indicators of readiness within some white mainline Protestant faith communities, they are not the means by which most communities identify and nurture their leaders.

We began to see that the programs themselves were designed precisely for the outcomes they achieved. Our underlying un-scrutinized design was the exact cause of the problem. Continuing in this mode of granting fellowships would, by design, continue attracting a mostly white applicant pool. The "best and brightest" bias, which had defined FTE's work for nearly six decades, had clear results in the flesh-and-blood world: well-resourced young people would continue to derive benefits from programs designed for them. Meanwhile, promising young leaders from non-mainline and nonwhite communities were largely excluded from our work. If our mission was truly to cultivate the next generation of diverse young leaders, we were falling flat. We were encountering a painful contradiction between our values and our practice. This contradiction was especially stark in light of demographic trends reshaping Christianity at the turn of the twenty-first century. The majority of Christians in the world live below the equator, and the fastest growing segments of Christianity in North America are in Black and Brown communities.[1]

Crises often emerge out of dissonances between the design of our endeavors and the realities of life on the ground. The persistent diversity deficit in our fellowship programs was just one internal element within a hive of disruptive forces. These forces demanded that we revisit the dynamics between who we say we are and how we go about our work. At the same time, issues outside our control added to the crisis. The 2008 recession slashed our financial footprint and caused massive destabilization among most of the religious institutions we serve. Shifts in higher education, generational trends among Millennials, and the emerging freelance economy combined with other factors to reveal a permanently changed environment. We found ourselves working on new ground with a severely outdated operating system. It was a time of massive destabilization in higher education, organized religion, and institutional life.

A choice loomed: Would we could continue to run our historic programs for a little while longer, until the wheels fell off? Or

[1]Pew Research Center's Forum on Religion & Public Life, "Global Christianity — A Report on the Size and Distribution of the World's Christian Population," https://www.pewforum.org/2011/12/19/global-christianity-exec/ and "Racial Landscape Study," https://www.pewforum.org/religious-landscape-study/racial-and-ethnic-composition.

would we explore a riskier, more uncertain path? The riskier path of transformation would require us to pursue a challenging alternative voluntarily. That leap toward change could mean our organization would crash and burn, but it might result in a renewed vision, structure, aligned values, and strategic direction better suited to the changing landscape of our field. While our crisis was particular, it echoed the reality of many organizations trying to find their way in uncertain times after the 2008 recession.

Stephen's inner monologue went something like this: *How are we now called to respond to this changing landscape and support a new generation of diverse leaders? There's got to be a way for us to thrive as we do this work. I know I don't have the answers. We can't invite people into an alternative that we have not seen or tasted ourselves.*

Holding this uncertainty, Stephen offered a reflection for the Board of Trustees' consideration. He noted: Each of the four Gospel writers records Jesus saying in some form, "Those who seek to save their own life, will lose it. But those who lose their life for my sake, and for the sake of the good news, will gain it."[2] Pausing to look at each face in the room in turn, Stephen asked: "What aspect of our institutional life are we willing to lose in order to gain the life into which God is now calling us?"

Creating Space to Explore the Question

Stephen's question catalyzed the work of FTE board and staff over the next two years. We eventually chose the riskier path. We pushed the pause button on almost all of the work that we typically conducted each year at breakneck speed. Sixty-year-old fellowship programs came to a halt.

Our daily work rhythm shifted. We slowed down. We made time to think together, time to engage in the kind of dialogue that enabled us to gather the collective wisdom of the whole organization, including staff and key stakeholders. This pause created space for us to ask deeper questions, to notice previously undetected patterns, and to make unlikely connections. We could do the kind of sense-making not possible amid the cacophony of the every day. We launched an eight-city listening tour, tuning our ears to our existing and potential partners in diverse corners of the United States and Canada.

We took the practices we had been developing to help individuals discern their next most faithful steps and now asked them of ourselves. We engaged in a process of organizational discernment.

[2]Matthew 10:39 and 16:25, Mark 8:35, Luke 9:24, and John 12:25.

All of this was to create space to explore the self-awakening question: What part of our lives are we willing to lose in order to gain the life into which God is now calling us?

We practiced what we lifted up in chapter 1: **Creating Hospitable Space**

- Sitting face to face
- Sharing silence and stillness
- Establishing shared guidelines
- Slowing down
- Turning to story

Asking Self-Awakening Questions

A year before that critical meeting with FTE's Board of Trustees, Stephen led a staff retreat at the Carter Center in Atlanta. As the staff entered the room, Stephen's inner monologue was going something like this: *All right, here we go. I wonder how this is going to go. They don't have any idea about what we're about to do. Will they get with it? Will they participate? I just need to trust the process.*

This was a meeting unlike any we had conducted before. Its purpose was to connect us to our personal longings and aspirations—to the deeply held values that might ground our vision. This was the first time we intentionally engaged the CARE practices ourselves as an entire staff.

Stephen began by asking the staff to draw their chairs into a circle around a table adorned with multiple folds of colorful cloth and a candle. As people begin to settle into being together, he invited them by name into the circle and thanked those who had traveled from afar. We spent a few moments turning off phones and inviting an ancestral muse, listening to a slow reading of an excerpt from Howard Thurman's "The Sound of the Genuine."

> There is something in every one of you that waits, listens for the sound of the genuine in yourself and if you cannot hear it, you will never find whatever it is for which you are searching and if you hear it and then do not follow it, it was better that you had never been born.[3]

[3]Howard Thurman, "The Sound of the Genuine" (Baccalaureate address, Spelman College, Atlanta, May 4, 1980). Speech edited by Jo Moore Stewart for *The Spelman Messenger* 96, no. 4 (Summer 1980): 2–3. The entire speech can be accessed here: www.uindy.edu/eip/files/reflection4.pdf.

We then enjoyed three full minutes of silence before turning to the Covenants of Presence. One at a time, we read them into the room, pausing at the end so we could all reckon with their implications and a form consensus around these agreements.

Stephen then explained his hope that we could create a shared vision.

A shared vision is an answer to the questions, Who are we called to become? and What future do we want to create? A shared vision derives its power from common caring and creates a common identity. It changes our relationship with the organization and each other. It encourages and requires risk-taking and experimentation. It compels courage, because we might not know the next steps. It takes time to emerge, and it evolves out of personal gifts. A shared vision requires ongoing conversation in which we feel free to express our dreams and learn to listen to each other's dreams. Out of this listening, new insights into what is possible will emerge. But it also requires extraordinary openness and willingness to entertain a diversity of ideas, to allow multiple visions to coexist, to listen for the right courses of action that transcend and unify all of our individual visions. Ultimately, our time together will be about listening to what wants to emerge through us. How is God calling this organization now for the sake of the world? After considering all of this, we must make sure we can articulate that shared vision in a compelling and beautiful way. Can we do this?

Over the next two days, we held a space of deep listening and sensing. We listened expressly for the Holy; we sensed Spirit moving through us; and we sought a collective, compelling vision that would emerge in our time together. Apart from the outcome of a shared vision, we began to sense the significance *of this process* for the future of FTE's work.

Because this was just the beginning of several conversations that would happen throughout the year, Stephen put everyone at ease: "Relax. We're not responsible for coming up with a complete and definitive vision right now that will carry the organization for the next decade. However, we are responsible for beginning to cultivate the conditions in which such a vision can be planted, received, nurtured, and can grow."

Matthew began to sense the significance of this process for the future of FTE's work. He reflected out loud on how this moment felt different than past attempts to think our way forward: "Yes. This is it! This is what we do. This type of dialogical process is in service to helping people discern their vocation and purpose. What if we do this work to help individuals and organizations find their way forward?"

We practiced what we lifted up in chapter 3: **Asking Self-Awakening Questions.**

Creating hospitable space by revisiting the first of the CARE practices, remembering that we gather with intentionality to invite silence, sit face to face, tell stories, slow down, and to reintroduce the Covenants of Presence if time has passed since their last introduction.

Employing a muse to invite in the simultaneously playful and serious expectation that we are connected to deep sources of wisdom and to something larger than ourselves, something to which our authentic selves desire to awaken.

Discerning questions that are truly self-awakening, questions that move us to a place of inner exploration, discovery, and creativity that we cannot access alone.

Letting the questions breathe in a way that holds the mystery and defies the desire to tidy up lingering uncertainties.

Catching what surfaces through journaling, holy listening, harvesting, or a dialogue-based process, such as World Café, Open Space Technology, and so on.

This process sparked a two-year journey in which our sixty-year-old organization transformed from the *Fund* for Theological *Education* to the *Forum* for Theological *Exploration*. Though still known as FTE, we redesigned our mission, vision, strategic direction, and organizational model to address the persistent leadership challenges in our field.

Reflecting Theologically Together

Our bodies cocreate a living tableau in the middle of a conference room at FTE's Atlanta office. Kimberly is playing the part of Jesus, on his way to the deathbed of Jairus's daughter. Patrick is the woman seeking Jesus's healing from a hemorrhage. Ched Myers and René August—activist/scholars we've invited to guide us—take turns reading Mark 5:21–39 as the rest of us find our places in the scene. Some of us become the surprised disciples, while others are members of the religious elite or of the throng of bystanders.

We freeze in place. Myers begins asking us questions about our scriptural scenario, questions such as: Where are there movements of power here? What social systems are present? What taboos or barriers exist? What are Jesus's actions here and how do they disrupt power?

We break out of our living sculpture and engage with the powerful feelings we experienced when embodying the exact moment when Jesus turns his attention away from the leader of the synagogue and toward the woman who has spent all of her money on physicians unable to heal a twelve-year-old problem.

You can almost hear a pin drop when Myers asks us: What would it mean for us to take up Jesus's action in our work? How do we transpose the biblical story onto our story in a way that takes seriously social systems and power?

In response, Dori's inner monologue went like this: *Holy cow! I'm finally getting it!* Then she said out loud. "Theological reflection is not a neutral practice of simply asking 'Where is God in this story?' It is always positioned! Unless it looks out for 'the least of these,' unless it pricks the conscience of those with power, it keeps us bound to the status quo."

At the end of the exercise, Stephen exhales and reflects on a lesson from the biblical story: "If the least of these get taken care of, there is enough to go around. Everyone got healed in the end."

Here, we practiced what we lifted up in chapter 6: **Reflecting Theologically Together**:

- Reckoning with intersections of systems, power, and agency
- Enlarging the "God question" from "How is God at work in our experience?" to include "What are the dominant notions of God at work here, and how are they shaping our thinking and action?"
- Asking, "What is our next most faithful step if we are to align our ongoing actions with this renewed view of who God is and how God is at work?"

As we learned in chapter 5, theological reflection done this way:

- Is communal, coming to life with, by, and for those who seek to lead change for good
- Is rooted in the lived reality of people whose lives hang in the balance because of unjust systems that create contexts of death-dealing inequity
- Excavates the histories, cultures, and faith traditions that inform our understandings of whom we serve, and helps us discern what we are called to do in the world
- Acknowledges that, yes, our understanding of self, God, community, and creation is shaped by Scripture, but it is also shaped by the many other written and unwritten "texts" that make us who we are
- Builds new muscle, allowing us to think beyond the world of the Bible, to better understand God's presence and agency in the midst of our lived realities

- Shifts our consciousness and our orientation toward God's relentless preference for the so-called "least" among us

Before dispersing from the room that day, we gathered up our learnings. Over the weeks ahead, those learnings evolved into a set of core theological and pedagogical principles and practices that now guide our work in vocational exploration and leadership formation with young people.

In this period of theological reflection on our organizational life, we gained a shared clarity that provided guidance—not once and for all, but for a little while. It will need to be revised again and again in the future. This shows what can happen when groups, organizations, and communities work and play with the practices of CARE in an ongoing way.

Enacting Our Next Most Faithful Step

Just because you find clarity does not mean you will act on that clarity. Haven't we all experienced a clarifying epiphany at a conference or retreat only to watch it dissipate in the real-world reality of deadlines, defaults, and lack of support? For this reason, we need practices for transforming insight into reflective action. The last step in CARE helps people move from clarity to action. Each action is incomplete in itself; it is merely a step on the way to another action in an ongoing process of becoming a learning organization or a learning leader.

"So what is our next most faithful step as an organization?" Stephen had asked in 2011. *Three years* later we emerged transformed: We had been a fellowship-granting organization working primarily with middle-class white mainline Protestant Christian communities. We were becoming a leadership incubator with a renewed mission: to partner with a diverse network of congregations and other faith-rooted organizations to cultivate a new generation of wise, faithful, courageous leaders seeking to participate in God's healing work in the world.

What got us from point A to point B? It was a five-step process that included the organizational disciplines lifted up in chapter 7: **Enacting the Next Most Faithful Steps**. Those practices are to:

Listen: Getting into close proximity with the folks most directly impacted by the problem and the potential solution.

Ideate: Imagining alternatives to the status quo that help create a future we long to inhabit.

Try something: Experiment with bringing ideas to life and test your assumptions in your context.

Reflect: Think and learn what happened with your experiment. Assess whether it gained any traction or solved the problem. Determine whether and what you may need to change in the next iteration of your experiment

Begin Again: Take the next step toward listening again to the people who will be most affected by the solution, ideate together with them, and try something to move closer to a viable solution that addresses the problem

We Listened—Even to the Hard Stuff

For us, listening is an essential leadership task. It includes paying attention to insights beyond and within us. Listening beyond us meant tuning our ears to our constituencies, to our organizations' history, and to the vocations of our organization and its people. Stephen visited and revisited the archives, listening to the musings of FTE's founders for places of consonance and dissonance. Where are the intersections? What were the key leadership problems FTE was addressing in 1954 in the midst of the civil rights era, and how do those problems differ today? In eight cities across North America, we convened stakeholders who had been walking alongside FTE for decades as well as potential new partners who had much to teach us about the future of the church and of theological education.

This kind of listening is hyper-local.[4] It is grounded in particularity, it uses holy listening and self-awakening questions, and it reflects theologically on real-life situations. At the end of each stop on the listening tour, Stephen had dozens of sheets of notes on large butcher block paper. He kept them on a long credenza near the window in his office, and he pored over them regularly. Bringing colleagues literally back to lines written in red Sharpie pen in Los Angeles, Vancouver, or Chicago, he continually sought connections between what we were hearing from our partners and inspirations bubbling up among our staff members.

Over time, we learned the importance of listening with more than just words. Our listening grew immeasurably richer with the addition of graphic notation. One artist in particular, Kate Morales (@crowcamino), came to be a regular at our events, setting up huge blank canvases. Kate would bring the canvases to life with colorful worlds of image and phrases reflecting key themes and the sometimes-quiet voices that rose to the surface to name a truth emerging from the wisdom in the room. Team members collected key portions of the art board, taking them back to their offices to inspire them in the days and months ahead.

Listening within means turning our attention inward and focusing on the history, practices, and assumptions we held about our organization,

[4]Deborah Frieze proposes a hyper-local approach to addressing big persistent problems. Listen to her TEDx talk here, "How I Became a Localist" at https://www.youtube.com/watch?v=2jTdZSPBRRE.

programs, and people. Often, this involves paying attention to what lies beneath the emotional waterline of our lives. This inward turn directs our listening toward the practice of surfacing the feelings beneath our actions. It attends to the energy of a room, the energy of a situation, or the energy between individuals. It considers the assumptions behind our words, feelings, and ideas. Such a practice invites us to become aware of and scrutinize the unexamined assumptions that either keep us from acting differently or drive us continually to recreate the same systems, although we say we desire different results. In our listening sessions we not only asked our partners and staff what was possible, we also welcomed their feelings and their unvarnished critiques about the implicit assumptions in the design of our programs.

We heard clearly and had to reckon with the fact that the fellowship model defining FTE's work for nearly six decades attended to the needs of the exact young people it consistently attracted—80 percent of applicants to those programs were predominantly white middle- to upper-class twenty-somethings who excelled in traditional academic institutions. By being designed to work specifically for this context, it did not work for others. Our work deepened the privilege of the privileged. These conversations conjured up a range of emotions and helped us to recognize that FTE's mental model of leadership was rooted in a "best and brightest" ideal that erected white middle-class cultural norms as a standard of leadership. These sobering diagnostic conversations reminded us that we could not leap into pursuing a new path, without first reckoning with the deeply held problematic assumptions baked into the very design of our programs. Honest dialogue and feedback then allowed us to assess the yawning gap between our "values in action" (read: privileging the privileged) and our espoused values of diversity and justice. More important, such dialogue and feedback gave us the opportunity to come to terms with our increasing awareness and emotions surrounding our programs. This was an important aspect of the decision-making process and the choice to redesign our programs in a way that would place equity, justice, and accessibility at the core of the organization's priorities and programmatic design.

The invitation to listen in these ways is often messy, difficult, conflict-ridden work. When discerning what parts of an institution or organization must die, we are doing the grueling but necessary work of grieving. Letting go is profoundly personal and emotional, and it is required in order to make space for what comes next.

We Ideated

Ideating takes on many forms, but one particular example stands out. In 2011 we retreated as a staff to envision a new organizational model for our work. We really didn't know what was on the other side of this meeting.

Team members arrived expecting to sit back and passively hear about our future direction from our executive leaders—business-as-usual. Imagine our surprise when instead Stephen invited us to watch a scene from the Pixar movie *Ratatouille*. In the clip, a rat named Remy gathers up scraps of food from the compost heap—bits of mushrooms, a strawberry, a little cheese, a crust of bread—and drags them to the rooftop to await the oncoming storm. When lightning strikes, the hodge-podge of over-ripe scraps melts and blends, becoming an innovative delicacy arising from a disciplined process of trial and error, iteration and reiteration. This story is about synthesis, creativity, and play—about putting things together that normally we haven't imagined would fit.

Could we as a team bring a similarly playful approach to our sources, resources, raw materials, and hoped-for outcomes? Stephen divided us into teams of three and turned over the next hour for us to mull three questions:

1. What is FTE's niche and scope of work given its limited resources, time, and capacity?
2. In the next twelve to eighteen months, who should FTE be convening, around what topics, and why?
3. What are viable ways in which FTE's program strategies could be fit together in order to pursue FTE's vision?

Then, for more inspiration on human-centered design, we watched the IDEO design-firm's process as depicted on an ABC Nightline special.[5] In it, IDEO designers set out to create a better shopping cart, leveraging the unique perspectives of practitioners from a variety of fields, and the wisdom of the very customers whose experience they hoped to improve. Most importantly, they experienced the creative freedom that comes when an engaged group works collaboratively on a problem from scratch with no predetermined ideas about what the finished product will look like.

Stephen invited us to "design a better shopping cart" in the work we do, engaging in a brief sample of a design process for how we might achieve our goals through reimagined strategies, programs, and offerings. After a couple of hours of working with this specific problem, team members pitched their new ideas to one another, and continued to refine these ideas over the next eighteen months.

[5]https://www.ideo.com/post/reimagining-the-shopping-cart.

Out of this longer process emerged a consensus. Given our unique access to a wide variety of players in the fields of graduate theological education, pastoral ministry, and faith-based volunteer service, we could do three things well. We could *convene* a diverse community of allies committed to the vocational exploration and development of transformative leadership. We could *consult* with organizational leaders to build their capacity to lead change within their institutions. And we could *cultivate* a new generation of wise, faithful, and courageous leaders. Convening, consulting, and cultivating became the watchwords that characterized our "better shopping cart."

In ideating, it is hard to get the "old shopping cart" out of our heads. Even when designers succeed in building a better shopping cart, they look up to discover they've built a tool that only works in a brick and mortar store. Meanwhile, people are increasingly shopping online with no need for a shopping cart at all. Similarly, if we're not carefully asking the big questions, paying attention to the changing environment as we generate ideas, we run the risk of painting ourselves into a corner of creative irrelevance.

> *We try something to learn what we still haven't figured out.*

In ideating change, we are often participating in social systems that were designed for the flourishing of some and the diminishment of others. While it pursues the possibilities of the world that could be, at its best ideation keeps track of the world as it is, and constantly tries to unmask the biases we carry from that world into our imagination. Ideation seeks alternatives that solve real world problems with real people, not alternatives merely for the sake of appearing new and different. That's why we come up with a prototype: we try something to learn what we still haven't figured out.

We Tried Some Things

Knowing that we wanted to shift from being a funding organization to being a forum for exploration, we changed the way we convened. Rather than inviting the "sage on stage"—an expert to deliver a keynote address—we started experimenting with convening in ways that embody the mantra the "smartest person in the room is the room itself."

We knew that diverse local communities were already brewing creative, innovative solutions to the fragmentation of the church and its academy. We also knew that most of them were disconnected, isolated, under-resourced, and sometimes feeling hopeless.

What would it mean to create a platform for the body to gain access to itself? What might it look like for people who were creating solutions to come together? Could they collectively address the problems plaguing young people, seminaries, church leaders, local communities, and academic guilds? Might that provide them access to each other for the sharing of resources, for collaboration?

The 2014 Christian Leadership Forum brought representatives of our whole FTE ecosystem together. This was our first "big tent" event, and it focused on embodying a forum.

What is a forum? A forum is unlike a conference, which assumes that there is knowledge to be taught and exchanged, primarily by talking heads. A forum is a space where meaning is created together. A forum assumes that everyone present brings wisdom to the table to share. A forum invites into the center of the gathering conversations that usually happen at the margins, and it assumes that the smartest person in the room isn't the individual standing in front of it—but the room itself.

A forum assumes that everyone present brings wisdom to the table to share.

In one plenary, Matthew and Dori described a theory of change that uses an old growth forest as a metaphor. Drawing two giant loops on the floor of a hotel ballroom, we described the cycle of emergence, influence, decline, hospice, compost, and new birth.[6] We invited leaders—ranging from college-aged seekers to seminary presidents— to walk around the visible metaphor. What does it feel like to accompany a dying institution? What does it feel like to steward the resources of a dominant system of influence? What does it feel like to walk out of the dysfunction of the dominant system and create new possibilities? What does it feel like to shine a light on others whose work is providing hope?

In other prototypes, we began to widen our pool of participants beyond fellowship recipients to include additional promising young leaders nominated by our partners. We piloted weekend discernment retreats to gather widely diverse young adults who were asking similar questions. We set up mini-grants for young people to get mentoring around niche ministries, and we set up a network for theological schools seeking to create institutional conditions in which students and scholars of color could thrive.

---

[6]For the Two Loop Theory of Change, see: https://berkana.org/about/our-theory-of-change/.

We Reflected

Testing involves forming relationships with the people you serve. We set up feedback loops that honored the voices of our participants, enlisting them in the process of design so that they would have a stake in the outcomes on the other side of the process. Testing is also about the stories to which we pay attention. We needed to stay open to hear about what's working and what's not working for the leaders FTE accompanies so we could continue codesigning solutions to problems they face and opportunities they seek.

Then We Began Again

We now know that redesigning an organization—like reorganizing one's life to respond to an emerging call—is not a once and for all process. We expect to get some things right and others terribly wrong. In hopes of creating change aligned with our institutional purpose, we are continuously trying to respond to the dynamic world that is changing around us.

As we looked toward 2019, we began the CARE process again. In the first six months of the year we paused again to:

Create space. We began planning a six-month sabbatical to discern our next most faithful steps toward a new strategic direction.

Ask self-awakening questions. How might we streamline our work to make room for what matters now given a changing world? How might we create a different organizational rhythm? How might we create more space that offers breathing room to reflect upon and write what we are learning? How might we develop resources and tools with partners, and to share our new knowledge with a wider audience?

Reflect theologically together. We continued to excavate the histories, cultures, and faith traditions that are rooted in the lived experience of the leaders we seek to serve. This informs our understandings and helps us to discern what we are now being called to do in the world.

Enact next faithful steps. We partnered with an organizational design strategy firm to help us see what we cannot see and help us design a new organizational and staffing model that will better equip us to work with, by, and for those who seek to live and lead change on purpose.

How CARE Changed Us

On the other side of our 2013 organizational sabbatical, we emerged with a renewed mission, a new strategic direction, and a new name. These changes signified that portions of our organization had died and had been composted to generate new life. We were no longer a fund but a forum—a living, learning organization that makes space for growth in conversation with many sources. We no longer focus on a single path to leadership, but regularly create spaces for young adults and institutional leaders who accompany them to explore diverse, contextual paths to leadership.

We are still iterating, still evolving, and we haven't figured it all out.

As a result of more than seven years of embodying CARE, FTE now sees itself as a living, breathing organism, exchanging nutrients with other parts of a living and dying system. We spend time in places that are nutrient-rich and cross-fertilize into places that are hungering and thirsting for ways the church and its leaders can enact change that benefits the least of these.

We consistently engage the rhythms of CARE, for example in the ways we design:

- staff meetings
- board meetings
- national gatherings
- exploratory initiatives
- discernment retreats
- external consultations on social entrepreneurship[7]
- facilitator preparation in the FTE way of convening and discerning[8]

We now live and breathe a kind of leadership development that roots itself in the interior life of communities. We retrieve individual life experiences, acknowledge the hidden worlds of our dreams, and foster connections to community, as we lifted up in chapters 2 and 4. We do so within broken systems—ones that were not designed for the flourishing of all—and we do so within systems in need of liberating, as lifted up in chapter 6.

When Matthew accepted Vincent Harding's invitation to pause, as related in the prelude to this book, a window opened into an alternative

---

[7]DOGOOD X is an eight-week start up accelerator for leaders working at the intersection of faith and social entrepreneurship. You can learn more at www.dogoodx.org.

[8]Co-CREATE is a national training in FTE's CARE practices as a way of facilitating for discernment. You can learn more about it at www.fteleaders.org

space, a space that allowed him to discern. When Stephen mines his dreams for seeds of intuition that echo the voices of his ancestors, time relaxes. When Dori asks a room full of strangers to sink into a few minutes of holy listening and self-awakening questions, energy shifts. We no longer act like hamsters on an endless wheel of activity. We reclaim time, and by doing so we invite ourselves to be whole people who engage the world humanely.

We don't have to wait for such moments to occur. We can create the conditions which lead to our flourishing—and we can bring others along. This is the effect of embodying the CARE practices. Not an ending, it is always again a first step toward welcoming ourselves as spiritual beings evolving and maturing into ways of being fully human. As we embrace the diverse expressions of God embodied and located in us, we learn how to embody what a new earth looks like.

We can create the conditions which lead to our flourishing—and we can bring others along.

We can create another way of being because we've been made in the image of the alternative one. Made in the image of the Creator, we, too, are called to create.

Another Way Manifesto

We open and close the book with a manifesto (from the Latin verb to *make clear* or *conspicuous*) that makes visible the values that guide the spirit and soul of our work. Because the ways of being and leading embedded in CARE approach are counterintuitive in most of the settings to which we show up, we begin our times together with these clarifications and revisit them regularly.

Our manifesto reminds us of what we know by heart. This is what we value deeply and what we can trust at our core as we do the work of leading change on purpose in ourselves, our organizations, and our world. [9]

---

[9]An artistic representation of this manifesto can be downloaded at www.leadanotherway.com

ANOTHER WAY MANIFESTO

THERE IS A FUTURE THAT MOURNS IF YOU AND I DO NOT STEP INTO OUR PURPOSE.

VOCATIONAL DISCERNMENT IS A DANGEROUS DANCE THAT REQUIRES RISK AND COURAGE. IT MAY LEAD YOU WHERE YOU DID NOT PLAN TO GO AND INSTIGATE PROFOUND CHANGE IN SELF, OTHERS, AND THE ENVIRONMENT.

CULTIVATE **YOUR OWN INTERIOR** LIFE AND ITS COMMUNAL SOURCES. LEADERS WHO LACK AWARENESS OF THEIR INNER SOURCES TEND TO REPRODUCE WHAT ALREADY EXISTS.

LEADERSHIP IS A COMMUNAL PRACTICE THAT BUILDS THE CAPACITY OF A TEAM, COMMUNITY, OR ORGANIZATION TO ENVISION AND ENACT A FUTURE INFORMED BY THE PAST AND THE DIVERSE PEOPLE AROUND US.

LEADERSHIP IS MORE ABOUT PUBLIC LISTENING THAN PUBLIC SPEAKING.

DIALOGUE IS AN ESSENTIAL LEADERSHIP PRACTICE AND A CORE PROCESS FOR CHANGE.

CREATE SETTINGS ON PURPOSE TO ENGAGE THE WISDOM OF THE ROOM VERSUS A "SAGE ON STAGE."

BETTER CHOICES EMERGE WHEN THE PARTS OF A LIVING ORGANISM ARE CONNECTED TO THE WHOLE.

STRENGTHEN YOUR **CAPACITY TO EMBRACE MYSTERY** BY THINKING ABOUT, PLAYING WITH, AND ADAPTING TO UNCERTAINTY, BECAUSE IT, LIKE DEATH, IS INEVITABLE.

IN THE FACE OF UNCERTAINTY AND DESTABILIZATION, GIVE YOURSELF PERMISSION TO PRIORITIZE **EXPERIMENTATION AND PROTOTYPING.** PAY ATTENTION TO HISTORY, POWER, JUSTICE, AND EQUITY OR YOU WILL MERELY MAKE CHANGE WITHOUT MAKING A DIFFERENCE.

EMBRACE MULTIPLE WAYS OF KNOWING: THEORY, PRACTICE, SENSING, AND INTUITING ARE LATENT BUT POWERFUL SOURCES FOR CREATING CHANGE ON PURPOSE.

SING, DANCE, MOVE, TAKE A MEDITATIVE WALK, AND ENGAGE OTHER EMBODIED PRACTICES. INTEGRATING THESE WAYS OF KNOWING MOVES US PAST THE PLACES WHERE WE GET STUCK.

THE **WISDOM OF OUR ANCESTORS AND DESCENDANTS IS ALWAYS PRESENT AND AVAILABLE TO US,** SO REMEMBER TO WELCOME THEM AS WE FACE THE MOST DIFFICULT TASKS OF OUR LIVES.

LEARN FROM MULTIPLICITY. MOST OF US ARE MORE THAN ANY ONE THING SIMULTANEOUSLY. **APPRECIATE THE COMPLEXITY OF OTHER STORIES AND PERSPECTIVES.**

CULTIVATE **NEW POSSIBILITIES THAT EMERGE BY RESISTING THE TYRANNY OF EITHER/OR.** HOLD THE PARADOXES THAT SHAPE OUR COMMUNAL LIFE WITH PATIENCE AND CURIOSITY.

Acknowledgments

Stephen writes: Deep appreciation for the powerful women and teenage girls in my life who have been my greatest supporters and teachers: my mother, Gloria Tiller; my wife, Tamu Toliver Lewis; my two daughters, Nya and Kai; and my mother in-law, Velma Love. To my family and a wider community of friends, mentors, and elders who helped cultivate my own sense of call and purpose. To the wise sages who have been important guides, ritualists, and conversation partners on matters concerning the Spirit, the ancestors, and vocation: Clifford A. Jones Sr., the late Mary Pearson, Alton B. Pollard III, Gregory C. Ellison II, Melva Sampson, the late Adenibi Ajamu, Falokun Fasegun, Fayomi Osundoyin Egbeyemi, and Malidoma Somé. And to Parker J. Palmer, Otto Scharmer, and Walter Earl Fluker, who invited me into their work and inspired me to see, imagine, and pursue another way that is ancient, ancestral, and a gift to those who dare to live and lead differently.

Matthew writes: I am eternally grateful for the wise women who called me to become myself at multiple moments in my journey. First and foremost in that queenly village are my mother, who now operates among the ancestors, Marcelle Hambrick Williams, and my wife, Alexis Edwards-Williams. My contemplative and mystical life has been enriched by the gift of my father, Reginald Wade Williams Sr., who bequeathed to me and my siblings a model of inner formation born of deep attention, discipline, and practice. To my siblings, Reggie and Joy, thank you for your unconditional love and affirmation—#WeWon! To my dear children, Sage Shepard and Zuri Alexis, your very being has created the space for me to rediscover my purpose, passion, and call. The leadership values expressed in this book are derived from elders and ancestors who helped me to learn how to prioritize character and integrity over talent and performance. I began to make my written contributions to this book while I was recovering and healing from a bout with cancer. I was only able to set aside the space and time to recover and write because of a village of innumerable angels that surrounded me and my family and made sure we did not want for anything. I have been blessed to be in relationship with mentors, models, and companions with whom I have conjured the consciousness and convictions that shaped my contributions to this book: Sharon Watson Fluker, Melissa Wiginton, Parker J. Palmer, Mark Ogunwale Lomax, Will Esuyemi Coleman, Randall C. Bailey, Jeremiah A. Wright, Jr., Iva E. Carruthers, Marsha Foster Boyd, Jeanette Foreman, James "JB" Brown, Joe S. Jones, Stephen Lewis, Romal J. Tune, and Gregory C. Ellison II.

Dori writes: Along the journey of writing this book, my greatest teachers have been my coauthors, Stephen and Matthew, who have generously and graciously shared their insights, stories, dreams, wisdom, and reading recommendations. Bookshelves groaning and heart enlarged, I am forever grateful. I am the beneficiary of wisdom that flows through relationships with hundreds of young adults whose paths I cross through FTE, through my young adult daughters, Erin and Olivia Baker, and through my local community of artist/activists in The Listening/Freedom School of Lynchburg, Virginia. Young people—men, women, non-gender conforming, transgender, transsexual, cis-gender, and queer—spoken word artists, community gardeners, hip-hop lyricists, beat-makers, craft beer brewers, bread-bakers, seminarians, climate activists, podcasters and more: I am watching you create a future you want to inhabit. I honor you and I appreciate the glimpses you give me of a future that wants to be born. A host of FTE friends added insights to this book. They include Chris McCain, Rimes McElveen, Callid Keefe-Perry, Brother Larry Whitney, and Tyler Sit. I also thank my ancestors Anna Anipen Grinenko, Andrew Grinenko, Bob and Jean Otte; my parents, Don and Dee Grinenko; and the conversation partners on my daily walk who nourish me body, mind, and soul: Keith Anderson, Diane Vie, Tasha Gillum, the Evanston tribe, Sunday night family dinner friends, the trees in my neighborhood, and my husband from forever, Lincoln.

Together, we thank conversation partners and those who read early versions of this work: Parker Palmer, emilie m. townes, Darlene Hutto, Christina Repoley, Patrick Reyes, Kimberly Daniel, Heather Wallace, Elsie Barnhart, Richard Havard (and his friends at the Inclusive Collective for contributing to our playlist), Cassidhe Hart, Stephanie Crumpton, Adam Bond, Ashley Cooper, Linda Kay Klein, Gregory C. Ellison II, Melissa Wiginton, Sharon Watson Fluker, and Elizabeth Mitchell Clement. Kate Morales patiently listened to us to create our cover design. We thank the Religion Division of the Lilly Endowment, Inc., including Chris Coble, Jessicah Duckworth, Chanon Ross, and Brian Williams. We work with amazing committed colleagues who have shared in the work we recount in this book. The cumulative learning that we share here is the fruit of our collective efforts. Thank you to our FTE colleagues and the many pastors, activists, and congregation members who provided laboratories for our work. Many thanks to the unsung heroes and sheroes, especially the ancestral mothers of the Black community and spirituality, who taught us another way to see, be with, and support each other, which is a time-honored, cultural, and communal practice we articulate here as the CARE practices.

Bibliography

Adams, John Hurst. 1991. "The Law Student Who Became Bishop," in William H. Myers, *The Irresistible Urge to Preach: A Collection of African American "Call" Stories*. Eugene, OR: Wipf and Stock.

Alexander, Michelle. 2010. *The New Jim Crow: Mass Incarceration in the Age of Colorblindness*. New York: The New Press.

Ani, Marimba. 1994. *Let the Circle Be Unbroken: The Implications of African Spirituality in the Diaspora*. Trenton, NJ: Red Sea Press.

Arao, Brian, and Kristi Clemens. 2013. "From Safe Spaces to Brave Spaces: A New Way to Frame Dialogue Around Diversity and Social Justice." In *The Art of Effective Facilitation*. Edited by Lisa M. Landreman, 135–50. Sterling, VA: Stylus Publishing.

Armah, Ayi Kwei. 2012. *The Healers*. Nairobi, Kenya: East African Publishing House.

Baker, Dori. 2005. *Doing Girlfriend Theology: God-Talk with Young Women*. Cleveland: The Pilgrim Press.

Baker, Ella. 1972. "Developing Community Leadership." In *Black Women in White America: A Documentary History*. Edited by Gerda Lerner, 345–51. New York: Pantheon Books.

Berry, Wendell. 2010. "Questionnaire." In *Leavings: Poems,* 14. Berkeley, CA: Counterpoint.

Block, Peter. 2009. *Community and the Structure of Belonging*. San Francisco: Berrett-Koehler.

Boulaga, Fabien Eboussi. 1984. *Christianity without Fetishes: An African Critique and Recapture of Christianity*. Maryknoll, NY: Orbis.

Brown, Juanita, and David Isaacs. 2005. *The World Café: Shaping our Futures Through Conversations that Matter*. San Francisco: Berrett-Koehler.

Brown Taylor, Barbara. 2010. Sermon at FTE's Calling Congregations Conference, October 9. : https://soundcloud.com/fteleaders/bbt-sermon-ftecc

——. Brown Taylor, Barbara. 2014. *Learning to Walk in The Dark*. San Francisco: Harper Collins.

Brueggemann, Walter. 2010. *Out of Babylon*. Nashville: Abingdon.

Carlyle, Thomas. 1888. *On Heroes, Hero-Worship and the Heroic in History.* New York: Fredrick A. Stokes & Brother.

Cunningham, David. 2016. *At This Time and In This Place: Vocation and Higher Education.* New York: Oxford.

Damon, William, Jenni Menon, and Kendall Cotton Bronk. 2003. "The Development of Purpose During Adolescence." *Applied Developmental Science* 7, no. 3: 119–128.

Davis, Viola. 2017. Academy Awards speech. www.huffingtonpost.com/entry/viola-davis-oscars-speech-totally-steals-the-show_us_58b05ae5e4b060480e073b3b.

Du Bois, W.E.B. 2013. *The Souls of Black Folk.* CreateSpace Kindle Edition. First published 1903 by A. C. McClurg & co. (Chicago).

Ellison, Gregory C., II. 2017. *Fearless Dialogues: A New Movement for Justice.* Louisville: Westminster John Knox Press.

Fluker, Walter. 2012. Preface. *The Papers of Howard Washington Thurman,* vol. 1. Columbia: University of South Carolina Press.

Gilbert, Elizabeth. 2006. *Eat, Pray, Love.* New York: Riverhead.

———. 2016. *Big Magic: Creative Living Beyond Fear.* New York: Riverhead.

———. 2018. "Choosing Curiosity over Fear." Interview with Krista Tippet, The On Being Project, May 24, 2018. https://onbeing.org/programs/elizabeth-gilbert-choosing-curiosity-over-fear-may2018/.

Gunning Francis, Leah. 2015. *Ferguson and Faith: Sparking Leadership and Awakening Community.* St. Louis: Chalice Press.

Holmes, Barbara. 2002. *Race and the Cosmos: An Invitation to View the World Differently.* Harrisburg, PA: Trinity Press International.

———. 2017. *Joy Unspeakable: Contemplative Practices of the Black Church.* Minneapolis: Fortress Press.

Hurtig Casbon, Caryl. 2011. *Framing Open Questions,* www.minnesotarising.org/2011/08/art-of-hosting-framing-open-questions.html

Jennings, Willie. 2010. *The Christian Imagination: Theology and the Origins of Race.* Hartford, CT: Yale University Press.

Jones, Miles. 1994. Unpublished lecture, "Digging Deeper Wells" delivered at Trinity United Church of Christ, Chicago, Illinois.

Kahane, Adam. 2007. *Solving Tough Problems.* San Francisco: Berrett Koehler.

Kinast, Robert L. 2005. "Pastoral Theology, Roman Catholic." In *Dictionary of Pastoral Care and Counseling*. Edited by Robert J. Hunter and Nancy J. Ramsay, 873. Nashville: Abingdon Press.

King, Martin Luther Jr. 1992. *I Have a Dream: Writings and Speeches that Changed the World*. Edited by James M. Washington. San Francisco: Harper Collins.

Lomax, Mark Ogunwalè. 2018. "Christian Theology And AfroCultures: Toward an Afrikan Centered Hermeneutic," Black Theology Project, February 27, 2018. www://btpbase.org/christian-theology-and-afrocultures-toward-an-afrikan-centered-hermeneutic.

Long, Charles. 1995. *Significations: Signs, Symbols and Images of Interpretation in Religion*. Minneapolis: Fortress.

Lorde, Audre. 2007. *Sister Outsider*. Berkeley, CA: Crossing Press.

———. 2017. *A Burst of Light and Other Essays*. Mineola, NY: Ixia.

Martinez, Juan. 2013. "What Does 2040 Mean for Doctoral Theological Education?" Speech given at FTE National Consultation on Doctoral Theological Education, Christian Theological Seminary, Indianapolis, April 18.

Moraga, Cherríe, and Gloria Anzaldúa, eds. 2015. T*his Bridge Called My Back: Writings by Radical Women of Color.* 4th ed. Albany: State University of New York.

Morton, Nelle. 1985. *The Journey is Home*. Boston: Beacon Press.

Myers, William H. 1991. *The Irresistible Urge to Preach: A Collection of African American "Call" Stories*. 2015 edition. Wipf and Stock.

———. 1994. *God's Yes Was Louder Than My No: Rethinking the African American Call to Ministry*. 2015 edition. Eugene, OR: Wipf and Stock.

O'Donahue, John. 2015. "The Inner Landscape of Beauty." Interview with Krista Tippet, The On Being Project, August 6, 2015. https://onbeing.org/programs/john-odonohue-the-inner-landscape-of-beauty-aug2017/.

Palmer, Parker J. 2004. *A Hidden Wholeness: The Journey Toward an Undivided Life*. San Francisco: Jossey-Bass.

Paris, Peter. 1995. *The Spirituality of African Peoples: The Search for a Common Moral Discourse*. Minneapolis: Augsburg.

Parks, Sharon Daloz. 1986. *The Critical Years: Young Adults and the Search for Meaning, Faith, and Community.* New York: Harper Collins.

———. 2011. *Big Questions, Worthy Dreams: Mentoring Emerging Adults in Their Search for Meaning, Purpose, and Faith.* San Francisco: Jossey-Bass.

Payne, Charles. 1989. "Ella Baker: Models of Social Change." *Signs* 14, no.4.

Pollard, Alton, III. 2003. Sermon preached at the ordination of Stephen Lewis, April 27.

Preskill, Stephen, and Stephen D. Brookfield. 2009. *Learning as a Way of Leading: Lessons from the Struggle for Social Justice.* San Francisco: Jossey-Bass.

Quashie,Kevin Everod. 2012. *The Sovereignty of Quiet: Beyond Resistance in Black Culture.* Rutgers University Press.

Ransby, Barbara. 2005. *Ella Baker and the Black Freedom Movement: A Radical Democratic Vision.* Chapel Hill, NC: The University of North Carolina Press.

Reyes, Patrick. 2016. *Nobody Cries When We Die: God, Community, and Surviving to Adulthood.* St. Louis: Chalice Press.

Rilke, Rainer Maria. 1984. *Letters to a Young Poet.* Translated by Stephen Mitchell. New York: Random House.

Rohr, Richard. 2009. *The Naked Now: Learning to See as the Mystics See.* New York: Crossroad.

———.2019. *The Universal Christ: How a Forgotten Reality Can Change Everything We See, Hope For, and Believe.* London: SPCK Publishing.

Santayana, George. 2010. *The Wisdom of George Santayana,* Philosophical Library. Kindle Edition.

Schreiner, Olive. 1890. *Dreams.* Matjesfontein, Cape Colony, South Africa. (The Project Gutenberg E-Book.) www.gutenberg.org/files/1439/1439-h/1439-h.htm#link2H_4_0005.

Senge, Peter M. 1990. "The Leader's New Work: Building Learning Organizations," *Sloan Management Review* (Fall 1990): 7–23.

Somé, Malidoma Patrice. 1998. *The Healing Wisdom of Africa: Finding Life Purpose Through Nature, Ritual, and Community.* New York: Penguin Putnam.

Steere, Douglas V. 1986. *Gleanings: A Random Harvest.* Nashville: Upper Room.

ter Kuile, Casper, and Angie Thurston. 2016. *How We Gather (report) and December Gathering: Notes from the Field.* howwegather.org/reports.

Thurman, Howard. 1962. *The Inward Journey.* Richmond, IN: Friends United Press.

———.1963. *Disciplines of the Spirit.* Richmond, IN: Friends United Press.

———.1979. *With Head and Heart: The Autobiography of Howard Thurman.* Orlando: Harcourt Brace.

———. 1980. Baccalaureate Address at Spelman College, May 4, 1980. Edited by Jo Moore Stewart, *The Spelman Messenger,* 96:4 (Summer 1980).

townes, emilie. m. 2011. "Ethics as an Art of Doing the Work Our Souls Must Have," in *Womanist Theological Ethics: A Reader.* Edited by Katie Geneva Cannon, emilie m. townes, and Angela D. Sims. Louisville: Westminster John Knox Press.

———. 2015. "womanist thoughts on vocation" speech given at Forum for Theological Exploration, April 13. www.leadanotherway.com

Tune, Romal. 2011. "What Are You Called to Do? Finding Spiritual Purpose in the Field." The Blog. September 24, 2011. HuffPost. https://www.huffingtonpost.com/rev-romal-j-tune/finding-purpose-in-the-fi_b_945786.html.

Tune, Romal. 2013. *God's Graffitti: Inspiring Stories for Teens.* King of Prussia, PA: Judson Press.

Wheatley, Margaret. 2009. *Turning to One Another: Simple Conversations to Restore Hope to the Future.* San Francisco: Berrett-Koehler.

Index

S

T

U

V

W

Y

About the Series

Cultivating Faithful, Wise, and Courageous Leaders for the Church and Academy

Welcome to a conversation at the intersection of young adults, faith, and leadership. The Forum for Theological Exploration (FTE) is a leadership incubator that inspires diverse young people to make a difference in the world through Christian communities. This series, published in partnership with Chalice Press, reimagines Christian leadership and creates innovative approaches to ministry and scholarship from diverse contexts.

These books are written by and for a growing network of:

- Partners seeking to cultivate the Christian leaders, pastors, and theological educators needed to renew and respond to a changing church.
- Young leaders exploring alternative paths to ministry and following traditional ways of serving the common good —both inside and beyond "the walls" of the church and theological academy.
- Christian leaders developing new ways to awaken the search for meaning and purpose in young adults who are inspired to shape the future.
- Members of faith communities creating innovative solutions to address the needs of their congregations, institutions, and the broader community.

This series offers an opportunity to discover what FTE is learning, widen the circle of conversation, and share ideas FTE believes are necessary for faith communities to shape a more hopeful future. Authors' expressed ideas and opinions in this series are their own and do not necessarily reflect the views of FTE.

Thank you for joining us!

Dori Baker, Series Editor
Stephen Lewis, FTE President

Other books from the Forum for Theological Exploration

Faith and Ferguson:
Sparking Leadership and Awakening Community
by Leah Gunning Francis

Nobody Cares When We Die:
God, Community, and Surviving to Adulthood
by Patrick Reyes

Stakes Is High:
Race, Faith, and Hope for America
by Michael W. Waters

About the Authors

Dori Grinenko Baker is Senior Fellow at the Forum for Theological Exploration (FTE). She is an ordained minister and holds a PhD in practical theology. Dori is passionate about enlarging the genre of stories, images, and artifacts for helping people find meaning and discover purpose. Her interests lie at the intersection of feminist theologies, young adult culture, leadership development, and spiritual practices that sustain activism. She is the author of *Doing Girlfriend Theology: God-Talk with Young Women* and several other books. www.doribaker.com

Stephen Lewis is the President of the Forum for Theological Exploration (FTE), which focuses on cultivating a new generation of Christian leaders. He is also the creator of DO GOOD X, a social good accelerator for diverse Christian social entrepreneurs. Stephen is an ordained minister with more than 15 years of experience in corporate and nonprofit leadership and strategy, organizational and program development, and group facilitation. His interest lies at the intersection of leadership, vocation, and leading change. He is passionate about helping the next generation of diverse leaders discover their purpose, passion, and calling to make the world a better place. www.fteleaders.org

Matthew Wesley Williams is the Interim President of the Interdenominational Theological Center (ITC) in Atlanta. Matthew is a strategist and facilitator who works through his consulting practice, Liberating Leadership, to build the capacity of cause-driven organizations and leaders to enact alternatives to the status quo. Matthew is a thriving cancer survivor, committed to utilizing his academic, activist, and pastoral background in the spirit of Ella Baker, who observed: "I have always thought that what is needed is the development of people who are interested not in being leaders as much as in developing leadership in others." www.liberatingleadership.org